That Fine Italian Hand

PAUL HOFMANN

A Donald Hutter Book

Henry Holt and Company   *New York*

Library of Congress Cataloging-in-Publication Data
Hofmann, Paul, 1912–
     That fine Italian hand / Paul Hofmann.—1st ed.
       p. cm.
     "A Donald Hutter book."
     ISBN 0-8050-0977-9
     1. National characteristics, Italian.   2. Italy—Civilization.
I. Title.
DG455.H64   1990
945—dc20   89-24601
                                                              CIP

Henry Holt books are available at special discounts
for bulk purchases for sales promotions, premiums,
fund-raising, or educational use. Special editions
or book excerpts can also be created to specification.
     For details contact:
     Special Sales Director
     Henry Holt and Company, Inc.
     115 West 18th Street
     New York, New York 10011

FIRST EDITION

Book design by Claire M. Naylon

Printed in the United States of America
Recognizing the importance of preserving
the written word, Henry Holt and Company, Inc.,
by policy, prints all of its first editions
on acid-free paper. ∞
10 9 8 7 6 5 4 3 2 1

CONTENTS

Introduction vii

1. The Two Italies 1

2. Pasta, Pizza, and Espresso 26

3. A Knack for Survival 45

4. Red Tape and Anarchy 65

5. The Art of Arrangement 86

6. All in the Family? 110

7. Mafia, Inc. 146

8. On Many Sides of the Law 170

9. The Question of Being Serious 192

10. Virtuosos Without Orchestra 213

Index 227

INTRODUCTION

Italy has attracted visitors since the earliest times of Western civilization. First came barbarian invaders who craved the lush South and its riches. They were followed by Saracen plunderers; northern pilgrims to the tombs of the Apostles in Rome; sages like Montaigne who toured the peninsula's spas and, "only to distract myself," made a point of looking at the courtesans in Venice, Florence, and Rome; English lords on their grand tour; Goethe, Stendhal, Byron, Ruskin, and Henry James; an endless line of artists from Dürer to Henry Moore; honeymooners from all over Europe and the Americas; and today's package tours from the United States and Japan.

The foreigner coming to Italy is baffled by conflicting impressions. "Sunny" Italy, especially Milan or Venice, may be shrouded in fog; an early spring week in such a celebrated resort as Taormina in Sicily may be rained out. Hotel guests in a presumedly quiet place off the beaten track, like Urbino, are kept awake half the night because of the whining motor scooters and roaring motorcycles in the street. Museums and churches that one wanted to see are closed. Airports look like refugee camps whenever one of the frequent strikes occurs, and railroad trains may be overcrowded and late when they are not halted by engineers clamoring for the same job conditions as airline pilots enjoy.

The tender contours of the Tuscan hills, with their villas, cypresses, and vineyards, and other beauty spots up and down the peninsula and on the islands, the majestic ruins from antiquity, the cathedrals and palaces, the lovely piazzas will nevertheless enchant the traveler. "All soft and mellow," as Henry James wrote. At mealtime almost any trattoria will provide a haven with tasty food and a genial atmosphere.

A visitor to Italy will be struck by how easy it is to communicate with most Italians. They are outgoing and articulate, ready to smile and engage in small talk or gossip. In conversation "one quickly reaches a note of intimacy in Italy, and speaks about personal matters," Stendhal noted. A simple request for directions by a traveler who hardly knows a dozen Italian words often loosens a cascade of explanations. Verbose many Italians tend to be, but they also make friends easily with strangers whom they met only half an hour earlier.

When Dickens visited the country in 1844, he was enthralled by the amiability amid all the "Italian shabbiness" he saw—"the smiling face of the attendant, man or woman; the courteous manner; the lighthearted, pleasant, simple air." He praised his Italian *corriere*, or travel manager, who struck up conversations with everyone they met along their route, won the sympathy of innkeepers and maidservants in a matter of minutes, managed to whip up a splendid meal in a kitchen in which he had never set foot before, and the morning after was able to entertain the famous author "with the private histories and family affairs of the whole party" with whom they had been traveling. A foreigner on a train trip or bus tour in present-day Italy might collect similar vignettes.

Most Italians underline what they are saying with eloquent gestures in the Mediterranean way of illustrating spoken words with the hands. Watch that manual language when some conversation takes place behind the plate-glass windows of a store or café. Even though you cannot hear what is being said and don't know whether the voices sound cordial or angry, you may be able to guess the drift of the dialogue from the play of the hands—who is persuasive and who skeptical, who wants to convey good faith (placing his hands on his chest) and who is accusing (pointing her forefinger at the other's face).

Some common Italian gestures will at first puzzle the newcomer: The thumb joined with the forefinger and middle finger while the hand is slowly shaken from a limp wrist expresses uncertainty, disbelief, or urgent inquiry. Striking the edges of one's hands together in a crosslike pattern means "I am off" or "Let's beat it!" Such manual messages probably go back to prehistory. The famous orators of antiquity reinforced the effect of their rhetoric with ample movements of their arms and hands, as prosecutors and defense counsel in southern courtrooms still do today.

Equally ancient are the multiform tactile skills of the Italians, their versatility and mastery in shaping, carving, crafting, refining, drawing, styling, painting, and lettering. Today's designers of elegant car bodies and casual wear are heirs to a long tradition that embraces the pottery and tomb frescoes of the Etruscans and the anatomical and engineering drawings by Leonardo da Vinci—indeed a host of celebrated or anonymous artists and artisans going back three thousand years.

The penmanship of Italian Renaissance scribes and copyists before printing became generalized—their "fine Italian hand"—was admired throughout Europe; Western handwriting as taught to first-graders today developed from early fourteenth-century Florentine cursive, a pencraft for speedily copying ancient manuscripts. The phrase *fine Italian hand* has long meant the particular way Italians like to do things, preferring adroitness to sheer force. Although the expression originally was a tribute to proverbial dexterity, ironical overtones suggesting manipulation and craftiness can now be detected whenever the "fine Italian hand" is mentioned.

There is another phrase that any visitor to Italy will soon hear—*all'italiana*, "the Italian way" or "Italian-style." It is no encomium, and the tactful foreigner should avoid it. Local people who are kept waiting in some office for an hour only to be told that the official they want to see has just knocked off for lunch will mutter "service *all'italiana*." *All'italiana* means haphazard, tacky, poorly improvised, confused, also shifty and underhanded. The newspapers all the time denounce things *all'italiana*—political decisions papering over conflicts without solving the underlying problems, bureaucratic idiocies, the mails that need a week or longer to deliver a letter to an address in the same city, or a criminal procedure that keeps defendants in jail for years and eventually frees them "for lack of evidence," without any compensation or apology.

Although the Italians, like other peoples, resent censures by foreigners, they have developed an uncommon proclivity for self-criticism, as their newspapers and everyday conversations prove. Italians are generally convinced that in other countries the judges are more impartial, government officials more honest and competent, businesspeople and workers more reliable, and the police more efficient. (Understandably, whenever Italians go abroad and run into corruption, bumbling, or fraud, they are astonished and disappointed, and will resignedly say, *"Tutto il mondo è paese,"* an adage that may be rendered as "People are all alike and things are rotten all over the world.")

This book is an attempt to exemplify how the "fine Italian hand" operates: the hand manner *all'italiana*, by one who has been observing it for most of his life.

I saw Italy for the first time as a hitchhiker after my freshman year at the University of Vienna. There were not yet a great many cars on the highways of the peninsula, but I did get picked up by some trucks; most of the time I walked. I spent nights in the diocesan seminary of Udine, in a monastery at Adria, in a farmer's barn at a village between Ferrara and Bologna oddly called Malalbergo (bad hotel), in similar places elsewhere, and in cheap inns. If there were any youth hostels then, I didn't find them. I met peasants, truck drivers, friars, nuns, soldiers, villagers, and townspeople, and was surprised by how sarcastically many of them talked about Mussolini's Fascist regime, then in its heyday. It helped that I had been learning Italian as a subscriber to a mail-order language course, but I encountered some difficulty grasping what was being said to me in Venetian or Ligurian dialect. From my first day I was captivated by the nearly general pleasantness, despite much poverty.

I returned to Italy a few times after that summer and eventually, having witnessed Hitler's triumphant entry into Vienna, moved from my native city to Rome. Self-exiled, I did not think of myself as being uprooted. From the very beginning I felt at home. My first job in Rome was in a third-class hotel near the railroad terminal, owned and run by a Sicilian who, as I found out only much later, was the godfather of an Agrigento Mafia family. I remember him as a droll and genial employer, who called the young, penniless foreigner he had hired as a receptionist Don Paul, pronouncing my first name the French way, the "don" being a Sicilian mark of esteem that neither my age nor any accomplishments warranted. After a few months I was able to resume work as a newspaperman. Following Italy's entry into World War II as an ally of Hitler, I was drafted into the German army.

I underwent basic training with an armored battalion in Bavaria and was sent to the Mediterranean Theater as an army interpreter with the simulated rank of sergeant. I saw Rome during Mussolini's downfall in July 1943 and under Nazi occupation. I kept in touch with the Italian anti-Nazi underground and was able to shed the hated Nazi uniform on the heady day of Rome's liberation by the Allied forces in June 1944. Shortly afterward I joined the staff of *The New York Times*. As a reporter and foreign correspondent, I served in the United States and in some forty other countries on all continents, but I always returned to Italy and eventually became chief of the Rome bureau of the *Times*.

I have visited all of Italy's ninety-five provinces (some may soon be subdivided), many of them often, and have spent varying periods in most of the country's major cities. I have seen Italy's quick transformation after World War II from a predominantly rural society into a modern industrial nation, neck and neck with Britain and France, and not too far behind West Germany in annual economic output.

While I was an on-and-off resident, Rome doubled in size; it now has a population of about 3 million, like Chicago. Milan has become a fashion and design center, an international beacon of taste and modernity. Most other Italian cities have grown impressively too. A remarkable exception is Venice, whose population shrank during the last few decades by at least one-third, to 80,000. The spread of urban areas (including Mestre on the Venetian mainland, administratively a part of the city of Venice with 250,000 inhabitants), the proliferation of second homes in the countryside and along the beaches that came with prosperity, the 4,000-mile network of roads built since the 1950s, the many new hotels and thousands of industrial plants all have covered much of Italy with layer upon layer of concrete, profoundly changing the scenery and environment.

Noble Florence has spawned unsightly new suburbs stretching across the northwestern plain toward Prato. Lombardy has become a clutter of factories that foul the region's air and rivers. Rome is ringed with a broad belt of mean new housing. Southern cities like Naples, Reggio di Calabria, Catania, and Palermo have become urban disasters in their incomparable natural settings. And garish hotels, villas, and condominiums have been closing in on the august Greek temples of Paestum and Agrigento.

All the time looters are despoiling Etruscan tombs and other archaeological troves, art thieves are plundering churches and museums, and many famous collections can be visited only at odd hours because they lack funds and personnel. Every now and then some foreign institution proudly displays a Greek sculpture or some other acquisition that probably has been smuggled out of Italy: There will be an outcry in the Italian media, and magistrates will open an inquiry, but the public is not told that the presumed theft was in all likelihood carried out by local specialists and facilitated by inadequate safeguards, and that the storerooms of Italian museums and galleries bulge with works of art and ancient artifacts that are rarely or never shown. Nobody has ever drawn up a complete inventory of the country's immense cultural riches.

Italy is slightly smaller than Japan, numbering less than half of that country's population, yet some of its metropolitan areas seem as congested as the Tokyo-Yokohama-Osaka corridor. The rickety Italian system of public transportation forces legions of commuters into their cars every working day to battle thrombotic rush-hour traffic. Italy is today among the world's most motorized countries, with 390 cars for every 1,000 inhabitants, as compared with 400 in West Germany and 460 in the United States; individual Italians spend more on their autos than do any other Europeans. The hill towns of Tuscany and Umbria are hemmed in by thickets of service stations and car repair shops.

After many years of living in Rome I have, I am told, adjusted to the local driving habits by practicing the blend of defensive maneuvering and cunning that is an Italian motorist's mental survival kit. I need a strong espresso in the morning and a few times later in the day; I eat plenty of pasta, vegetables, and fruits; and I prefer olive oil to any other fat (the now-vaunted "Mediterranean diet"); I also drink wine moderately with my meals and am not averse to a brief siesta. I have acquired Italian relatives with whom I speak in their language, and I sometimes dream in Italian.

Yet I am not an Italian. This fact will explain the conflicting feelings this book may mirror—affection for the country and its hospitable people, to whom I owe much gratitude, and a stranger's occasional irritation at local peculiarities that natives accept without questioning, including some sleights of that fine Italian hand. Longtime foreign residents who profess to be, and are considered, *italianisants* will sometimes confide to visitors from abroad that Italy would be a splendid country—its natural beauty, the climate, the food, the architecture and the art!—if only it weren't populated by Italians. This is an old, stale chestnut, served up with slight variations by expatriates in host countries from Mexico to the nations of East Asia.

Italy may no longer be the "paradise of exiles" of which Shelley wrote in Venice in 1819. The recent refugees from Eastern European countries generally consider it a transit place and try to reach the Western Hemisphere or Australia as soon as possible. Some expatriates who years ago thought they had found the perfect haven in Italy are also moving on or at least talk about leaving.

The bustling and at times disconcerting country that Italy is today is no quaint idyll or permanent comedy or aesthete's dream. It must be taken on the Italians' own terms. It is essentially the product of a smiling nature and of the keen minds and skilled hands of the Italians who through the centuries tilled the land; cut down (alas!) most of the forests; built the towns and cities (and rebuilt them after each of many calamities); laid out the highways, canals, railroads, and *autostrade*; and created an artistic patrimony without paragon on earth.

The same resilience that enabled the Italian people to survive the recurrent catastrophes their country endured in the course of its turbulent history was displayed after the disaster of World War II. It was a tribute to both Italy's past and the nation's recent show of vitality that the birth certificate of the European Community was issued and signed in Rome in 1957. A confederation based on the Rome Protocols, Western Europe with its Mediterranean appendages is today bidding for superpower status, and the Italians, senior partners in the grouping, are among the staunchest advocates of further integration and cooperation within the Community. That fine Italian hand is helping also to shape European dealings with the world at large. At the same time Italy—at least the country's North—is quickly becoming more "European" than it used to be. The future of the country's South remains its biggest problem and challenge.

We begin with this fundamental division of the country.

That Fine Italian Hand

1.

The Two
Italies

The traveler journeying from Italy's North to the South passes from the Alps through the broad Po Valley before gentle, tidy Tuscany and the green slopes of Umbria yield to a more sullen landscape in the lower Tiber Valley, with high mountains—the wilds of the Abruzzi—to the east. After Rome, palms and orange trees come into sight, and the roads and railroad tracks are bordered with prickly-pear shrubs. The sea, where it is visible, seems a deeper blue than in the North. Naples looks much more crowded, disorderly, and scruffy than Milan or Bologna. The state railroads management seems to have sent all of its superannuated coaches and sleepers to the South, and they are not only old but also dirty. The motorist is warned to be doubly careful while driving through, say, Brindisi or Catania: At intersections gangs of young hoodlums might break car windows to snatch bags.

Palermo may be the only city in Europe where buildings bombed out during World War II were not yet repaired or replaced by the late 1980s—not because the ruins at the center of the island capital were meant as a memorial but because nobody had gotten around to eliminating the eyesores. In the espresso bars and piazzas of southern cities and towns, groups of youths who have nothing else to do hang out for many hours every day, languidly talking about girls or the performance of the local soccer team. Naples is as chaotic as Cairo, and many of its neighborhoods are outright squalid, yet the Napoli soccer club easily raises a few million dollars to buy another famous Brazilian or Argentinian player who will help it maintain its standing in the first division of the national soccer league or even recapture the dizzying triumph of 1987, when the team won the Italian championship, defeating the clubs from the rich North.

In rocky Calabria or in Sicily, some hill towns look like the white medinas of the Arab cities on the opposite shore of the Mediterranean. But in the slums of Reggio di Calabria or Trapani, new Mercedeses or BMWs may be seen plowing through the teeming, narrow lanes, and Filipino maids look out from the steel grilles of pretentious villas on the sprawling outskirts of Cosenza or Agrigento.

This is the Mezzogiorno. The word means "midday," also "land of the midday sun." The region runs down the Italian peninsula south of an imaginary line somewhere between Rome and Naples to about Ancona on the Adriatic Sea, and it includes Sicily. To romantic foreigners *Mezzogiorno* may conjure up visions of a land drenched in the light and heat of the high noon; Greek ruins; Mount Vesuvius and Mount Etna surmounted by plumes of smoke when they are not belching lava in the periodic eruptions of Europe's only active volcanoes (although Vesuvius has long been dormant, and few people think of the junior volcanoes on the islands of Vulcano and Stromboli); golden oranges and robust wines; outdoor life all year round until late into the night, when the strumming of mandolins may be heard; good-looking men and sensual women; *dolce far niente*. To Italians in the North, Mezzogiorno also means Mafia, appalling crime statistics, economic stagnation, an alien mentality, clannish and feudal, a reservoir of future policemen and government officials for the entire country, and a permanent burden to be shouldered by the taxpayer.

Northern and Central Italy on the one hand and the Mezzogiorno on the other are in fact two distinct cultures and societies that have much in common but are also divided by many things. Instead of becoming more closely integrated, they appear to be drifting further apart—the North becoming more "European," the South more Mediterranean or Oriental. Many northerners would today assign the national capital, Rome, to the Mezzogiorno rather than to their "European" portion of Italy.

True, all Italians from the Alps to Sicily want their pasta al dente, watch the same television programs, and vote for the same political parties in the national elections, when usually an astounding 90 percent or so of the enfranchised population go to the polls without any coercion. Most Italian men and quite a few women follow the soccer championships with passion. Northerners and southerners drink espresso, hum the same pop songs, and read the same kinds of newspapers and magazines. It is hard to tell southerners from northerners before they open their mouths and identify themselves by accent or dialect. There are tall, lanky, blond, horse-faced Sicilians who look like Britons and may be descended from their island's Norman overlords of the twelfth century; and there are short, chubby, black-haired and dark-eyed Florentines and Mantuans whose bloodlines may go back to the Etruscans. How people tackle life—that is what distinguishes Northern Italy from the Mezzogiorno.

Take teenagers in a place like Bergamo or Parma or Siena today. Asked what they intend to do with themselves, most of them will answer "make money." They want to become architects, engineers, or physicians, go into industry or public relations, perhaps start their own businesses one day. Young men and women of the same age in Catanzaro or Caltanissetta will think of becoming lawyers or teachers if their parents can afford their schooling. Until quite recently, teaching was the only profession that a southern girl was allowed to choose if she did not want to stay in her parents' home until marriage and raise a family afterward; for a Calabrian or Sicilian woman to work in an office or some other job was long felt to be faintly immoral—she would be in touch with a lot of men who weren't her husband!

Poorer southern males who meet the height and literacy qualifications can always enlist in one of the nation's several police forces. (Few northerners care to.) The foremost goal in life for many young people in the South is to land some job in the state bureaucracy. It pays little, but it provides security and a shred of prestige, even power. Prestige and power are highly valued in the Mezzogiorno. The old men who sit on chairs in the street of a Sicilian town outside some tawdry storefront "Club of Notables," drinking coffee or wine and watching what's going on in the neighborhood, may wear rumpled suits and cloth caps, and not have shaved for a couple of days, but they will be greeted with deference by passersby—even by the elegant chief of the local bank branch, the parish priest, and the carabinieri sergeant. Before every election, candidates from the provincial capital or even from Palermo or Rome will seek these men out and humbly ask for their support; youngsters in need of a job, or their fathers, will try to catch these men's eyes and maybe talk to them. The old men wield influence in mysterious ways, are able to settle disputes, get some girl hired by the post office, and swing hundreds of votes for a politician. My mafioso employer at the hotel near the railroad terminal in Rome was dressed so badly that unwary foreigners who entered our cramped lobby mistook him for a menial, yet the guests arriving from Agrigento and the nearby towns treated him with marked respect, even awe.

Today many influential southerners wear diamond rings, ride in flashy cars, have offices with computers and blond secretaries. Still, the important thing in the South is not so much wealth and ostentation but power. It does not necessarily have to be Mafia power, with the veiled threat that anyone opposing it may get killed. What is common to these relationships based on prestige and influence is that they seem to belong to an archaic world of lord and vassal, patron and follower. Such ties, an intangible reality throughout the Mezzogiorno, are called *clientela*; the word has come down straight from the Latin of Cicero. *Clientela*, that web of connections between influential personages and hangers-on, of favors rendered and due, is what distinguishes the society of the Mezzogiorno from that of Northern and Central Italy, where the individual does not need to fawn on some *capo* (although it never hurts).

The cultural differences between the industrial North and the still semifeudal South of Italy are so deep that sociologists have spoken of "two nations." I prefer to view Italy as a system of two interlocking cultures and societies. What, then, is *the* Italian nation?

Metternich, who is always quoted in this context, could still say that "Italy is a geographical expression," meaning that there is no such thing as an Italian nation. Large parts of the country had, in fact, been subjected to foreign domination for centuries by Metternich's time. Italian as spoken in Tuscany had slowly been recognized as the linguistic standard, but the populace in other regions clung to their local dialects: The Sicilian could not understand the Venetian or Piedmontese, and vice versa. A common idiom, as distinct from stilted book Italian, has developed only recently through films, radio, and television. It is essentially a mixture of Tuscan and the Roman vernacular; the circumstance that the national capital is also the center of the Italian film industry and houses the headquarters of the state broadcasting system has helped Roman accents and expressions slip into everyday speech throughout the country.

Not only has television influenced and unified the way the Italians speak today, it has also exercised an immeasurable cultural impact. It has even helped change the country's laws: The courtroom episodes of the American television serials that Italian networks buy and rebroadcast continuously have acquainted provincial audiences with the oratorical and procedural duels between prosecutor and defense counsel that mark criminal trials in the United States. To Italians, this adversary system based on common law has been a fascinating novelty; their country's penal procedures are derived from Roman law, giving the prosecution preponderance. When the Italian Parliament in 1988 passed legislation introducing features of the Anglo-Saxon system of criminal justice, including a broader possibility for cross-examination in court, lawmakers and lawyers spoke about the new "Perry Mason trial." Italians, finding themselves defendants or witnesses in a court of law for the first time in their lives, addressed the presiding judge as *"Vostro Onore,"* the video translation of "Your Honor." This is not the way to speak to an Italian magistrate, who expects to be called "Mr. President" or "Your Excellency." Often the smiling or annoyed judge would tell the defendant: "You are not Perry Mason, and we are not on TV here!"

Roman law is one of the many historic strands that interlace the fabric of Italian national identity. Reminiscences of the Roman Empire and the cultural heritage from the Middle Ages and the Renaissance have always made educated Italians aware, however dimly, of common bonds and a common destiny. To the masses of the population in Northern Italy who had been living in several distinct states for hundreds of years, Napoleon gave the first brief taste of a unified Italy, albeit one held within his French Empire and with his viceroy in Milan.

During the Italians' nineteenth-century struggle for liberation from foreign rule and for national unity—the Risorgimento—plots were hatched, secret societies founded, uprisings organized and quelled, diplomatic intrigues spun, battles won and lost. Yet French and Prussian military help was needed to achieve, at last, the political unification of 1860 to 1870. The Risorgimento was in the main a movement of political and intellectual elites. Byron, who lived for years in Italy, sympathized with them but did not take them too seriously. In his diary he noted that the well-to-do young people who were members of the outlawed Carbonari alternated between conspiratorial activities and hunting parties. (*Carbonari*—meaning "coal burners," people living in the forests—was a romantic name assumed by secret revolutionary groups in the early nineteenth century.) The masses of the population, particularly the farmers, were apathetic and played almost no role in the Risorgimento. Surveying the last few centuries, Luigi Barzini, Jr., has pointed out the "mediocre quality of Italian history."

At the height of the Risorgimento, in May 1860, Giuseppe Garibaldi, already famous as a guerrilla leader in South America and Italy, sailed with 1,162 volunteers (The Thousand) from Genoa to the Mezzogiorno. He used the word *Mezzogiorno* in a letter to an associate, Biagio Caranti, on the eve of his fateful expedition. Officially the Mezzogiorno was then known as the Kingdom of the Two Sicilies and embraced the realm of the Bourbon kings who had reigned in Naples since 1816. The Thousand, many of them wearing the red shirts that Garibaldi had fancied since his days in Latin America, landed near Marsala, at the westernmost tip of Sicily. Four months later Garibaldi was the master of the entire Mezzogiorno: The Kingdom of the Two Sicilies had toppled like a rotten tree, its soldiers laying down their weapons or going over to The Thousand. Garibaldi styled himself The Dictator and for a few dizzying months wielded supreme power, first from Palermo and then from the former royal palace at Caserta near Naples (where he slept like a soldier, on his saddle, covered by a coarse blanket).

The romantic flavor of the enterprise undertaken by The Thousand brought Alexandre Dumas, the celebrated author of *The Three Musketeers*, to the scene; he joined Garibaldi in Sicily and followed him to Naples, where The Dictator named him director of the city's museums and the excavations in Pompeii. Dumas *père* was to spend four years in Naples, where he published a liberal newspaper, *L'Indipendente*.

In the autumn of 1860 King Victor Emmanuel II, the ruler of Piedmont and Sardinia, in whose name (and with whose connivance) Garibaldi had attacked the southern kingdom, proclaimed himself king of Italy. The quick and easy conquest of Sicily and the southern part of the peninsula had shown how ripe the Mezzogiorno had been for takeover by the dynamic North. National unification was almost completed—except for the Italians still under Austrian rule in the Alps and Trieste—when the king's *bersaglieri* (sharpshooters), sporting rooster feathers on their helmets, stormed into papal Rome in 1870 without encountering any resistance. Pope Pius IX proclaimed himself a "prisoner in the Vatican," and his priests and their followers boycotted the new unified state for decades. The papacy was not to make peace with Italy until 1929, when Mussolini, in the Lateran Treaties, paid it off for church properties seized nearly sixty years earlier and carved a tiny sovereign entity, the State of Vatican City, out of Rome.

Upper-class enthusiasm for the Risorgimento faded after 1870. The practical problems of nationhood had to be tackled, and the exhortation of the Piedmontese prime minister and writer Massimo d'Azeglio, "Italy is made, now let us make the Italians!" became a common catchphrase, though translating it into reality proved arduous. Although Italy's North and South had been politically united, their cultural, economic, and social differences remained. At the end of the nineteenth century and during the first two decades of the twentieth, nationalistic politicians and intellectuals whipped up Italian chauvinism rather than focus on the nation's North-South tensions. And Mussolini duly reinforced that chauvinism.

The experience of World War II was sobering, however, and today, well over a century after national unification, Italians are no longer flag wavers. Many of them seem not even sure whether their country's tricolor (adopted during the Risorgimento) is green-white-red (the correct sequence) or red-white-green. Whenever homeowners put flags out of their apartment windows—as happens almost exclusively on days when the national soccer eleven plays against a foreign team—the colors are often reversed. Army barracks and other military installations fly the tricolor daily, but schools, factories, department stores, and service stations, which in many countries routinely display the national colors, almost never do so in Italy. Even government members and other high officials have only lately taken to adorning their offices with their country's flag, and then only because they have seen it done in Washington and other capitals.

Today's Italy incorporates a few ethnic minorities—French-speaking inhabitants of the Aosta Valley, German and Ladin speakers in South Tyrol, Slovenians in the Trieste area—yet the biggest minority is not ethnic but cultural: the people of the Mezzogiorno.

Whenever the lingering backwardness of the Deep South is discussed, educated Southern Italians will usually remind one that their land saw a brilliant civilization 2,500 years ago. Greek settlers had built large urban centers and religious shrines; city states like Taras (now Taranto), Syracuse, and Akragas (now Agrigento) were flourishing; Sybaris, at the spot in the instep of the Italian boot where the small town of Sibari today perpetuates the name, was a Greek byword for "sybaritic" luxury. To the inhabitants of mainland Greece and the Greek islands, Greater Greece (in Latin *Magna Graecia*) beyond the Ionian Sea was the golden West—a new world and fabled land where traders and adventurers could quickly make a fortune and where artists and intellectuals from the old Greek cities would find eager audiences and disciples. Pythagoras, Herodotus, Aeschylus, Euripides, and Plato visited at various times what is now called the Mezzogiorno in much the same way European artists and scholars tour the United States today. The philosopher Empedocles belonged to the ruling clan of Akragas and, according to legend, ended his life by throwing himself into the crater of Mount Etna. Archimedes, the greatest mathematician of antiquity, was a native of Syracuse; he was slain when Roman soldiers looted the once-powerful city in 212 B.C.

Under Roman rule the Deep South became an expanse of enormous farming estates, the latifundia, where a slave population worked the soil, enabling the absentee landlords to regale themselves in Rome. Then came raids and invasions by Germanic tribes and centuries of domination by Byzantines and Arabs, and by Norman, German, French, and Spanish rulers. Feudal barons and chieftains, and eventually the viceroys and officials of the kings in Naples, maintained a flimsy surface control while vast stretches of Sicily, Calabria, and Basilicata slipped into near barbarism. Banditry and clannish vendettas were for many centuries everyday occurrences. (They have not been completely rooted out even now. An old blood feud between the Raso-Albanese and Facchineri families in the town of Cittanova in Calabria resulted in four-teen murders during just fifty-five days in 1987; by 1989 the toll of those killed had reached fifty-nine.) Christianity sur-vived in the Mezzogiorno only by making compromises with the archaic superstitions of the populace.

Most of the great Italians, from St. Francis of Assisi and Giotto to Puccini and Marconi, were of Northern or Central Italian stock—a truth that remains unpopular in Rome and to its south. Dante, Leonardo da Vinci, Michelangelo, and a glittering galaxy of other poets, novelists, sculptors, painters, thinkers, scholars, and scientists were Tuscans; Raphael al-ways spoke of Urbino as his "fatherland"; the many Vene-tians who achieved fame or notoriety include Marco Polo and the adventurer Casanova; Verdi was born in the village of Roncole near Parma. And Garibaldi, who came from Nice, never did get to like the Neapolitans toadying to him and his Thousand.

The Piedmontese officials who took stock of the Mez-zogiorno territories that Garibaldi had conquered for their king were appalled by what they saw. They reported on the Deep South as if it were located on a different, dark conti-nent. Count Camillo Benso di Cavour, the diplomatic archi-tect of Italy's unification, never even bothered to visit the Mezzogiorno. (Cavour spoke French much better than he did Italian.) The southerners, on the other hand, quickly gained the feeling that they were not citizens of a new Italian state with the same rights and opportunities as the northerners but had become subjects in a colony.

To Italians from the North who were sent to the Deep South as administrators, tax collectors, police officers, build-ers, and salesmen, the region often meant exile in dusty vil-lages, a diffident local population, chronic scarcity of water, and an atmosphere of stagnancy and provincialism with the pervasive though shadowy presence of a daunting power called Camorra in Naples, 'Ndrangheta in Calabria, and Mafia in Sicily.

The national governments that succeeded one another in Rome, including Mussolini's, all promised to tackle the "Southern Question." But despite some spotty reforms under Il Duce, the Mezzogiorno continued to lag. When Fascist authorities decided that the Piedmontese doctor, painter, and writer Carlo Levi was a security risk and relegated him to a village in Basilicata, Levi was stunned by the primitive society and patterns of life he found there. The result of his experience was the forceful book *Christ Stopped in Eboli* (1945). The Jewish exile took the title from a local proverb implying that Christian civilization had never reached Basilicata but had halted at the town of Eboli near the Bay of Salerno.

After the collapse of Fascism and the end of World War II, the new Italian Republic also undertook to solve the "Southern Question," and by now public funds estimated at $150 billion (in 1989 dollars) have been poured into the Mezzogiorno. Several hundred miles of new streets and hundreds of bridges, many new schools and hospitals, and a network of modern hotels and service stations have been built, along with a few large, new industries, like the Taranto steel mills and the petrochemical complexes at Brindisi and on Sicily's east coast. Infant mortality and illiteracy have declined sharply (although in 1988 some 3 million adult southerners still could not read and write), and while the overall character of the Deep South has remained rural, its principal cities have greatly expanded. Their historic cores are now surrounded by vast belts of condominiums and new housing projects, many built in brazen defiance of zoning regulations; their streets are choked with traffic, and their air is acrid with exhaust fumes.

Nevertheless, the economic gap between the Mezzogiorno and prosperous Northern and Central Italy has widened. The per capita income in Southern Italy is still barely 60 percent of the average in the rest of Italy. At first the new industries in the South provided jobs for a few thousand workers, at least for a few years, but their products still lack a local market. Expectations that the new plants would generate many ancillary small and medium-sized enterprises in their areas have been disappointed. Italians speak of the solitary industrial giants in the Mezzogiorno as their "cathedrals in the desert." Some factories in the South were apparently built only to collect the lavish state subsidies for economic development in the region; they closed down after a few months or years, while the Mafia continued to siphon off billions of dollars in the form of kickbacks and protection money. Such illegal profits explain in part the many new cars and the garish new villas in the supposedly impoverished Deep South.

Today the Mezzogiorno—an area the size of Greece, inhabited by more than one-third of the 57 million Italians—has an official unemployment rate of nearly 20 percent of the labor force, against 8 percent in the North. The South accounts for only one-fourth, in value, of the goods and services Italy is turning out, its gross domestic product. Only Apulia, the flat and fertile "heel" of Italy, shows signs of an economic takeoff, spurred by thriving agriculture and many diversified small businesses. Perhaps most important, Mafia power is weak or absent in the area. Campania (the Naples region), Calabria, Basilicata, Sicily, and Sardinia, on the other hand, have remained stagnant and are infested by criminal gangs.

Many southerners are nevertheless convinced that they are smarter than the people in the country's North, whom they often view as plodding, mercantile, arrogant, and maybe really not too bright. *Cà nisciuno è fesso* (nobody is dumb here) is a Neapolitan saying. People from the Mezzogiorno make shrewd lawyers, able administrators, sharp police investigators, and consummate diplomats; they may also excel in philosophical speculation or mathematical theory. The plays and novels of Luigi Pirandello, the Sicilian who won the 1934 Nobel Prize in literature, provide penetrating psychological insights into the Mezzogiorno.

Emigration has long seemed the best way of escaping the torpor, misery, hunger, and hopelessness of the Deep South. In the late 1940s I heard Alcide de Gasperi, then premier of Italy, remark in Rome one day that he could advise southern people only to "learn languages and seek a new life abroad." De Gasperi, one of the pioneers of the European Community, along with Robert Schuman of France and Konrad Adenauer of West Germany, was a native of the Trentino in the Alps and had little understanding of the Mezzogiorno. Before and during World War I he had been a deputy to the Austrian Parliament in Vienna; when his region became a part of Italy, he helped found the church-backed Popular party, and he weathered the Fascist dictatorship as a librarian in the Vatican. As Italian government chief from 1945 to 1953, he rarely visited the Mezzogiorno and seemed to distrust its potential for economic and cultural development, even though southern specialists, known at home as *meridionalisti*, kept insisting that the Mezzogiorno might one day become the "California of Italy."

Individual Italians, especially from the North and the center of the country, have always been intrepid travelers. The Franciscan friar Giovanni da Pian del Carpino, sent by Pope Innocent IV to the Tartary court in 1245, rode on horseback across Russia and Central Asia for more than three months to reach Karakorum in Mongolia and brought back astonishing news about the immense East. Thirty years later the Venetian Marco Polo made it to China, traveling on the system of tracks, paths, and mountain passes that since antiquity had been known as the Silk Road of East-West trade. Polo lived at the court of Kublai Khan as a favorite of the Mongol emperor, but when he returned home in 1295 and told about Cathay, few people would believe him. The great Jesuit missionary and savant Matteo Ricci (1552–1610), a native of Macerata near Ancona, impressed the court of China's emperor by his learning and tact, and laid the groundwork for an eventually futile effort to reconcile Christianity and Confucianism. (The Vatican vetoed the Jesuit project, and the Roman Catholic church thereupon "lost China.")

Christopher Columbus was only the best known of many Italians who, in the service of various European powers, sailed uncharted seas. Columbus, probably a native of Genoa, knew about Polo's discoveries, and when he was exploring the coast of Honduras during his fourth voyage (1502) he believed himself to be in Cathay near the residence of the Grand Khan. Another navigator, the Florentine Amerigo Vespucci, also sailed from Spain and was to describe the "earthly paradise" that he said he had found on the Atlantic coast of South America. Amerigo was associated with the Medici clan and knew Leonardo da Vinci; his name was already in his lifetime (first in 1509) used to denote the lands of the Western Hemisphere.

Before and after the great Atlantic expeditions, Italians helped build the Kremlin in Moscow and erect churches and palaces all over Europe. Other Italians found employment as diplomats or artists with the Holy Roman emperor and at many royal and princely courts. In the Baroque age royalty and other wealthy patrons from Madrid to St. Petersburg employed Italian musicians, poets, singers, artists, goldsmiths, stucco workers, and other artisans. Pietro Metastasio, a native of Rome, refined the Italian language during his long, productive years as the court poet in Vienna; the young Haydn learned much from the Neapolitan émigré composer Niccolò Porpora; Antonio Salieri, from Legnago near Verona, the fortunate rival and ambiguous friend of Mozart, was the teacher of Beethoven, Schubert, and Liszt; the Jewish-born Venetian Lorenzo Da Ponte wrote the libretti for three Mozart operas. Da Ponte eventually reached New York, taught Italian at Columbia College, helped found the first opera in the American metropolis, and died there in 1838.

By that time a trickle of Italian immigrants—a few hundred each year—were arriving in the United States. Like Garibaldi, who lived briefly in New York, many of the newcomers were Ligurians, and quite a few of them went to California, especially during the gold rush. Northern Italians founded wineries, fruit-packing businesses, and banks in that western state.

A mass exodus from Italy's Deep South started after national unification. Of the 4 million Italians who entered the United States in huge immigration waves from 1880 to 1914, and again from 1920 to 1927, three-fourths came from the Mezzogiorno. The immigrants from Italy took pick-and-shovel jobs, entered the building trades in force, provided manpower for the waterfronts, worked for municipal sanitation departments, became hairdressers or waiters (some scraped together enough money to open small restaurants or groceries—*grosserie* in their patois); the women became seamstresses in the sweatshops and factories of the garment industry.

Many of the men from the Mezzogiorno who had sailed in steerage to America had left their families behind, and a great number of them returned, sometimes twenty or more years later, when the children they had last seen as infants were adults. The hope of going back to the old country one day to buy some property in the native village with one's American savings prompted most of the immigrants to settle near the East Coast seaports. Quite a few eventually changed their minds and had their wives and children join them. Although the bulk of the newcomers were originally from rural areas, they tended in the United States to cluster in cities and suburbs, forming Little Italies.

There were, to be sure, also thousands of immigrants from Northern Italy, especially from economically depressed parts of the Friuli, Venetia, Romagna, and Liguria regions. Yet the American perception of the immigrants from Italy, indeed of their entire nation, was above all shaped by the poor Sicilians, Calabrians, and Campanians. Most of them had lived in some village before embarking in Palermo or Naples and had never really known big-city life before they arrived in New York, went through the immigration mill on Ellis Island, and started looking for a cousin in one of the Little Italies, someone they had probably never met before but who would let them sleep on a mattress in the kitchen for a few weeks.

The Italian enclaves in American cities were themselves subdivided by invisible walls: Sicilians were wary of people from Avellino in Campania, and immigrants from one Calabrian village would not trust those from a village in the next valley. Statues of hometown saints were revered in the Little Italies like tribal totems and were carried around the neighborhood on the saints' feast days in parades that might attract curious and amused outsiders but annoy the local Roman Catholic bishop, usually an Irishman, and most of his clergy, who viewed the celebrations as relics of paganism. The dialects spoken in the Little Italies were incomprehensible to people from Northern Italy.

Many of the immigrants from the Mezzogiorno were total or virtual illiterates. Rome, Florence, Venice, Milan, the national government and Parliament, and the country's cultural heritage had no meaning for them. Their "Italy" was their own corner of the Deep South, and a local baron who owned the land, a carabinieri sergeant who would round up lads for induction into military service, the parish priest, a miraculous image of the Madonna, the traditional way of garnishing spaghetti with olives or seafood, and memories of family alliances and feuds.

"They are not Italians because they have never been," wrote Giuseppe Prezzolini in New York in 1931. "Here they have taken on certain American habits, but basically they have remained southern peasants, without culture, without schooling, without language. . . . They left Italy before being Italians. They have been here, and have not become true Americans." Prezzolini was a journalist and author, born in Perugia, who lived in New York for many years and taught at Columbia University; his observations betrayed the disdain of an Umbrian intellectual for uneducated southerners.

Many Italian visitors to the United States today who want to have a look at what has remained of the Little Italies make similar judgments. An Italian consul general in New York told me in the 1970s that because of his assignment he had to ride the ethnic circuit in the metropolitan area, attending Italian baptisms, graduation ceremonies, weddings, and funerals. "You wouldn't believe what I see and hear," he reported. "I don't understand those Italo-Americans when they start talking in what they think is Italian and actually is the dialect of some mountain village in Sicily or Calabria that their grandparents used to speak, interlarded with hybrids like *carro* [car] or *giobbe* [job]. They offer me espresso, and a bit of lemon peel is swimming in it!" The old Sicilian custom of having black coffee with a slice of lemon peel is largely unknown on the Italian mainland.

At first, many Americans were convinced that a sizable number of the Italian immigrants were in some way mixed up with secret and criminal societies, the Black Hand or the Mafia. Italian men were said to be insanely jealous, and one was advised never to glance too long at their wives, sisters, or daughters unless one wanted trouble. Unlike the Jewish immigrants from Eastern and Central Europe, the newcomers from the Mezzogiorno seemed to care little for education and books. Hence the stereotype of the "dumb Italian."

As for the Irish, who also had to cope with much prejudice in the United States, when the Italians started arriving in force they found the Irish already entrenched in formidable political machines, in police forces, and, above all, in the Roman Catholic church. Southern Italians never had much clout in the Vatican, and the immigrants from the Mezzogiorno were producing few priests and even fewer prelates; the church hierarchy was almost exclusively Irish. Italian-Americans did get together in a maze of hometown, regional, and fraternal organizations, but there was never a united front. Political scientists from the old country who have surveyed the Italian-American communities point out that even now there is no such thing as an "Italian lobby" or an Italian-bloc vote in the United States.

Italian-American leaders often sound defensive, seemingly anxious to negate any tie to the mob; or they simply insist that "there is no Mafia." American media indeed dropped the term *Mafia* during the 1960s and 1970s, although it was at the time being officially used in Italy in a parliamentary investigation of Sicilian-based organized crime. In the 1980s the ominous word crept back in the United States, alternating with the phrase *Cosa Nostra*, an American coinage that at first sounded unfamiliar to people in Italy but through the press and films eventually found acceptance there too.

Glamorized by books like Mario Puzo's *The Godfather* and derivative movies, the fictional or real crime families with their Sicilian roots, their sinister patriarchs, pettifogging counselors, arrogant henchmen, and lethal "soldiers" seem to have filled some Italian-Americans with perverse pride. The offspring of immigrants from the Mezzogiorno had from their childhood been smarting from more or less jocular allusions to their presumed mob connections; now it seems the macho thing for some to swagger like a movie don. A few Italian restaurants call themselves "The Godfather." (Back in Italy, too, *trattorie* in various cities have sprouted such business signs as "Il Padrino"—Italian for godfather—or "Il Mafioso.")

The mafioso with a bulge in the jacket of his sharp pin-striped suit has undoubtedly remained a stereotype for Italian-Americans among their fellow citizens, along with those of the Italian waiter, pizza cook, tailor, hairdresser, longshoreman, and sanitation worker. Never mind that thousands of second- and third-generation Italian-Americans have become prominent in the arts and literature, in the media, in the judiciary, in industry and finance, and in politics.

True to the pattern observable in other ethnic groups, many children of Italian immigrants became uncomfortable with the outlandish ways and the accents of their elders. Sons and daughters of immigrants who would not speak Italian strove to drift into the American mainstream, to move out of the Little Italies, and often to marry outside their ethnic group. In the third generation of Italian-Americans, a nostalgic search for roots can often be observed: Some start to learn Italian as a foreign but faintly familiar language, follow Italian cultural activities, maybe travel to the old country to visit grandfather's hometown . . . and are outraged if they get stranded in one of the frequent Italian aviation or railroad strikes.

The old Italian neighborhoods that the socially mobile offspring of immigrants abandoned have not completely disappeared. In Manhattan, it is true, Mulberry Street has been all but taken over by an expanding Chinatown, but other Little Italies continue to prosper as newcomers from the old country fill the vacancies. Some traditionally Italian districts, like Greenwich Village in Manhattan or Park Slope in Brooklyn, have become trendy, attracting affluent people from other ethnic groups. "There is no street crime here," prospective home buyers are told. "The mob takes care of punks and muggers; these blocks are safe." Presumed Mafia control of an area has become a selling point in the real-estate market.

The quota system adopted by United States immigration legislation in 1924 restricted the influx of Italians, and Mussolini wanted his people to colonize his African empire rather than sail for America. After World War II there was a new large-scale exodus from the Deep South, but in a different direction. In a silent mass migration that made no headlines either at home or abroad, 6 million Southern Italians—nearly one-third of the population of the Mezzogiorno—moved northward. Most of them found jobs in Northern Italy, but hundreds of thousands went to Switzerland, West Germany, France, Belgium, and other European countries. There they provided manpower for big and small industries, went down into the coal mines, worked as ditchdiggers and bricklayers, as hotel maids and waiters, as cooks and gelato makers. Some—the *magliari*, from the Italian word for undershirt, *maglia*—sold cheap underwear from house to house, even if they knew only a few words of the language of their new countries. Many made good and became foremen in factories and construction firms, or were able to open their own pizzerias or restaurants. A few came as racketeers to extend the Mafia's tentacles into new territory.

During the 1950s, when the "Italian miracle" of explosive industrial development started in earnest, companies in the country's North sent recruiters to the Mezzogiorno to hire cheap labor for Piedmont and Lombardy. The subsequent arrival of millions of people from the Deep South irked many northerners. The newcomers complained about discrimination in the factories, where they seemed to get only the most tedious jobs, and about difficulties in finding any but substandard dwellings. In their new homes, the heads of these immigrant families were told by their children of hard times in school and by their wives of unpleasantness in shops and markets. All southerners in Turin, Milan, and the other industrial cities in the North seemed to have their stories of unfriendliness, of slights or outright hostility from the local population. In Italy's North the standard disparaging nickname for any native of the Mezzogiorno became—and still is—*terrone*, a word derived from *terra* (soil). The term is imperfectly rendered as "clodhopper." *Terrone* suggests less a yokel than an uncivilized but cunning fellow with dirty habits, a man who is clannish and may be a mafioso; a *terrona* is, to northerners, a primitive woman who doesn't use much soap. Because most of the civil servants and the personnel of the police forces in the North have roots in the Mezzogiorno, the dislike and distrust of the *terroni* blended with the general disaffection for the central government in Rome. In fact, for many natives of Milan, Turin, Genoa, Venice, or Bologna, *terronia*, the despised South, begins south of Florence. As early as the 1960s, sociologists and newspapers in Rome and in the real Mezzogiorno started denouncing northern "racism" and "intolerance," and today these ethnic antagonisms are a prime theme of public discussion throughout Italy. Northern Italy's antipathy for the Mezzogiorno finds increasingly less subtle expressions. Newspapers in Turin, Milan, or Venice usually make a point of noting that an arrested robbery, burglary, murder, or rape suspect was born in Palermo or Reggio di Calabria and regularly theorize that a Sardinian-Calabrian crime syndicate was again at work whenever another of the North's frequent kidnappings is reported. (And these explanations all too often turn out to be correct.) When Mount Etna was once again spewing lava in the early 1980s, large graffiti reading FORZA ETNA! (Go Etna!) appeared on overpasses spanning highways near Venice. To the foreign traveler the inscriptions might have been puzzling, but every Italian understood the message: "Come on, Mount Etna, blow up real good and knock off a few thousand Sicilians!" One Sunday in September 1989, the crowded Verona soccer stadium erupted in an anti-Naples demonstration when the local Veronese team was playing the visiting Napoli eleven. The fans chanted: *"Terroni, terroni!"* And there were banners in the bleachers reading "Napoli, Welcome to Italy!" To gauge the depth of antisouthern feeling in the North, talk at random to a few native people there: You will be struck by the distaste with which many, even casual acquaintances, speak about their compatriots in the Mezzogiorno and about the Romans. The blandest comment will be that the inhabitants of the Deep South and of the nation's capital steal and squander the tax money that northerners contribute out of what they earn through their efficiency and hard work.

Several politicians in Northern Italy have tried to channel the widespread aversion to the Mezzogiorno into organized movements. Home-rule parties with such names as Ticket for Trieste, Venetian League, Lombard League, and Piedmontese League have sprung up since the 1970s and have won sizable slices of the popular vote in administrative elections. In their official propaganda such factions never use the term *terroni* but stress instead their determination to see to it that the bumbling and corrupt government in Rome no longer meddle in local affairs.

The founder of the "Lombard League," Senator Umberto Bossi, explained the movement's drive for greater autonomy of the Milan region in a recent interview: "Think of our schools, the public administration: the southern ethnic group represents the majority there, monopolizing the structures of the centralistic state, the political forces, the government. . . . The bulk of the Treasury revenues comes from Lombardy. We have every right to protest when we see that these funds are being thrown out of the window to join the immense river of billions [of lire] that so far have not benefited the Mezzogiorno but the southern [criminal] gangs. It's as if Lombardy were handing its wallet to the Deep South."

Compassion swept much of such rancor aside in 1980 when a catastrophic earthquake hit a large area in the south of the peninsula, most heavily Campania and Basilicata. Television showed the ancient, poor towns on the harsh southern mountain slopes reduced to rubble, and old women, wrapped in black scarves, weeping for their dead. As if for the first time, northern viewers had to realize that not all of Italy was prosperous. In an outpouring of idealism and national solidarity, young people set out from Milan, Florence, and other northern cities to bring aid to the earthquake victims, and in some remote villages the northern volunteers were on the spot before the official rescue parties arrived.

The following years of reconstruction were less inspiring. The central government earmarked huge amounts of funds for the rehabilitation of the stricken areas—perhaps as much as $50 billion, although nobody seems to know the exact amount—and a good deal of the money seems to have been misappropriated. Local banks multiplied their assets and reaped interest, contractors profited, and politicians favored their *clientela*. Nor is the sequel to the 1980 earthquake the only example of the squandering of taxpayers' money in the Mezzogiorno, and today impatience with that part of the country appears to be spreading in Italy's north, threatening to weaken further Italy's ever fragile national cohesion.

2.

Pasta, Pizza, and Espresso

On hearing the name *Italy*, foreigners are apt to think first of food: of pasta, pizza, espresso, gelato, and wine from straw-clad flasks. Italians themselves, when abroad, are likely to have similar associations as they think of their own country. A deft publicity spot for a spaghetti company, shown on Italian television, presents an Italian business executive in a hotel room, the Manhattan skyline visible through the window, pulling a short piece of dry pasta, his good-luck charm, out of his pocket and wistfully looking at it. The viewer gets the message: The man is pining for his family back in Italy and for the spaghetti on their table. The voice-over: "Pasta Barilla means home." The brand name is stressed, but the accent should really be on *pasta*.

The French have long been scoffing at their southeastern neighbors as *les macaronis* or *les spaghettis*. To Italians themselves, a craving for pasta as a staple food that one can pleasurably eat every day the way Asians fill up on rice is as natural as their melodious language. Fondness for pasta is indeed an important facet of *italianità*, the essence of being Italian. Although cultured Italians wince at the hoary stereotype of "macaroni and mandolins," pasta is a test of collective identity for a people who until very recently had only a vague sense of nationhood.

When an Italian comes home from a trip abroad the first question from relatives and friends is likely to be "How did you eat?" The usual response is a grimace. And Italian newcomers arriving in a foreign city will always ask "Where can I get a decent plate of pasta?" If they don't find it they will be uncomfortable.

From the oldest times cereals have been an essential element in the diet of people living in what today is Italy. The ancient Romans enjoyed a kind of porridge, and ordinary people in antiquity subsisted for long periods on bread and cheese, figs, or grapes, and ate meat or fish only on special occasions. Slices of bread toasted with olive oil and seasoned with salt, garlic, or some other spice are probably a very ancient snack; as *bruschetta* this concoction is still offered as an appetizer by many simple eating places in Italy, and lately by a few fancy ones too.

One always hears that spaghetti (literally, "little strings") was brought from Cathay to Italy toward the end of the thirteenth century. The story that Marco Polo was the pioneer of pasta is dubious, but there are reasons to assume that thin noodles, a Chinese invention, did first become known to the West in his city on the lagoon. (Thanks to its far-flung trade relations, Venice introduced into Italy other exotic food items as well, such as artichokes, and it imported the first coffee beans.) The taste for spaghetti and kindred starchy dishes spread quickly throughout the peninsula and Sicily. Old prints show Neapolitan urchins happily eating thin noodles with their bare, and probably unwashed, hands; what they are so visibly enjoying is called vermicelli ("little worms").

Italian inventiveness has through the centuries created uncounted pasta variations, in ever new shapes and with new garnishings. Fettuccine, ribbons of egg pasta, often served drenched in butter, is said to have been invented by the court cooks of Duke Ercole I d'Este as a culinary tribute to Lucrezia Borgia, the daughter of Pope Alexander VI, when she arrived in Ferrara in 1501 to become the wife of the duke's son Alfonso: The golden ribbons were meant to celebrate the blond hair of the beautiful bride (who at the age of twenty-one already had two marriages behind her). Pasta factories were among Italy's first industries.

Today pasta is on the table of many, maybe most, Italian households at least once a day; some have the national dish for both lunch and dinner. To a friend who is down on his luck or to a poor relative one says, "There will always be a plate of pasta for you in my house." Even Italian cats will, though disdainfully, eat spaghetti if they are hungry and there is nothing else for them.

Sit down in any eating place in Italy, whether a truckers' haven or a two-star restaurant, and you will be asked, "Pasta?" Some patrons deem it necessary to justify their choice of, say, a clear soup, pleading a delicate or upset stomach. But then, minestrone and most other soups also contain pasta elements. And whenever Italian restaurants offer fixed-price meals for foreigners, their so-called tourist menu lists pasta as a first course.

Most Italians need filling pasta for lunch because they have eaten nothing or very little since the night before. Italian breakfasts are notoriously skimpy; many people have just a cup of espresso after they get out of bed and follow it with a cappuccino and a *cornetto* (croissant) later in the morning. By the time they sit down for lunch at 1:00 or 2:00 P.M., they are ravenous and will devour a heaped plate of spaghetti or ravioli as a starter.

Such insistence on pasta makes the normal Italian meal top-heavy; there are few choices for hors d'oeuvres, and the appetite for, and interest in, entrées is blunted. Gourmets often accuse the Italian cuisine of offering few options outside its classic first course. Yet within the family of pasta dishes, the variety is endless. Each region has developed its own specialties: ravioli in the North, lasagne in "fat" Bologna, pappardelle with venison-based sauce in Tuscany, tortellini in Latium, macaroni and linguine in Naples, cannelloni in Sicily. Trimmings and seasonings range from greenish pesto—finely chopped basil, other herbs, and garlic mixed with cheese and pine nuts—in Genoa to clams in Naples and eggplant in Palermo. The town of Amatrice, just northeast of Rome, is famous for its *spaghetti all'amatriciana*, with bacon and pepper. In their search for gastronomic innovation to justify higher figures on the check, many restaurants are now dousing their pasta in whiskey or vodka, garnishing their dishes with salmon, or greasing them with Gorgonzola or Roquefort. Orthodox eaters will nevertheless request their spaghetti served just with fresh tomato pulp, the basic Neapolitan recipe.

Pasta should come al dente—somewhat chewy. Italians who order their national staple in eating places abroad always complain that what they get is *pasta scotta*—overcooked pasta, a mushy abomination. The Italian housewife or pasta cook often fishes out a length of spaghetti from the boiling pot and bites it to see whether it has reached the right consistency. Purists eat spaghetti, macaroni, or vermicelli with their fork alone, without needing a spoon to roll the strands into a neat bundle that they can shove into their mouth without unseemly sucking noises. Using a spoon with one's fork betrays fussiness; foreigners who do so are, however, regarded with indulgence. Cutting spaghetti with a knife is like putting catsup on a fruit salad.

Italians miss their pasta even if they are offered plenty of other food. After Rome was liberated from Nazi occupation in June 1944, the United States supplied K rations and other available provisions—but little pasta—for the hungry population. In the meantime the chief of the Allied provisional military administration of the Italian capital, Colonel Charles Poletti, an Italian-American, broadcast frequent pep talks, suggesting among other things that the Romans ought to use more soap than, according to him, they were doing. Soon a satiric couplet appeared on local house walls in the tradition of the Roman pasquinades:

> *Dear Colonel Poletti,*
> *Less prattle and more spaghetti!*

When shipments of hard wheat arrived at last, Italian pasta factories resumed turning out the national staple in pre-war quality. In 1967 Italy enacted Law No. 580, providing that pasta must be made only of durum wheat. Twenty-one years later the European Court of Justice in Luxembourg, invoking its supranational powers, voided Italy's genuine-pasta legislation as an illegal restraint of trade within the European Community. A West German noodle company had run afoul of Italian customs authorities when it tried to market its soft-wheat products in the land of pasta al dente; the firm took the case to the Luxembourg court and won. The ruling ordered Italy to allow the importation of German-made pasta but told Rome it might require that the soft-wheat base be clearly stated in labeling. *Corriere della Sera* of Milan disgustedly headlined its report of the Luxembourg verdict: "Now We Have the Invasion of Overcooked Spaghetti."

Northern Italians eat other cereal dishes as well: risottos in Milan and Turin; and polenta (cornmeal mush) in Venice, the Friuli region, and Bergamo. But only pasta is the truly national dish. The closest runner-up is pizza, a Neapolitan invention that in a few decades has won popularity all over Italy and far beyond the country's frontiers.

.   .   .

What was nourishment for humble people in antiquity has become a trendy symbol of modern informality and youthful merriment. Maybe Sophia Loren, as a *pizzaiola* (pizza cook) bowing deep over her counter to offer her generous décolletage to best effect in the film *The Gold of Naples*, has made a decisive contribution to the global fortunes of the dish. Pizza is deceptively simple; a fine Italian hand is needed to make it come out just right.

There is archaeological evidence that in the Greek colony Neapolis, the "New City" that today is Naples, ovens in which pizza may have been baked were burning as early as 500 B.C. Hot pies, the prototypes of pizza, were surely eaten in nearby Pompeii before that prosperous town and resort for wealthy Romans was smothered by the ashes of Mount Vesuvius in A.D. 79. Horace had a name for the popular dish, *laganum*, the Latin form of a Greek word. *Pizza* is apparently derived from the Latin *picea*, "of pitch," which may have referred to either the texture or the color of the well-baked cake.

Already in the Middle Ages the flat pies were apparently often garnished with cheese. Tomato pulp became a standard condiment when the "golden apples," as the plump fruits were first called, reached Naples from Peru by way of Mexico in the late sixteenth century. The oldest mention of "pizza" in literature is found in a cycle of fantastic stories in the Neapolitan dialect that Giambattista Basile wrote in the early seventeenth century, a late echo of *The Thousand and One Nights.*

The first commercial pizzeria is said to have been opened in Naples by one Antonio Testa in the Salita Santa Teresa, a sloping alley in the old town, early in the nineteenth century. Ferdinand II, king of the Two Sicilies, reportedly asked for the products of the new shop to be sent to the royal palace from time to time and eventually titled Testa's son *monsù,* the Neapolitan form of the French *monsieur*, which in the Naples of the Bourbon kings was almost like raising the *pizzaiolo* to knighthood. Still today, old Neapolitans will say of an exceptionally crisp pizza that it "seems made by Monsù Testa."

About half a century later, in 1889, another renowned Neapolitan pizza cook, Raffaele Esposito, was summoned to the royal residence to prepare the local culinary specialty for Queen Margherita, who was visiting the city with her husband (and cousin) King Umberto I. Esposito, eager to demonstrate his devotion to the queen and his loyalty to the new ruling dynasty, the Savoys, composed a pizza in the colors of unified Italy: green (basil leaves), white (mozzarella cheese), and red (tomato pulp). Testa's patriotic palette has been popular ever since as pizza Margherita. Unlike his Bourbon predecessor, the Savoy king did not confer any special honor on the pizza purveyor.

To Queen Margherita, a northerner with intellectual pretensions, the Neapolitan dish may have seemed an exotic experience, but for Neapolitans long before and after her time pizza has been a staple—often the only nourishment in their day. "A monument to misery" is how the writer and publisher Leo Longanesi characterized pizza.

The age-old poverty and forced frugality of the Neapolitan populace is epitomized by the famous institution of the *pizza a otto*, or eight-day pizza. It is the most elementary form of consumer credit: Eat now, pay a week later. The only collateral for such an interest-free edible loan is the goodwill of the *vicolo*, the slum alley. Hungry Neapolitan households have for generations weathered hard times by buying dinner from the pizzeria at the corner with payment deferred. The *pizzaiolo* was pretty sure he would get the money eventually. The promissory-note pizza was thought to belong to the realm of folklore—until the earthquake of November 1980 hit Naples and *pizza a otto* again helped poor slum dwellers survive the chaotic first few days after the disaster.

Esposito's tricolor recipe fit for a queen was one of the many embroideries on the canon of pizza making, which basically calls for just four elements: flour, leavening, water, and salt. Neapolitans are convinced that whatever housewives or even amateur gourmet cooks can get up in their home kitchens, not to mention the products of the modern frozen-food industry, will always be inferior to a pizza baked over a wood fire in the brick oven of a traditional pizzeria. Expert handling of the dough is the secret of any good pizza. Customarily the dough is allowed to "rest" and rise in a wooden trough overnight before it is thoroughly worked manually. It is shaped into a round cake with a strong rim and a thin center and put with a wooden spoon directly on the hot floor of the furnace, where it bakes for two to three minutes; poplar wood is said to be best for the fire. The condiments are quickly put on the pizza, and the end product should be served piping hot.

Mozzarella, now regularly a fifth pizza ingredient, should be made from the curd of buffalo milk and, like the dough, is best if worked by hand in the old-fashioned way. The buffalo in question is the domesticated Asian water buffalo, which is still being bred in the wet plains around Naples. The soft and moist curd of its milk is squeezed, pulled, and stretched until it becomes rubbery and satiny; the cheese tastes best when consumed within twenty-four hours. Nowadays almost all mozzarella marketed in Italy and practically any mozzarella available in other countries is produced industrially from bovine milk or even powdered milk. It is not the same as buffalo mozzarella; it is saltier and lacks the delicate flavor that Queen Margherita found on her pizza.

The Southern Italians who started emigrating in great numbers to the United States, Canada, Argentina, Brazil, and other countries in the Western Hemisphere in the days of Queen Margherita took their taste for pizza with them, and some of the newcomers were professional *pizzaioli*. In America the dish caught on and evolved, eventually breaking out of the Little Italies to become a broadly accepted snack, like hot dogs or bagels. Italians who today arrive for the first time in the United States are startled to see neon signs saying things like THE TOWER OF PIZZA and are baffled when they are offered a slice from a giant wheel of dough instead of the individual flat pie to which they are accustomed. (On the other hand, heaps of minipizzas as small as silver dollars, and sometimes nearly as hard, are carried around on platters at American cocktail parties.)

International pizza today comes in as many varieties as do sandwiches. In addition to mozzarella (or, in its place, ricotta), mushrooms, anchovies, shellfish and other seafood, herring, eggs, ham, bacon, green or black olives, eggplant, basil, oregano, garlic, capers, and slices of pineapple or banana are being lavished in kaleidoscopic patterns on the old pizza. In Japan rice flour is used for making pizza that is doused with catsup. Germans go in for pizza garnished with wurst and mustard.

In pizza's homeland, the ambience where it is eaten has changed too. Until well after World War II, *pizzerie* in Italy were mostly cramped little places with naked tables facing the oven. Walls were tiled or whitewashed, or maybe bore a clumsy fresco of the Bay of Naples with Mount Vesuvius in the background. Soldiers, still hungry after their barracks rations, used to be regulars in the evening hours. During the day young couples would drop in, and on Sunday afternoons clusters of maids, alone or with boyfriends, would chatter and giggle. Cheap wine out of ceramic jugs or beer was regularly drunk with pizza, but soft drinks as an accompaniment are now advancing.

While the *pizzerie* are still havens for people who cannot

or will not treat themselves to a full restaurant meal, many of these emporiums have been gussied up with wood paneling, plastic decor in bright colors, and garish lighting, and are staffed with young attendants in red or white uniforms. This is the Italian answer to the fast-food vogue. When one of these new luncheonettes was opened in Rome's center under the sign PIZZA POINT, it sounded like an echo of "hamburger joint." Even in Naples, quite a few of the three hundred *pizzerie* existing today use electric ovens and put industrial mozzarella on deep-frozen or precooked disks of dough. Old-timers have told me they've found better pizza in New York or San Francisco.

If the pizzeria is a piece of Naples in any corner of the world, the espresso machine has become a truly ubiquitous emblem of Italy. In Italy itself the smallest village has at least one, and in cities like Rome, Milan, and Naples many thousands are operated from early morning until late at night. One might conclude that Italians drink more coffee than anyone on earth, but the statistical truth is that Americans, Swedes, and Germans, among others, outrank Italians in per capita consumption of the beverage. Yet Italian espresso contains three to four times more caffeine than does the same quantity of American coffee.

A cup of espresso provides an instant injection of well-being and energy, a small rush that, alas, will last only twenty minutes or so. Espresso is a benign stimulant, a very soft drug. Darkly roasted, shiny, oily coffee beans are used, and a mixture of steam and water is forced by high pressure to extract the utmost strength from the finely ground beans. The word *espresso,* understood throughout the world today, means both that the potent brew is squeezed out of the grind and that it is done on the spot and quickly.

Although machine-made espresso is no older than the

twentieth century, coffee has been popular in Italy for hundreds of years. Like other good things, the beverage was introduced from Turkey by way of Venice, where coffeehouses already flourished around the middle of the seventeenth century. The upper Adriatic seaports and cities have remained the main coffee importing and roasting centers, and their famous old coffeehouses—the Caffè Florian on St. Mark's Square in Venice, the Caffè Pedrocchi in Padua, and the Caffè degli Specchi in Trieste—perpetuate an old tradition. Stendhal was a regular of the Pedrocchi.

The first espresso machines made their sibilant appearance around 1900. In 1907 an Italian patent was granted to Desiderio Pavoni of Milan for a contraption that through steam filtration could provide 150 cups of coffee an hour. Teresio Arduino in 1909 introduced his Victoria Arduino machine with a capacity of 1,000 cups per hour. These and similar early espresso *apparati* were upright metal urns, not unlike the Russian samovar, with gauges and handles that allowed boiling water and steam to be channeled to individual spigots equipped with filters that could be rapidly detached for replacement of the grinds. Improved models came with special pipes to inject steam into milk, both to heat it and to make it frothy for cappuccino.

The Victoria Arduino machine was surmounted by an eagle and became a beloved symbol of the espresso subculture. Installed in coffee bars all over Italy and in similar shops in Italian neighborhoods of cities in North and South America, such antiques are still in use, and other espresso bars have lately, in a nostalgic mood, ordered handcrafted replicas of the original model.

After World War II the upright urns were replaced by a new generation of low-slung espresso machines that looked like precision tools—lathes, maybe, or computers. The principle of filtering a mixture of hot water and steam under high pressure through coffee grinds remained unchanged, however.

The sight of the gleaming espresso machine with its dials, handles, tubes, and spigots, and the characteristic noise of hissing steam, the thump of filters being emptied and, with new loads, quickly put back in place, and the trickling of coffee from the spouts into the cups is as invigorating to Italians as is the aromatic brew itself. Operating a big unit in an espresso bar that may serve 10,000 cups a day requires the deftness and stamina of a virtuoso—that fine Italian hand again—to make sure the optimum mix of steam and water goes to the right spigots, the sensitive grinds are not overheated, and excessive filtering that would result in unpleasant bitterness is avoided. Countermen in smaller places cannot concentrate on the espresso machine alone; they must also serve other drinks, pastry, rolls, and snacks, not to mention maintain the flow of gossip and banter with regulars, some of them even patrons, that is an essential part of the espresso atmosphere.

Coffee bars all over Italy are as a rule sparkling with chromium, bright marble, clear colors, and garish neon lighting, and they are very clean. They represent the environment that most Italians like best—modernity, rational design, brilliant light, cheerfulness, loud voices, noncommittal badinage, and quick action. Italians do not usually feel comfortable in an English pub with its musty coziness, or in the heavy conviviality of a German beer hall, and they usually complain about the poor quality of coffee and the high consumption of alcohol in French cafés. Much of the coffee in Italy is drunk standing up at an espresso counter. One does not linger: five minutes for a cup is enough, ten minutes ample. Most espresso bars offer a wide range of refreshments besides coffee—soft drinks, beer, hard liquor, sandwiches, hamburgers, small pizzas, and gelato. However, coffee purists shun places where warm snacks are also served because the toasting or cooking odors spoil the heavenly smell of their nectar.

Many customers will not just order an espresso but add

specifications: *ristretto* (short and dense), *lungo* (diluted), *al vetro* (in a glass instead of in the customary ceramic cup), *macchiato* ("spotted" with a drop of hot or cold milk), *freddo* (iced, especially in summer), *corretto* (with a shot of brandy or grappa), or *senza schiuma* (without the ring of foam that most people like). If patrons do not sugar their coffee themselves, the counterman will ask them how sweet they want it, or whether they spurn sugar (*amaro*, bitter).

The operator of the espresso machine is called the *barista*, a term derived from the word *bar*, which the Italians long ago adopted from English. The *barista* is most often a young man who, in immaculate white, goes through the automatic motions of his trade and has the quick reflexes of a professional driver. He can field orders that half a dozen patrons shout at him at the same time, slam cups under the spouts of his machine, offer his contribution to a loud debate on the soccer championship, and still wink at a woman customer whose appearances have lately become frequent. Many Italians turn up at their favorite espresso bar three or four times every day, or are regulars at more than one such place—one around the corner from their business or office, another near their home, and maybe a third where they go on Sundays to discuss the soccer game they have just been watching on television. Scores of Italians who live abroad have told me that among the things they miss most is the possibility of dashing out of their home or place of work to a coffee bar for a quick cup of real espresso and a group of friendly faces.

In Italy itself some shops are especially renowned for the quality of their coffee. Local skills may have something to do with such excellence, but the main reason is believed to be the special properties of the water. Step into any espresso bar in Naples—under the central Galleria, in the warren of the Spanish Quarter, on the waterfront, or around the railroad terminal—and the counterman will take a small cup, preheated in a bath of warm water, put it under a spigot of his machine, let plenty of steam pass through the freshly deep-roasted and ground coffee, and put before you a tiny quantity of dark, dense liquid with a thin wreath of brown foam at the top. Instant euphoria!

In Rome the coffee bars around the Pantheon are reputed to serve the best espresso and cappuccino because they are using the Aqua Virgo (Virgin Water). This water flows out of faucets and fountains in the city's core from an often-repaired and still functioning aqueduct that M. Vipsanius Agrippa, general and son-in-law of Emperor Augustus, built. According to the legend, a maiden discovered a clear spring in the hills east of Rome and led thirsty legionnaires to the site. The "virgin's water" was then harnessed, and Agrippa in 19 B.C. had it funneled through a ten-mile conduit to Rome to supply the Pantheon complex, including the famous circular temple and a system of baths, that his architects had erected ten years earlier. (The soft water is said also to be unequaled for cooking pasta.)

In Italian restaurants espresso usually completes a meal, coming after dessert or substituting for it. Many establishments operate their own machines, others send out to a nearby coffee bar if patrons order espresso. Whenever visitors are invited to a private home in Italy, they are likely to be offered Aunt Silvia's or Grandma Giovanna's famous espresso. They will be expected to smack their lips and proclaim it infinitely superior to the products of any coffee bar. Maybe it is, maybe not. Appliance and hardware stores do carry many newfangled models of espresso makers for the home, but the old, simple *macchinetta napoletana* (little Neapolitan machine)—comprising a metal container in which water is boiled and steam rises, a compartment in which the ground coffee is placed, and a filter through which the espresso oozes into a chamber, to be poured out through a spout—remains unsurpassed.

Gelato, an added money-maker for many coffee bars today, has in its various forms been an Italian delight for a long time and has lately won legions of new aficionados in America who prefer it to industrially made ice cream.

In ancient Rome, rich epicures had snow brought in baskets from the high mountains of the country's interior to cool their drinks and fruits, and probably also to make some kinds of sherbets, but the real art of concocting sweet, icy drinks (and perhaps producing semisolid sweet and cold confections) was refined by Arabs, Persians, and Turks, whose Moslem religion forbade alcohol. The Sicilians, who were under Arab rule from the ninth to the eleventh century, were affected in their tastes by the sweet tooth of their Moslem masters and learned from them to turn out cold delicacies, often enriched with such local goodies as almonds and dried grapes. Sicilians are to this day the wizards of elaborate gelato, and of even more complex specialties such as *cassata.*

Soft, creamy gelato seems to have first been made in Italy in the seventeenth century. By the end of the eighteenth century, Italian *gelatai* (gelato vendors) had established themselves in various European cities, and in Paris, especially, Italian ices became the rage. *Gelatai* were among the founders of small Italian colonies in various places on the continent, and ever since their arrival Italians who have settled in other European countries, or who periodically arrive, with the swallows, in the warm season, have supplied Europeans with cold comfort during their more or less short summers.

For at least three thousand years, the Apennine Peninsula and Sicily have shared in the ancient Mediterranean and Middle Eastern wine civilization, already present in the Book of Genesis. The Romans learned viticulture from the Etruscans, whose fondness for carousing is attested to by the wall paintings in their burial chambers, and from the Greeks. In classical Rome Horace praised the Falernian vintages from Campania, while soldiers and even slaves were given less select wine with their food rations. In Italy wine has always been drunk for nourishment (it does, after all, provide calories and traces of minerals) as well as for pleasure.

At present, depending on the weather and the vagaries of the statistics, Italy is in some years just ahead of France or just behind as world leader in wine production. It also reports one of the highest per capita rates of wine consumption, although the quantity, which in the mid-1980s was still a remarkable 23 gallons annually for every man, woman, and child, is continually diminishing. Drunkenness in public places can nevertheless be observed in Italy much less frequently than in, say, Britain or the Soviet Union. With the new Italian affluence, it has become fashionable to drink imported hard liquor, and the nation has become one of the major markets for Scotch whiskeys.

The once ubiquitous wine flask, its bottom and belly covered with plaited straw to protect it from breakage (such flasks were also used for olive oil), has become a rarity. Apparent reappearances today are likely to be faked: What looks like straw is plastic. At the same time, Italians have become increasingly discriminating with regard to their country's vintages.

Connoisseurs from abroad, especially if they are French, may still dismiss most Italian wines as mediocre (with a few exceptions—some Barolos from Piedmont, Soaves from Verona, Valpolicelli from Venetia, some Chiantis, and perhaps white Capri), even though tankers full of heavy Apulian wine have been sailing, without much ado since World War II, to Southern France, where the *vino primitivo* (coarse wine) has been used to reinforce local vintages. Until recently such apparent indifference to wine quality was shared by Italians themselves; patrons in most *trattorie*, and even some of the more pretentious restaurants, would routinely be asked by the waiter, often before they had had a chance to order their meal, "White or red [wine]?" Now even simple eating places will tell their guests where the wine comes from and offer a few bottled vintages. Many wine dealers have taken to calling their shops *enoteche* (a neologism suggesting a library with bottles instead of books on its shelves) and displaying hundreds of labels. Wineries have generally upgraded their products and developed new vintages. There has been some criminal doctoring too: In 1986 at least twenty-five Italians died from poisoning by wine spiked with methanol (methyl alcohol) to make it more potent. But despite such scandals, to be a vintner in Italy today is a glamorous profession, or it can be a hobby with snob cachet. Some practitioners of the age-old art of winemaking now turn out hundreds of thousands of bottles with fancy labels; others produce just a few thousand bottles that they painstakingly number and sign—designer vintages.

In just a few heady years the Italian wine industry has won new markets abroad, especially in the United States. Whereas once only the homey straw flasks with Chianti and some bottled Sicilian wines could be found in Little Italies and in Italian restaurants, a wide range of vintages from all regions of Italy are now sold in American liquor stores. (One anecdote has it that the owner of a winery near Modena showed a visitor three huge vats filled with Lambrusco, the sparkling red wine that should have a bouquet evocative of violets; the containers were labeled "Sweet," "Dry," and "America"—the plonk was destined for export to the United States.) In fact, the new American interest in Italian vintages is generally credited as a factor in changing the United States' perception of Italy—it is now seen as a country where people know how to get the best out of life.

That changed perception can also be appreciated in the

recent fortunes of Italian cuisine. Dishes that had for generations been commonplace in Italian homes, like risotto with mushrooms or spaghetti with clams, have made their appearance in deluxe restaurants abroad, while Italian cookbooks have started to crowd the shelves of American bookstores. The "Mediterranean diet"—lots of pasta, olive oil, little meat, and plenty of vegetables and fruits—has been touted by nutritionists in more "advanced" countries (even as the consumption of meat, butter, and sugar has been rising in Italy). For some years now international marathon runners have been filling up on pasta, and in 1988 Britain's Royal Army substituted spaghetti in plastic bags for the traditional cans of meat and beans as its field and combat rations.

Key to the exportation and international popularity of Italian gastronomy have been well-heeled Italian tourists—familiar characters everywhere, always asking for pasta, wine, and espresso; impressing, amusing, and occasionally annoying the natives with their panache, their cheerfulness, the stylishness of their women, their readiness to spend money in order to cut a fine figure (*far buona figura*, an important Italian phrase and concept).

Not so elegantly, but with no less aplomb, other Italians have been making money all over the world as contractors—all the while also hankering for pasta, wine, and espresso. Having profited and gathered experience at home through reconstruction work—largely financed by the Marshall Plan—after the ravages of World War II, they branched out into other countries and continents, building dams and roads in Africa and submitting winning bids for large-scale projects in distant places. Since antiquity, Italians have excelled in construction work—the flagstones of Roman roads are still found from Britain to Morocco to the Black Sea, and ruins of ancient triumphal arches, aqueducts, and amphitheaters from Spain to the Rhine, from the Danube to the Middle East, speak not only of past grandeur but also of architectural and engineering mastery. By volume of business, Italian contracting firms are today in the world's vanguard.

I think of such Italian builders and contractors, helping to spread the customs and manners of their home country, when I recall a visit to Iran during the last months of the shah's rule. Driving across a barren, remote stretch of countryside, I was startled to notice a road sign reading ESPRESSO. I followed the sign and reached a rudimentary coffee bar run by a camp follower for an Italian oil-drilling crew. And there it stood: a late-model coffee machine in the near desert—maybe Marco Polo had passed through here seven hundred years earlier?—marking an outpost of that expanding realm of Italianate tastes, the espresso empire.

3.
A Knack
for Survival

More than four centuries ago, Benvenuto Cellini, that master goldsmith, sculptor, hothead, adventurer, sensualist, braggart, and quintessential Renaissance man, barely escaped from yet another hair-raising scrape in which he'd risked being robbed and perhaps murdered. Right afterward, he tells in his *Life*, he sat down to a merry supper with friends, "laughing over those great blows that Fortune strikes, for good as well as evil, and which, whenever they don't hit the mark, are just the same as though they had never happened."

Cellini's sanguine philosophy that adversity has to be laughed off and that the worst does not always come to pass still distinguishes the Italian character. With their gift for snapping back after catastrophe and for making do with whatever is at hand, the inhabitants of Italy have outlived the fall of the Roman Empire; barbarian invasions; raids by Saracens, Normans, and Turks; incessant wars; communal strife; pestilences and floods; famines and earthquakes—and come out all right again and again, their way of life and their closely knit family structure intact.

One evening in the winter of 1945–46, I took an English journalist friend, Alexander Clifford, to Alfredo's in Rome, then still in its original premises on the Via della Scrofa. The place was crowded with local people, who all appeared to be in high spirits. Alfredo di Lelio, the owner, personally served us his famous fettuccine, using the gold-plated fork and spoon that he said Douglas Fairbanks and Mary Pickford had given him in the 1930s. The fettuccine came with double portions of butter and was followed by tender artichokes, succulent lamb, and a high-calorie *zuppa inglese*. Clifford, who had been a war correspondent and had just arrived from a dark, hungry, and shivering London, licked the whipped cream from his dessert fork, looked around the room while drinking up the amber Frascati wine before sipping his strong coffee, and asked, "Now, who has won the war?"

Italy, like Britain, had gone through terrifying years— the devastating Allied air raids on industrial centers, railroad hubs, seaports, and eventually on Rome; the naval bombardment of Genoa; the loss of a major part of its merchant fleet and the disaster of the warships sunk in the harbor of Taranto by torpedo-equipped planes; hundreds of thousands of soldiers in prison camps, if not dead; the battles from Sicily to the Po River, with many civilian casualties and innumerable bridges blown up and buildings destroyed; atrocious Nazi reprisals for acts of sabotage and resistance. When the country recovered from World War II with surprising speed, foreigners voiced admiration for the "Italian miracle."

The miracle of Alfredo's fettuccine had been achieved thanks to a flourishing black market that was able to supply high-grade flour stolen from American Liberty ships, and fresh eggs, butter, meat, cream, and Brazilian coffee beans from a variety of sources. The black market was also keeping millions alive who could not afford to dine at Alfredo's. It was operating outside the official rationing system, was completely illegal and at times even criminal, but was widely tolerated and singularly efficient—a convincing demonstration of the Italian talent for survival.

We were halfway through our meal when two men entered the restaurant; the younger one started singing popular Roman and Neapolitan tunes, accompanied on the violin by his elderly companion. After the plate had gone around, the pair treated the diners to a last number, a song often heard in those days:

Chi ha avuto, avuto, avuto	Some have got, got, got
Chi ha dato, dato, dato	Others have given,
Scordiamoci il passato . . .	given, given
	Let's forget the past . . .

In the decades since that night at Alfredo's, the national knack for survival has enabled the Italians—a large part of them, at any rate—to thrive despite a sclerotic bureaucracy, a rapid succession of governments, continual strikes, a brittle infrastructure, and the terrorism of the Red Brigades. The country's overall performance in the 1970s and 1980s, though not so dramatic as the postwar "miracle" of Japan, was no less astonishing in view of the odds. Like the other losers of World War II, the former junior partner of the Axis found itself a generation later in the select club of the world's foremost industrial powers, a country discussing, among other weighty themes, what could be done to prop up the sickly U.S. dollar.

Many Italians were surprised and incredulous when told that their economy was abreast of Britain's and France's, and possibly had even surpassed one or both. Statistical indicators did not tell the whole story. Per capita incomes were much higher in Switzerland and Sweden, but if Northern Italy alone had been in the running, it would have been recognized as one of the most prosperous and dynamic areas in Europe, whereas much of the Mezzogiorno had Third World aspects and pulled down the statistics for Italy as a whole.

The international success of Italy's economy and creativity was unplanned. Markets, customers, and audiences throughout the world were not conquered by disciplined legions of salesmen and propagandists that a Roman economic and cultural empire might have ordered to march out on strategic roads; nor was there a Vatican of Italian *dolce vita* sending missionaries to the corners of the earth to convert remote peoples to its creed. There was nothing that could be compared with the aggressive export strategy of Japan's Ministry of International Trade and Industry.

The businessmen, financiers, movie directors, restaurant chefs, pizza cooks, couturiers, designers, wine shippers, and gelato makers who won foreigners over to their products and services had, unlike their Japanese counterparts, received scant if any help and encouragement from their home authorities. In Italy itself anyone who has a new idea, who tries to leave the well-trodden paths and wants to set up a novel enterprise, must ignore or circumvent the thickets of laws and regulations that postwar Italy has been cultivating as if to make sure all personal initiative is thwarted, and moreover must cope with the most ramshackle of infrastructures.

The Italian bureaucratic machineries—both public and private—are as enervating as the sirocco wind that frequently dumps Sahara sand on the country, and as baroque as a dilapidated Neapolitan palazzo. The nation's battered railroads are almost always late. Italian mails are outrageously unreliable and the telephones capricious and expensive. Local banks need a month to clear a check written elsewhere in the same country. Cities from Turin to Palermo are plagued by perpetual traffic jams; in Naples they are as vicious as those in Lagos, Nigeria. To top it all, Italy has for decades held the world record in numbers of working hours lost through strikes, and its public services are chronically disrupted by labor conflicts.

Add to this an all-pervasive political patronage system, proverbially weak and unstable governments, widespread corruption as evidenced by an unending chain of scandals, and the sinister power of the Mafia, and one can see how an entrepreneur requires uncommon energy, resourcefulness, and courage, besides a good deal of cynicism, to thrive in Italy. These are, it is true, qualities that Italians have honed through the ages. And they may be equally useful to someone trying today to establish a foothold in duller countries.

An outstanding industrialist and financier, Carlo De Benedetti, describes Italy as schizophrenic—one aspect of its split personality is its cumbersome government machinery, the other the dynamism of its private business. Each nation on earth, to be sure, groans under its own burden of bureaucrats, and Italians who ought to know will tell you that the red tape in any leading democracy is at times no less daunting than are the mechanisms of repression in dictatorships or the incompetence, greed, and arrogance of the panjandrums in newly independent countries. But Italians are also justifiably convinced that they are shackled by the most inept state apparatus of any large industrial society outside the Communist orbit—by administrative structures and practices far less efficient than those in the United States, Japan, West Germany, Britain, and France. An Italian premier, Giovanni Goria, addressing the editors in chief of leading newsmagazines in various countries, candidly admitted, "Our bureaucracy is slow, costly, useless. . . . Italy is not a modern nation," at least, he added, not outside its well-run industrial plants.

Because of the long and checkered history of Italy, many traditions, inveterate habits, and ingrained attitudes are invisibly stifling the atmosphere of offices that may today be air-conditioned and equipped with state-of-the-art electronic gadgetry. The legalism of ancient Rome; the Byzantine mania for impressive titles and procedural flourishes; the majestic slowness and hierarchical paternalism of the Holy See; the quirks of French, Spanish, and Austrian rulers; and the insolence of homegrown despots and oligarchies up and down the peninsula and in the islands all are strands in the bureaucratic webs of present-day Italy.

Distaste for an officialdom that for hundreds of years has served alien masters or—in the former States of the Church—a self-centered and bumbling theocracy is innate in most Italians; in contrast, many of the nation's bureaucrats betray something like distrust if not contempt for the citizenry. Anyone who is forced to deal with the drab machinery of the Italian state, if only at the post office, ends up in a bad mood. One is kept waiting in long lines, snarled at, and often sent away empty-handed; underlings are usually surly or outright rude, higher-ups inaccessible.

Foreign tourists who have the none-too-rare misfortune of discovering that their wallet has been lifted by a pickpocket on a crowded bus, or of having their handbag snatched by a youngster on a motor scooter, and who then go to the police station to report what has happened, are in for a shock. They will be asked to supply the place and date of their birth, the name of their father and maybe also the maiden name of their mother (still alive? dead?), all of which will be laboriously recorded; they will also be questioned about what they are doing in Italy anyway, and may get the feeling of being vaguely considered suspects. Eventually the *brigadiere* (sergeant) who has conducted the interrogation will nonchalantly put the new file on top of a high stack of similar ones.

The majority of Italian administrators, judges, police officers, and other public functionaries are today being recruited from the nation's South, where feudal patterns of life die hard. All too often southerners raised in modest circumstances who with great efforts and thanks to intricate maneuvers conquer the tiniest crumb of official power will by instinct regard the ordinary citizen as a subject who must be made to feel the weight of authority, ought to show proper respect to its representatives, and had better learn to be humble and patient. The cliché of the always good-natured Italian (whose embodiments can be met often enough) does not normally apply to the sunny country's morose public employees.

Many of the higher positions in the bureaucratic hierarchy require a law degree, and as far as that qualification is concerned Southern Italy is able to fill any demand. Families in the Mezzogiorno who can afford college education for their children will most often urge them to attend law school as a stepping-stone toward a decorous post in the state apparatus. Comparatively few young people from Northern Italy (other than southern immigrants or their offspring) seek government employment. Southerners are thus usually left to compete with one another in the scramble to get on the public payroll.

Every so often the newspapers report on the contests for vacant state, regional, or municipal jobs that have to be held, at least pro forma, to comply with the law; they sound like the New York Marathon. For 411 subaltern posts in the city administration of Messina, 50,450 candidates apply; tests to narrow down the field to 5 competitors for each opening take place during three weeks; the finals to select the winners among the remaining 2,055 take another week; the results won't be known for months. For, say, a handful of vacancies in the sanitation department in Catanzaro or for the police in Cagliari, thousands of applicants will turn up. Sometimes the throng of job seekers is so vast that the authorities rent the local stadium for the elimination quizzes.

Before being admitted to the tests all candidates will have filled out lengthy questionnaires and submitted many pieces of paper—birth and residence certificates, school reports, police statements that they have never had any trouble with the law, and, for the men, attestations that they have fulfilled their military obligations. Some applicants won't mention that they have a degree in law or the humanities when they put in for a street cleaner's or gravedigger's job; they reckon that once they are hired they will eventually worm into some bureaucratic niche with its own desk on the strength of their academic education and, much more important, with the backing of powerful sponsors. No wonder that from time to time the nation learns again, without surprise, that of the thousands of employees in the sanitation departments of Naples or Palermo only a couple of hundred are actually in the streets on any given day, while the others may be found in the offices and corridors of city departments, or simply have better things to do and will show up only to collect their pay.

Publications containing nothing but information on forthcoming contests for civil service and other official positions, and on the conditions for participating in them, are prominently displayed by virtually every newsstand from Rome southward. One of these sheets, a fortnightly, carries the lapidary name *Il Posto*; the Italian word conveys a sense of job security even though "the post" may be a lowly one. Not only thousands of job hunters in their twenties and thirties but also the parents and girlfriends or boyfriends of unemployed young people buy every issue of *Il Posto*: "Instead of watching television and listening to rock music all day, why don't you put in for one of those jobs in the Bari city hall? You have nothing to lose, and, who knows, you may win!"

Thousands of young Italians, above all in the South, are listed as applicants in half a dozen employment contests at the same time. To bone up for the tests, many candidates buy or borrow manuals with sample questions and answers: Name three outstanding Italian poets! (Dante, Ariosto, and Leopardi will do.) Write three sentences describing the tasks of the national Parliament! What does the expression *air pollution* mean? Multiply 849 by 63! The quizzes usually have little to do with the job at stake, but the idea is that a gravedigger too should possess a minimum of intelligence and knowledge.

In nearly every contest a few competitors seem to know beforehand what they will be asked, and everybody is convinced that the quizzes are an empty rite, a tedious and costly charade that has to be played out even though the winners are actually picked under ancient rules of influence and patronage. Thus, as job seekers file their birth certificates and school reports, their relatives and friends are enlisting the help of powerful personages—politicians, generals, prelates of the church, maybe mafiosi—directly or through friends of friends. Who will deny a *raccomandazione*, a few lines of introduction and character reference, to a voter whose daughter aspires to a high-school teacher's job in Frosinone? Leaders of political parties and ministers in the government keep platoons of secretaries busy writing such letters. The trouble is that the tens of thousands of such "recommendations" always being showered on the organizers of job contests cancel one another out.

A labor leader, Daniele Mengoni, recalls that when he, earlier in his career, was chief of the personnel department of the prime minister's office, five messenger jobs were to be filled in the usual competitive process; he received fifty-six letters recommending individual candidates—all signed by the prime minister. A sponsor who really wants to get results will at the least have to make a personal follow-up telephone call, indicating readiness to trade favor for favor.

Periodically some newspaper crusader or would-be reformer denounces the plague of "recommendations" and fails to stir up public outrage. After all, virtually everybody has at least a cousin who got hired by the national health service, the Carabinieri Corps, or the state broadcasting system through the intervention of an archbishop, a member of Parliament, or some other power broker. Remo Gaspari, a Christian Democratic politician who by diligent and unstinting patronage over many years built a formidable voting machine in his native Abruzzi region and served as a minister in a number of national governments, told an interviewer that he didn't get jobs for any protégés of his; all he did, he explained, was to "reassure people, for instance by informing a candidate in some job competition of the favorable outcome of the tests, possibly a minute before the official announcement." It should be noted that the several government departments that Gaspari headed during his long service in public life included the Ministry of Bureaucratic Reform.

Not all contests for state jobs are rigged. A friend of mine who lived in the United States for years and earned a master's degree in history from New York University applied for a post as an English teacher at a high school in a town near Venice after returning home. She was first hired on a temporary basis and after a few years was admitted to a competition for a tenured position as a language teacher in the school system. In a written test she had to produce an essay on the American Revolution, and in an oral examination a full year later she was asked questions about Italian history from antiquity to the present. "I passed and won the job," she told me, "without any *raccomandazione* but with plenty of suspense and cramming for the orals—all for 1,100,000 lire a month [about $900 at the time]."

Private corporations also test job applicants, but far fewer candidates turn up for these tests than for the contests for public employment, even though the pay at stake is considerably higher. Every weekend the country's newspapers are filled with advertisements whereby industrial firms search for graduates from technical colleges, systems analysts, accountants, and other specialists. Most of those who answer the want ads are eliminated in the screening process because they lack the necessary qualifications. A multinational computer firm looking for technical personnel in Milan quizzed thirty applicants, all recent graduates from polytechnic colleges; when they were asked the comparatively simple question How does a transistor work? only one of them gave a satisfactory answer. She was immediately hired. Other industrial companies have similar experiences: In a country where almost every young person who carries a briefcase is styled a *dottore* (doctor), marketable advanced skills are rare. A *dottore* may have a degree in medicine, law, or psychology or may be a graduate from any one of scores of other academic courses. The title means very little.

Only in the mid-1980s did Italy's bloated system of higher education attempt to overcome the national crisis that had started with the European student rebellions of 1968. From France, academic unrest spilled quickly into Italy that year, leading to rioting, sit-ins, and violent protests. Partly as a result, the Italian Parliament in 1969 passed legislation aimed at wiping out social-class distinctions in education: It permitted any high-school graduate to go on to any state college or university without an entrance exam. The consequence was an academic explosion. Whereas there were 270,000 university students in Italy in 1960, their number a quarter of a century later had quadrupled.

A good deal of Italy's school violence in the late 1960s occurred in the graffiti-covered high schools, but the effects were soon felt in the universities too. Teenage student radicals fought for years for what was to become a system of virtually automatic passing grades. Militants engaged in a sociocultural revolution, so the ultraleft argument went, should not be bothered with *nozionismo*, the accumulation of such allegedly useless knowledge as the dates of the battle of Cannae or Waterloo or the formula for determining the area of a triangle. In numerous circulars after 1968, the government's education authorities directed high-school teachers to take into consideration the entire personality, intellectual commitment, and mental process of a student, not just his or her performance on a specific test. This was an implicit rejection of *nozionismo*, and it encouraged students to cultivate the old Italian penchant for rhetoric—if you don't know the correct answer to a question, keep talking, talking; maybe you will convince the examiner that you are smart.

The "maturity examination," the once-dreaded set of tests for high-school graduation, became a mere formality, and the increasingly large proportion of students who easily sailed through it went on to institutions of higher learning. Overcrowding strained all academic facilities. In the mid-1980s the State University of Rome, which carries the historic name La Sapienza (Wisdom), had an enrollment of 160,000. Some professors lectured to audiences of more than 1,000. Rome's medical school was supposed to train 23,000 students concurrently; many of them never made it to the dissecting table during exercises. To secure a library seat, students had to line up early. Most of the 160,000 enrolled in La Sapienza found it wise to show up only for tests, for which they had prepared at home, learning by rote every word in mimeographed aids that provided an extra income to university teachers. Things were not very different in other college towns in the country.

Only one-third of all students who enroll in Italian institutions of higher learning ever graduate; the other two-thirds remain "professional students," eventually dropping out to look for some job or swell the unemployment statistics. Nevertheless, there are legions of fresh *dottori* every year, especially doctors of law and of economy and commerce (a catchall degree). Prospective employers evaluate diplomas the way wine connoisseurs read the labels of Chianti or Bordeaux vintages: Any degree granted before 1968 is acceptable, and some issued from the mid-1980s on are passable too, because academic requirements have been tightened again. On the other hand, parchments attesting that a physician, lawyer, or other *dottore* was studying and taking exams in the decade and a half that followed 1968 are accorded a low rating.

The temporary decline in academic standards caused Italy—which had produced Galileo, Volta, Marconi, and Fermi—to fall back in the sciences. The extent to which research suffered can be deduced from the small number of new Italian patents registered abroad: Only 1.0 percent of all patents granted in the United States are Italian, against a Japanese share of 7.5 percent. In Europe, 26.0 percent of all registered patents are American, 23.6 percent German, 15.0 percent Japanese, and 3.1 percent Italian. Many Italian pharmaceutical, chemical, and other companies pay licensing fees to foreign patent owners because they are using technical processes and designs that were developed abroad.

Research and development have lately been stepped up in Italy in an effort to catch up with advanced technology, but institutions of higher learning keep churning out *dottori* in law, philosophy, political science, and economy and commerce, especially in the Mezzogiorno. All too many of them expect the taxpayers to support them for the rest of their lives, as do many thousands of new high-school graduates who look for public employment right away.

Some of the innumerable southerners who seek posts in the state administration apply for admission to job contests in Northern Italy, where a real demand for mail and railroad employees, teachers, and other public personnel exists. Yet many of those who—thanks usually to the interventions of influential personages—succeed won't stay long in the North.

After a year or so they will petition their superiors for transfer to their hometowns in Calabria or Sicily to rejoin their families (aged parents and unmarried sisters left behind, or spouses acquired during a vacation and already producing and raising children). There is no legal provision entitling Italian state employees to serve where they were born, grew up, or have a family, yet people on the public payroll regard it as their right to be sent back to their province or even their town of origin. Their requests to be moved will be reinforced by new avalanches of "recommendations" from sponsors old and new. "To deal with those demands has in some notoriously disorganized branches of the government services, like the mails, the railroads, and the schools, become a predominant task," says Massimo Severo Giannini, who also once served as minister of bureaucratic reform. Railroad workers have staged strikes to win official recognition of their claims to be retransferred to their hometowns.

The results of all these maneuvers are many post offices in the South populated by staffs far too large for what little mail there is to sort and distribute, southern schools with more teachers than students, and railroad stations that see only a few local trains passing through every day staffed by half a dozen signalmen and another half a dozen ticket agents. And all the while, business executives in the North keep complaining that important letters are being delayed or lost, only to be told, alas, their post office is shorthanded right now but don't worry, another contest for selecting new employees will be held soon.

With 200,000 transfer petitions from teachers pending at any time, 100,000 from postal employees, and 20,000 from railroad workers, as well as many more from other government personnel, it looks as if a major—maybe the main—task of Italy's awesome bureaucratic machinery is to administer itself. Nobody knows even approximately how many people the Italian taxpayer has to maintain—estimates run to at least 4 million, or one out of every five or six Italian wage earners. Yet the nation that on paper seems overadministered is suffering, as leading Italians point out almost every day, from deplorable public services. Whenever the state television devotes a few minutes to the country's bureaucracy, it shows some post office or tax center, the camera zooming over long lines or thick clusters of people—video shorthand for the frustrations of ordinary citizens who have to deal with a state apparatus that seems sadistic but is only inept. While the residents of Communist countries are all the time lining up to secure a few oranges, sausages, or stockings because the central planners are incapable of foreseeing and fulfilling consumer needs, Italians, who don't have to worry about food or apparel, stand in line for many hours to pay or receive money or to trade pieces of paper with the authorities.

Youngsters are initiated to the rites of the Italian *fila* (line) when they line up during long and noisy hours for college registration or induction into the armed forces. They will have to learn patience and cunning to survive the innumerable lines in which they will be wasting time over the rest of their lives—lines for paying fees, utility bills, and taxes; for getting the many official certificates they will then have to hand to other bureaucrats after waiting in other lines; for cashing checks or withdrawing money from their bank accounts; for buying railroad tickets or checking in at airports; for sending registered letters, getting building permits or business licenses, seeing a doctor or being admitted to a hospital; and once retired, for collecting their monthly pensions. Even the dead have to wait, because many big-city cemeteries are overcrowded and a *raccomandazione* is needed to get a burial plot weeks or even months after a person's demise.

Lining up comes harder to Italians, a vivacious and undisciplined people, than it does, for instance, to Britons or

Germans. Watch any bus stop: At rush hour there is a throng, and everybody pushes and shoves to get in before passengers waiting to get off have a chance. This is, with little variation, the normal scene from San Remo in the northwest to Syracuse in Sicily's southeast. In Valletta, the capital of Malta, just 60 miles from Syracuse, people form orderly lines at bus stops the way it is done in London. The Maltese are ethnically and culturally close to the Sicilians, but their island was a British colony and naval base for a century and a half.

Lately lines have been proliferating in Italy, for its people too have to learn, however reluctantly, to stand in line and wait their turn instead of crowding and bickering. Yet someone in every post office or bank will always jockey for a better position, try to outflank others in line, or brazenly rush forward to the counter and barge in on whatever business is being transacted to ask "just a quick question" or breathlessly announce an emergency. The other people in the line will protest loudly, and a shouting argument may ensue, causing everybody to waste additional time. At toll plazas along the highways some car will inevitably surge from behind to squeeze into the front of the line.

The victims of the *fila* are not only the applicants, who have to spend hours lining up in understaffed offices, but also the few employees behind the windows or counters, who soon become gruff and irritable. If one of them has to take a break for a couple of minutes, there is exasperated muttering among the people outside. Small wonder that some functionaries seem to take delight in telling a customer that his postal order is improperly filled in and cannot be accepted, that her appeal against the income tax assessment has to be presented on the floor above, or that the duplicate of a driver's license lost or stolen a year ago still isn't ready. The nasty mood in many offices intended to serve the public is a piece of Italy that tourists usually don't see.

Many foreigners who settle in the country because they like the climate, the art, the food, and the jovial people never get around to registering as they should after staying for three months, when they can no longer claim to be tourists. They are supposed to report to the *questura*, the police headquarters in cities and major towns. (The word *questura* is one of several echoes from antiquity that still reverberate in present-day Italy's bureaucratic language. In classical times the *quaestores* dealt principally with financial affairs rather than police matters.)

At the foreigners' office of the *questura*, the newcomer will find scores, maybe hundreds, of other aliens who have been told, as official parlance puts it, to "regularize their position" and get their residence permits. There will be maids and nannies from the Philippines and the Cape Verde Islands, pizza cooks from Tunisia or Egypt, au pair girls from Britain or the Netherlands who have found an Italian boyfriend and want to stay on indefinitely, Brazilian dancers, farm workers from Eritrea or Sri Lanka, souvenir peddlers from Senegal, and refugees from Eastern Europe. Theoretically, all need a residence permit to be allowed to work, and a work permit to obtain a residence permit. Many of the applicants will have been illegally harvesting artichokes or tomatoes for farmers, or washing dishes in restaurant kitchens for months and years, and are no longer willing to do tedious work at miserable nonunion wages. They may also be after the free medical treatment available under the national health plan, for which one also needs residence papers.

More than a million foreigners are now living permanently in Italy, and several hundred thousand of them—nobody knows how many—do not officially exist because they have never shown up at a *questura*. The majority of these belong to the army of immigrants from the Third World who arrive as "tourists," then stay on and take jobs that most

Italians spurn even if unemployed. The authorities leave the clandestine workers and their families alone most of the time and do not object if they send their children to local schools. Every so often police catch a drug runner from Colombia, an exotic pickpocket or robber (most of the pickpockets that the Rome police catch red-handed on the city's buses turn out to be foreigners), a prostitute or pimp from Latin America, or a gypsy thief who has come in a battered car from Yugoslavia. They lock them up for some time and order them to leave the country; many are back within weeks.

Expatriates from Western countries who have never registered and are therefore technically outside the law may pick up a few lire as baby-sitters, language teachers, models, tourist guides, or in other temporary jobs. Nonpersons to the tax office, the health service, and other branches of the bureaucracy, they enjoy one advantage, not having to wait countless hours in line.

Italy's most authoritative sociological research institution, CENSIS (Center for Social Investment Studies), has tried to put a price tag on the time wasted by lining up in the nation's public offices. After interviewing sample groups of citizens, CENSIS experts concluded that tens of billions of dollars' worth of working time was lost by standing in the *fila* every year. In 1968 Parliament passed a law whereby a citizen is entitled to "self-certification" by substituting a single affidavit for the many documents that bureaucrats usually want to see. The law has never really gone into effect, although there have been several attempts to make it work. Parents must still line up in half a dozen offices for the necessary certificates to have a child admitted to kindergarten.

Further, nobody has yet tried to quantify the waste of time and the accumulating frustrations caused by the many invisible waiting lines in which millions of Italians are trapped. If you sue somebody for payment of a debt or become a party to some other legal proceeding, you are lucky if a verdict is forthcoming in thirty months; even then there will usually be an appeal. Many court matters—civil actions and criminal cases alike—drag on for ten years or longer. In one judicial grotesquerie a court in Catanzaro (in Italy's toe) was in 1989 still trying defendants accused of having perpetrated a 1969 bombing in a Milan bank in which sixteen people died. After long pretrial investigations the hearings opened in Rome in 1972, soon moved to Milan, and eventually were transferred to Catanzaro, 760 miles to the south, because the judges in Milan were deemed possibly biased. Six years later the Catanzaro court imposed life sentences on two defendants; an appeals court annulled the verdict and acquitted the accused for "lack of evidence." The highest tribunal in criminal matters, the Court of Cassation, ordered a retrial in the southern city of Bari, but the defendants were again acquitted in 1984. Meanwhile, investigators had come up with a new set of suspects, and the Catanzaro court started trying *them*, apparently unconcerned about the reliability of witnesses and other evidence two decades after the fact.

Almost two-thirds of the 30,000 to 40,000 people crowding Italian prisons at any one time have not been tried, and many of these who are eventually cleared won't receive any compensation for the time they have served. Of 203,000 defendants in criminal trials in 1986, fewer than 114,000 were found guilty and received prison sentences or were fined; more than 89,000 were acquitted. A reform law enacted in the early 1980s established that prisoners who had not been given a final sentence after four years of detention must be set free without bail pending the disposition of their cases. Thus thousands of alleged criminals who had never been tried or had appealed to higher courts regained their liberty, and the police got the additional task of keeping an eye on them.

Most other societies afflicted with a cumbersome state machinery have sunk into stagnation and sullenness, as has happened under the world's Marxist regimes. The Italians, with their knack for coping with adversity, have instead been thriving—not only despite the *fila* and horrendous bureaucratic delays but also in the teeth of social and governmental structures seemingly designed to frustrate efficiency.

4.

Red Tape
and Anarchy

The Italian citizen who requests an income tax refund may have to wait four years before hearing from the fiscal authorities; their shelves bulge with 12 million unexamined claims. Getting money out of the government is always hard, even if it has long been promised or allocated. Public-works contractors whose bills remain unpaid often have to run to banks or other lenders to keep going, as do Italy's thirteen state-supported opera houses and symphony orchestras when the funds to which they are entitled are late. Civil servants and teachers who have retired may have to wait ten or more years to learn the exact amount of the pensions due them (meanwhile, they get periodic advances).

State pensions are paid by the post offices in cash toward the end of each month. Occasionally some postal branch office will be closed because of a strike, or it will run out of funds, or the armored truck with the money will be waylaid and robbed (it does happen once in a while). The pensioners are told to come back some other day.

Italy's public and private bureaucracies are by and large equipped with data-processing systems, but people keep complaining that the computers of the labyrinthine Social Welfare Agency and many of the state-controlled banks seem to have slowed down rather than speeded operations, and to have lowered productivity. The sellers of mainframe computers have little trouble persuading government administrators and corporate executives to order ever larger and more sophisticated systems—Italians love up-to-date gadgetry—but getting the equipment to work is another matter.

Every automobile registered in Italy, regardless of whether it is on the road day and night or indefinitely stored in a garage, must have a tax badge affixed to the windshield. The tax is increased nearly every year—as motorists have come to expect—but what really exasperates them is that they are supposed to find out exactly how much they have to pay from an official tabulation that lists 324 amounts depending on the "fiscal" horsepower of the engine (different from the actual power), the kind of fuel on which it runs (gasoline, diesel oil, methane gas, or a mixture), and the province of registration. Most of the amounts on the tax table end with figures such as 805 or 640, but the post offices where payments must be made reject any deposit slips with numbers that are not rounded off to the next higher (not the nearest!) 100-lire amount (for instance, 805 to 900 or 640 to 700). The hapless car owner who makes a mistake has to go to an office of the Italian Automobile Club and stand in another endless line to obtain a duplicate form. (In France the car tax badge, *la plaquette*, can be bought at any tobacco store. Whenever administrative obtuseness presents yet another vexation to the citizenry, people shake their heads and remark with a sigh, "Methods *all'italiana*.")

A foreigner who buys a condominium, a house, or a plot of land in Italy will make jarring acquaintance with the *catasto*, the real-estate register. Any change of property has to be entered into it, titles to ownership depend on it, and real-estate and succession taxes are assessed on its basis. The trouble is that almost everywhere in the country the cadastral registers are hopelessly out of date. Title searches, tax controversies, applications for building permits, inheritance proceedings, and other business involving real estate are an ordeal because of the cadastral mess. In Florence, lawyers and land surveyors park their cars near the *catasto* office and sleep in them overnight to make sure of a good place in the waiting line that forms at dawn. In Rome alone, some 200,000 apartments in buildings erected in violation of zoning rules are not registered at all.

Italy's Court of Accounts, an independent government agency with roughly the same functions as the General Accounting Office in the United States, keeps denouncing the shortcomings of the state machinery. Its annual audits, usually a couple of thousand pages long, always note that its earlier criticisms and recommendations have remained unheeded. In 1962 Italy set up a new government department charged with revamping the civil service, calling it the Ministry of Bureaucratic Reform. It has survived all the many cabinet changes since its founding, has been headed by many ministers, and has never succeeded in making the administrative apparatus work faster, better, or more cheaply. The department is now called the Ministry of the Public Function, and its main task is to deal with government workers' multifarious demands for higher pay and transfers home, as well as their other grievances, strikes, and strike threats—an acknowledgment of the fact that Italy's public bureaucracy is first and foremost concerned with its own well-being. Government salaries and personnel costs take up 85 percent of the Italian state budget, leaving a measly 15 percent for building new schools and hospitals and improving decrepit ones, for repairing crumbling monuments, and for the many other investments the government of a modern country ought to make.

Why is there so much red tape and bureaucratic inertia

today in a nation that in earlier ages brought forth the Florentine and Lombard bankers, the brilliant diplomats of the Republic of Venice, Leonardo da Vinci and Michelangelo, great artists and musicians—a nation otherwise envied for its inventiveness, vitality, and relaxed ways?

One reason is that Italy, united only in the 1860s, lacks a strong tradition of a dedicated civil service such as, for instance, Britain and France can boast. Moreover, two decades of Fascist dictatorship, from 1922 to 1943, weakened the state machinery it claimed to be strengthening. Mussolini, to be sure, had imperial-style post offices, courthouses, and police barracks built all over the country, but what was going on inside them was another matter. During some periods of his rule Il Duce personally held half a dozen cabinet posts along with the premiership. With yes-men installed in all government departments, he must have been convinced he was in full control. Yet the Fascist regime, hypnotized by its own rhetoric, became increasingly eroded by corruption, and only military defeats and the rubble in the bombed cities brought home to the Italian people the fact that the new Roman Empire had been a sham.

The fragile administrative apparatus that the postwar Italian Republic inherited teemed with bureaucrats who asserted that they had been secret anti-Fascists all the time. These were soon joined by protégés of the democratic parties in power, creating a patronage system that inevitably politicized the public administration: To get certain desirable posts, or even any state or city job, one had to have the right *tessera* (party membership card).

Another cause of administrative incompetence is the scarcity of specialists. Most leading positions are filled by law graduates, few of whom have taken the bar examination and most of whom are incompetent to deal with special crises. Thus Italy, a country that is periodically struck by earthquakes, landslides, and floods and—alone in Europe—must keep an eye on active volcanoes, employs only a handful of geologists in public service. Government departments are also short of medical doctors, engineering experts, systems analysts, and linguists. Whenever some technical problem arises, even if only a translation is needed, outside consultants must be called in and paid extra.

While millions of private enterprises have long been flourishing, and any espresso bar is staffed with untiring countermen who serve customers quickly, expertly, and cheerfully, the Italian state has for generations proved unable to train and motivate its myriad employees. The listlessness of the public apparatus is most striking in the national capital. The personnel of the government departments in Rome are supposed to work thirty-six hours a week, from 8:00 A.M. to 2:00 P.M. Monday through Saturday. The offices actually remain empty until 8:30 A.M. because of an official half-hour grace period for latecomers, and the larger part of the staffs won't show up before 9:00 A.M. Once the employees have signed in, hung up their coats, and read the morning newspapers, virtually all of them desert their desks for their morning cappuccino. Almost every government agency has its in-house espresso bar (else the personnel would swarm out into the neighborhood and stay away even longer). If the telephone rings and somebody asks for Counsellor Rossi or Dottoressa Grande, a lone holdout will explain that they are "in conference" and may be expected back by noon. They are in fact conferring with colleagues—discussing the chances of the soccer pool or last night's television show over coffee and fresh *cornetti*. Or they are looking over the merchandise the espresso concessionaire is displaying that week: women's underwear, pullovers, handbags, pots and pans, toys, Parmesan cheese, encyclopedias, or perfumes.

Every now and then a new department chief clamps

down on the espresso operator, ordering him to stick to coffee and get rid of his miniature department store, and all personnel are warned by mimeographed circular that they are allowed just one coffee break a day and that it must not exceed twenty minutes. But governments come and go in quick succession, another minister or undersecretary who knows from earlier experience that new-broom attitudes are futile takes office, and the in-house bar is again crowded all morning.

Often government employees ask their supervisors for a special permit to stay away from the office for, say, three hours or an entire day because of urgent private business—they themselves have to wait in line at a branch office of the national health service for a medical test, or they have been summoned by the principal of their children's school. Maybe they won't need all three hours or the entire day and can do a little shopping in their spare time.

"The Italian state," an undersecretary in the Public Works Ministry, Raffaele Costa, observes, "has struck a deal with its employees, saying, 'I pay you little, and in return let you do whatever you want.'" The undersecretary points out that during an outbreak of the flu twice as many government workers, proportionally, report sick as do employees of private firms, and that members of the state bureaucracy stay away from their jobs an average of twenty-five days every year, in addition to their regular vacations. Costa estimates that low productivity and absenteeism cost taxpayers $30 billion annually. A trade-union leader, Francesco Piu, says that Italy is offering its citizens services typical of a Third World country: "Lebanon comes to mind."

When the Italian national soccer team played Sweden in a European Cup game in Naples, the 400 patients of the city's run-down San Gennaro Hospital were practically left to themselves—almost the entire male staff and quite a few female nurses were at the stadium. The police arrested thirty-nine hospital workers, including two supervisors, who were supposed to see that nobody was goofing off, and brought criminal charges against two hundred more who had also disappeared. Elsewhere sanitation workers are from time to time found driving cabs or doing odd jobs instead of cleaning the streets, and government employees on sick leave are discovered frolicking on Adriatic beaches or visiting with relatives in distant towns when they were reported to be at home with a high fever.

The bulk of Italy's state, regional, and municipal personnel clearly gets away with a good deal of lassitude, and little can apparently be done about it, even though once in a while some state prosecutor makes headlines by investigating the absenteeism of public employees. A few years after getting on the public payroll, one has a good chance of joining the *organico*, the hierarchy of tenured bureaucrats. The pay is low, but one cannot be fired, is entitled to periodic promotions and salary raises, and will eventually get a pension. One may even pick up extra money by taking an outside job afternoons or by volunteering for after-hours work in one's own office. (Urgent matters are taken care of in many government departments by skeleton staffs on overtime between 5:00 and 9:00 P.M.)

The changelessness of the state bureaucracy seems to contrast with the instability of the nation's governments. The life span of the Italian cabinets that have succeeded each other since the foundation of the Republic at the end of World War II averages ten months. But look more closely: Many faces in the posed pictures taken each time the head of state swears in a new government are familiar, the features have just become pastier and the bodies heavier over the years. A young undersecretary will, a couple of decades after his administration falls, be again in the government as a minister or even as its head; he will have become paunchy and gray but still be in power. Giulio Andreotti was twenty-eight years old when he won his first cabinet post as undersecretary in the premier's office; forty-two years later he was premier for the sixth time after having served, between earlier stretches at the top of the government, as chief of several departments and as foreign minister. Similar examples of ministerial longevity are numerous.

Most of the politicians in these revolving-door governments are Christian Democrats; their moderately conservative party has been in power, alone or in coalition with other middle-of-the-road groups or Socialists, uninterruptedly since 1946. Similarly, many cities and towns, like Bologna or Siena, have for decades been run by local Communist machines. Although most Italian premiers stay in office for short periods and government departments change hands often, the political establishment is remarkably stable, and it knows better than to interfere with the glacial pace of the civil service.

The general lethargy of Italian bureaucrats is not the only reason most of the country's public services are lamentable. With so much money being wasted on people who do not work very hard to earn it, there is not much left to spend on equipment, new computer systems notwithstanding. Many offices of the judiciary are cramped and lack enough desks, typewriters, file cabinets, and even chairs. When lawyers confer with judges they often have to stand in a corner of some crowded office. Bundles of dossiers are piled on floors, along corridors, and in basements. Even if funds for buying a desk or a computer have at last been appropriated, it may take more than a year before all the signatures necessary for the actual purchase have been collected and delivery can take place.

The average age of the state railroads' locomotives and cars exceeds twenty years, the tracks and much other equipment are similarly antiquated, and maintenance is poor. No wonder there are frequent breakdowns and chronic delays. Yet Italy maintains 215,000 railroad employees, twice as many per mile of track as in France.

Three of Italy's four continental neighbors—France, Switzerland, and Austria—offer excellent rail services (only Yugoslavia compares unfavorably with Italy). France especially, with its 170-mph Train à Grande Vitesse, is generations ahead in rail technology. Railroad travelers from Switzerland to Italy must brace themselves for instantly crowded coaches and erratic schedules. Crossing the frontier between the two countries, says the British writer Anthony Burgess, who lives near Lugano, is like entering Mexico from the United States. South of Rome, the trains are even slower and more tightly packed than those in the country's North.

The state railroads' freight service is so unsatisfactory that today less than one-eighth of all goods moving in Italy are shipped by rail. (In the rest of Western Europe more than half of all freight transportation is by rail.) Yet 30,000 Italian freight cars stand permanently idle, taking up 180 miles of sidings. Trucking in Italy costs three times as much as shipping by freight train, but farmers and manufacturers usually put up with the higher expense for the sake of speed and reliability. Sicilian oranges cannot be sent by rail to northern markets because the journey, 1,000 miles or so, may take three weeks. Entire freight trains get lost for days before being found stranded on a siding in some obscure Calabrian station.

At a time when mail services are deteriorating in other industrial nations, the slackness in Italian post offices is no longer as startling as it used to be. If a resident of Rome receives an airmail letter that was sent, correctly addressed, from Los Angeles a month earlier and notes a rubber-stamp mark in English on the envelope reading "Sent by Mistake to Jakarta," he will praise the diligence of the Indonesian mails rather than blame the U.S. or Italian postal workers for sloppiness. Yet the Italian press still voices outrage every so often when a postcard mailed twenty-eight years ago is delivered, or when a survey shows that the postal system needs an average of five days to transport a letter across Rome.

Telephones, also operated by state-controlled companies, make up to some extent for the unreliable mails—if one is a subscriber. It takes more than a year to get a phone. Lines are often overloaded, crackle ominously, and are cut suddenly; or one hears other people's conversations. But the chief complaint by subscribers who line up at the post office to pay their phone bills is the cost. Telephone service in Italy is more expensive than it is in the United States, Britain, France, West Germany, or Switzerland. What's more, however, when a whopping long-distance charge appears on your bill, you are kept in the dark as to the number and destination called; if you insist on knowing, you must pay the full amount first, and afterward go to the telephone company, pay an extra fee, and ask for the information, which may or may not be forthcoming after a long wait. Not everybody has the stomach to take on the telephone bureaucracy. One group of customers who did pursue investigation brought forth the discovery of a racket in which phone employees let some people call Singapore or Australia free of charge except for a small personal consideration, then debited someone else's number with the entire amount due.

The national health service that Italy set up in the late 1970s on the welfare-state models of Britain and the Scandinavian countries has grown into a bureaucratic monster. "It is a national disgrace," Premier Ciriaco De Mita admitted in 1988. Newspapers, politicians, labor spokespeople, and civic groups denounce its inefficiency, waste, and corruption almost every day, and hardly a week passes without a magistrate somewhere in the nation starting a probe into suspected wrongdoing.

Trade-union statisticians have estimated that in Rome alone 14 million working hours are being lost annually by patients who have to line up to obtain a doctor's or laboratory appointment and again, after weeks or months, to undergo actual examination. Even then, the results can be unreliable. In one secret check, specimens of the same person's blood were simultaneously sent to four different laboratories for testing. The cholesterol readings ranged from a safe 199 to a high 240. A Turin laboratory noted the absence of albumin in a urinalysis report while failing to discover that the liquid it was examining was tea.

In Rome it took a health-service clinic fifty hours to notice that one of its patients had died. In Genoa's 3,800-bed San Martino Hospital, one of Italy's largest, investigators found a cat prowling the house pharmacy; "we are keeping him to catch the mice," the staff explained candidly. The police have reported many other irregularites and cases of outright thievery at San Martino, considered to be among the country's best institutions of its kind.

Health Minister Carlo Donat-Cattin stated publicly that in Turin hospitals patients were dying during the night because they were left without assistance. The paramedics of Turin's Le Molinette Hospital distributed leaflets warning the citizenry to shun the institution's first-aid station if they wanted to survive in an emergency. In Rome the head of the physicians' union at the big San Giovanni Hospital remarked: "We regard patients as a pain in the neck. We hate them because with their demands they force us into a collision course with the bureaucracy." On the street outside the same hospital, a mother had to give birth in a car because the doctor on duty in the admission ward had refused to assist her on the ground that he was not obliged to perform obstetric services. The Deep South continually provides even worse horror stories.

Many hospitals are chronically overcrowded, with beds lining the corridors, each bed costing the taxpayer as much as a room in a five-star hotel. The total cost of the national health service takes up at least 6 percent of the gross national product. Patients who can afford it consult expensive physicians in private practice, undergo treatment or surgery in luxury-class clinics (some of which are excellent), or seek admittance to renowned institutions in Switzerland, France, Belgium, Britain, or the United States.

A survey of Italy's shaky infrastructures is not complete without a mention of its banks, which are also state controlled. Bank employees once regarded themselves as the aristocracy of white-collar workers and were widely envied because they received two or even three months' extra pay every year. Now, a generation later, they are no longer so privileged, have lost prestige, and often appear listless. The scene in many bank branches is the same as in government offices: long lines of irritable customers and unhelpful staff behind the counters. Every now and then some teller will leave for a smoke or a chat with colleagues on the pretext of having to check a back-room file. Transactions are slow and mistakes frequent; "the computer is down" has become a handy explanation for delays.

Occasionally, mistakes work in the customer's favor. A lower-middle-class Roman woman I know one day found a credit of 6 million lire (then about $5,000) on her bank statement. There was no explanation, and she knew she was not entitled to the amount. The balances of subsequent statements all remained 6 million lire too high, and the woman eventually said to herself, what the hell! and cashed the windfall. The bank paid it without any trouble and four years later still has not caught up with its error. Probably it never will.

Whose money did it give away? How many such slipups go undetected?

Banks, like other services in Italy, are frequently paralyzed by strikes—sometimes for an hour or two every morning over a week or longer, sometimes for three or four days on end. It is all part of the liturgy of Italy's ever-militant labor. The Italian worker's propensity for walking out is an aspect of his *conflittualità*, proneness to conflict. It is most pronounced today in the service industries—mails, railroads, civil aviation, hospitals, schools, credit institutions, and the information media—where the public becomes a hostage in the struggle between management and labor.

Every strike or work slowdown by postal employees, no matter how short or limited in area, further disrupts the precarious mail system for weeks afterward. Letters and packages pile up, and it takes forever for the backlog to dwindle. One celebrated strike some years ago resulted in such mountains of undelivered mail that post offices ran out of storage space; many thousands of mailbags were loaded on state railroad freight cars, forming ghost trains that kept traveling leisurely up and down the peninsula until some time after the mail employees had returned to their jobs.

In transportation, strikes by the crews of ferryboats linking the Italian mainland with Sicily and Sardinia have long been a travel-season tradition. The second half of August and early September, when many thousands of vacationers, most of them with their cars, have to get back home is the favorite period. Messina in Sicily and the Sardinian seaports of Cagliari, Olbia, and Porto Torres rerun the familiar scenes of frustrated multitudes camping near the waterfront—crying children, distraught parents, people fighting over who gets first on some boat manned by strike breakers.

Weary travelers stranded for hours or even days in railroad stations and air terminals can be seen on Italian television fairly regularly. Nationwide unions, their local chapters, and wildcat "rank-and-file committees" often vie with one another in calling walkouts. Whipsaw techniques are recurrent: One day the railroad engineers stop all or most trains for twenty-four hours, the next day station personnel stay off their jobs, achieving the same effect. Pilots, air-traffic controllers, and other ground staffs take turns going on strike for a few hours or an entire day or two throughout the country or in scattered airports. At times the railroads and air traffic are simultaneously hit by such sectional or checkerboard stoppages, leaving only the highways for urgent travel. Striking schoolteachers stay away from classes at the beginning of the academic year as they do in other countries but then also in spring, when graduation exams are to be held and students run the risk of finding no one to test them. As one or another branch of the country's basic services is knocked out almost every week by some labor conflict, the press and the news broadcasts routinely warn the public of the next round of *disagi.* The word means "discomforts."

Strikes in the service industries, especially those that are publicly controlled, obviously inconvenience other workers much more than they do their managements. But the teachers, air-traffic controllers, railroad engineers, doctors of public hospitals, or magistrates who walk out apparently do not care much for the solidarity of the working class that is the official philosophy of the nationwide trade-union confederations. Teachers, aviation personnel, doctors, and magistrates, to be sure, are earning more than do secretaries, drivers, and most manual workers, but that doesn't keep them from feeling that their interests have been neglected and that they should earn much more in view of their training and responsibilities.

The big unions have, for their part, fought successfully since the end of World War II to improve the workers' lot. As Italy within two or three decades transformed itself from a still predominantly agricultural nation into a leading industrial power, labor won relatively high minimum wages and advanced social legislation. Union pressure prompted Parliament in 1969 to pass an industrial relations bill that has become known as the Workers' Statute. The bill made it very difficult for an employer to fire anybody for laziness or absenteeism, and it gave unions additional powers in factories and offices. Workers can refuse to be transferred to other jobs. If litigation ensues, pro-labor judges often decide against the employer. Most industrial workers are doing quite nicely.

Filippo, for example, had been a young, discontented farmhand before he emigrated from a dusty village in Apulia in 1952 to work on the assembly line of a Fiat Motor Company plant in Turin. Thirty-five years later he was driving a new car, owned a four-room apartment on the city outskirts, and was able to spend a three-week beach vacation near Genoa in August after a brief visit to his brothers and sisters who had remained in the Deep South. He married a woman from the North, and their two boys have both become electricians and found jobs in factories near Turin.

Filippo was active early on in the Metal Workers' Union and remembers the noisy parades on the plant floor and the strike pickets outside the gates during his first years with Fiat. He must have developed into a good mechanic too, for after eighteen years with the company he was promoted to foreman. In 1980, when the Metal Workers' Union called out all Fiat personnel on another strike, Filippo was one of 40,000 who paraded in the streets of Turin in a back-to-work demonstration. That "March of the 40,000" broke the strike and marked a turning point in the history of the Italian labor movement. "We at Fiat seem to have become Japanese," Filippo said ruefully soon before he was to retire, meaning that he and like-minded comrades may little by little have turned into company men, paying only lip service to their old vision of class struggle. Filippo roots for the Juventus soccer team of Turin, which is identified with Fiat, instead of for his old hometown club, Leccese, but he keeps voting Communist in elections because he hates the government.

Fiat, Italy's largest private corporation, had surprisingly little trouble from labor in the early 1980s, when it replaced many unskilled workers with machines and gradually laid off one-third of its work force. The big automaker and other industries were able to get rid of unneeded hands because they could disguise dismissals under guarantees that the newly jobless would be paid for not working. This ingenious government mechanism for bribing labor to make no fuss when companies are restructuring or automating plants or when they have to be shored up in some crisis situation is the Earnings Integration Fund. The institution, born during World War II, now ensures a minimum income for two years and even longer to workers who in effect have been laid off. Such payments, distinct from ordinary unemployment compensation, are financed in part by industry and to a much larger extent by the government.

Many workers like to be taken care of by the Earnings Integration Fund, even though they may be obliged to attend retraining classes to qualify for jobs requiring new skills. During their many free hours they can get busy as handymen, fixing leaky faucets or painting kitchens for neighbors and acquaintances, and quite a few of the former factory workers who receive periodic payments from the fund are earning additional money selling textiles or appliances from house to house, or pulling off real-estate deals, all without paying any income tax.

While labor militancy seems to have abated in Italy's manufacturing plants, it has become increasingly virulent in the broadening service sector. Short of militarizing the striking personnel of airport control towers, streetcar networks, the state railroads, or other vital services, the government has lacked any means of curbing these periodic disruptions. Italy's Constitution of 1948 declares in Article 40: "The right to strike [will be] exercised within the framework of the laws that regulate it." Such laws were slow to materialize because left-wing parties automatically opposed them, leaving the right to strike unrestricted for a long time. Only in 1988 did Parliament start to consider a bill that would lay down rules for calling strikes; the proposed legislation, however, envisages no penalties other than fines for noncompliance.

There are many weapons in labor's arsenal today. After negotiations with management have broken down, or even before they have started, unions or ad hoc groups may tell staffs to stand by for a fight. Such a warning is known in Italian labor parlance as a "call for a state of agitation." Work slowdowns or work-to-rule periods come next. The musicians of the Rome Opera House wear turtlenecks in the orchestra pit, won't play any encores, and stay seated when the conductor motions them to acknowledge applause. Bank personnel become even gruffer than usual. The final step is an actual walkout.

Employees prefer intermittent and checkerboard stoppages to long-drawn-out strikes because they can create a lot of confusion and discomforts *(disagi)* with a minimum of pay loss. One clever way of halting work for a couple of hours or even an entire morning without having to forgo wages is to hold an "internal assembly" of an enterprise's staff to discuss their grievances; it's legal and is not considered a strike.

Labor leaders who want to stage a one-day walkout usually pick a Friday or a Monday in order to give workers a long weekend as a means of assuring obedience to union commands. Once in a while all three allied labor confederations agree on ordering a nationwide general strike for a few hours or an entire day to make some political point, or to prove that they are still in control of the country's workers. Despite its truculent purpose, such a strike isn't usually a grim affair; it's more like a national holiday. The power plants keep working, supplying electricity to households and television stations, and sometimes the railroads and public transportation in the cities also remain exempt from the strike orders, or halt only for a few hours. Almost all stores remain open, small firms keep working, and few people care if the government offices stay closed. Meanwhile, in the major centers, national labor leaders address workers' rallies; their speeches sound combative, as do the slogans on the signs and streamers that paraders carry, but the crowds are good-natured. There is more genuine passion in the soccer stadiums every Sunday afternoon. Other so-called general strikes are often proclaimed locally whenever a spectacular Mafia murder has occurred, a gas leak or other accident in some industrial plant has killed workers, or some other event demands a show of labor outrage in the judgment of trade unionists.

The Italians' exceptional proclivity for walking off their jobs may spring from a deep-seated strain of anarchism. At its root lies a distrust and hatred of authority that Italians in many parts of the country have been nursing for centuries. Individually often brilliant, the inhabitants of Italy have always shown distaste for discipline and regimentation . . . until chaos became so threatening that the populace felt compelled to invoke the strong man who would restore order, the way Dante invoked the emperor. Foreign invaders have usually been loathed and feared, but sometimes they have been welcomed (at least for a while) because their rule would curb the arrogance of local chieftains, punish thieves and robbers, and guarantee a minimum of justice.

Fighting state authority instead of collaborating with it

and tormenting the rich and powerful without getting caught have long been admired in Italy. Rebels, conspirators, outlaws, bandits, even common highwaymen have for centuries enjoyed great prestige among the populace. When Mikhail Bakunin set himself up as a champion of anarchism and advocated revolutionary violence everywhere, he found many followers in Italy, where he lived between 1864 and 1867. Italians, together with Spaniards, French-speaking Swiss, and Russians, were foremost in the anarchist movement. An Italian anarchist, Luigi Luccheni, senselessly murdered Empress Elisabeth of Austria-Hungary in Geneva in 1898, and another Italian follower of Bakunin, Gaetano Bresci, traveled from Paterson, New Jersey, to the old country in 1900 to assassinate King Umberto I in Monza. (Bresci died in jail. In the late 1970s anarchists in Tuscany commissioned a statue to honor the regicide but were prevented by the government from erecting it in Bresci's hometown, Turigliano, near Carrara.)

Anarchism imported from Italy and other European countries has long frightened the United States, and it contributed to early American diffidence toward organized labor. Worldwide attention was attracted by the six-year case of the shoemaker Nicola Sacco and the fishmonger Bartolomeo Vanzetti, both anarchists. The Commonwealth of Massachusetts executed them in 1927 for a murder they probably did not commit.

Today anarchist clubs and cells in Italy still churn out earnest propaganda for the abolition of the state and of private property in a society based on free associations; oldtimers wave the red-and-black anarchist banner and keep alive the memory of their martyrs. The headquarters of Italian anarchism is in Massa-Carrara, the twin towns near the quarries from which Michelangelo and many lesser sculptors and builders got their marble blocks. The miners there have always had great familiarity with explosives, which of course can be used for more than blowing up rock.

Marx and Engels discredited Bakunin, ridiculed his ideas, and had him drummed out of the International Working Men's Association (the First International); thereafter, Italian Marxists would officially never have anything to do with anarchists. Still, the Italian Socialist movement and its 1921 offshoot, the Italian Communist party, had to cope repeatedly with their own anarchist fringes. The strike waves that swept the country after World War I were felt to be an outbreak of anarchism. The frightened capitalists, landowners, and middle class hailed Mussolini's Blackshirts when they were battling strikers because Mussolini promised law and order.

This presumed savior of the nation owed his given name, Benito, to the revolutionary-anarchist enthusiasm of his father, a village blacksmith and later tavern owner and mayor at Dovia, near Predappio in the fiery Romagna region. The elder Mussolini revered not only Bakunin but also Benito Juárez, Mexico's national hero, who had the foreign-imposed Emperor Maximilian shot by a firing squad in 1867.

Benito Mussolini was a radical socialist before he turned nationalist and founded the Fascist movement. He was convinced that the Italian people needed iron discipline, and for quite some time he apparently thought it possible to mold them to his will. Yet Il Duce is supposed to have remarked to a foreign visitor one day that, no, it wasn't difficult at all to govern Italians, "only it is useless." That aphorism is attributed also to Giovanni Giolitti, a left-wing moderate and renowned cynic who several times served as Italian premier before the Fascist dictatorship. Maybe the self-taught son of the village blacksmith plagiarized Giolitti, as he did so many other sources.

The first two decades after the collapse of the Mussolini regime were marked by frequent and widespread strikes, many of them politically motivated, and new generations of Italians again got used to the strategies and rituals of labor militancy. From the late 1960s onward, left-wing extremists—more often intellectuals than workers—went underground and, in the traditions of revolutionary anarchism, engineering bombings, industrial or military sabotage, kidnappings, and assassinations. Small neo-Fascist groups had started committing terrorist acts even earlier. The Red Brigades and other clandestine organizations vowing to destroy the Italian state through revolutionary violence will be discussed in chapter 8. The Italians were to ride out that neoanarchist storm too.

5.

The Art of

Arrangement

Toward the end of each month, one out of every ten Italians trudges to the post office and, if there is enough cash on hand and the staff does not happen to be on strike, lines up to collect the pension that the state pays to its army of invalids. The amount is modest—some get as little as the equivalent of $100 a month—but it helps the beneficiaries and their families to have their pasta on the table every day.

With 5.5 million certified *invalidi* (including 700,000 people officially found to have suffered bodily harm in the nation's last war, which ended in 1945), Italy would seem to be one of the world's most hazardous countries, writhing under plagues like biblical Egypt, endangered by accidents lurking in homes, fields, and factories, and racked by crippling diseases. Catastrophe is indeed familiar to Italy. Five deaths out of every 100,000 are caused by one of the frequent floods, earthquakes, or other natural calamities; the statistical average for most other Western countries is about one death in 100,000. Gunfire and bombings by terrorists, mafiosi, and other criminals punctuate life in Italy, and the hectic motor traffic exacts its daily toll of casualties. Yet Italians live on average longer than do Britons, French, or West Germans. Spry and lucid octogenarians abound. In the Alps, great-grandmothers walk for hours to and from church; in Rome, old men hold sway in the national government and in the Vatican; in Sicily, aged godfathers call the tune. The longevity and vitality of the Italians is enviable—convincing proof of their knack for survival.

Few of the 5.5 million supposedly handicapped Italians are permanently disabled, and many are chipper as the birds in the trees. The overwhelming majority of those who receive monthly invalidity pensions are nursing questionable if not imaginary ailments that do not prevent them from tackling life as everybody else does, and from getting old. By far the major part of the spurious infirm live in the sunny Mezzogiorno, where, one would think, the environment is healthier than in the foggy, industrial North. Southerners, to be sure, have a hard time finding jobs; to be pronounced an invalid by an official commission and thus become entitled to a state pension is a substitute for a guaranteed minimum wage or unemployment compensation. "In the North they have the Earnings Integration Fund, and the South has the invalidity pensions," said Ciriaco De Mita, a Christian Democratic leader whose rocklike political base is Avellino near Naples. He was soon to become government chief.

For decades candidates for elective office, mayors, members of Parliament, and cabinet ministers have been busy obtaining pensions for reputedly disabled constituents—a small favor like handing out candy to children or cigars to their fathers. If the officially attested impairment is not—exceptionally—a serious one, the person claiming to be afflicted with it may even get a job, because the law obliges some public employers, like the state railroads, to set aside a quota for *invalidi* when they hire new personnel.

Despite all the interventions by powerful personages, the procedures for getting an invalidity pension are slow and complicated, of course. In 1988 the Court of Accounts in

Rome reported about 10,000 pending claims that referred to injuries said to have been suffered or diseases contracted during military service in World War I. Probably few of the original would-be *invalidi* were still alive, but their spouses and children had kept pressing their cases. The backlog from World War II was 180,000 claims.

The monthly payment from the state that helps millions of Italians, especially in the South, in the business of surviving is, unsurprisingly, a handy tool for assembling and operating political machines. It is also a prime example of the Italian art of arrangement—a technique for taking life's hurdles, surviving by one's wits, coasting along, making ends meet, and striking deals that are not exactly illegal, or only slightly so, and may bring advantages to more than one party (even though less clever people, the anonymous ranks of taxpayers, and the even vaguer interests of the national community might be directly or indirectly damaged).

Arrangiarsi, a verb that uncounted Italians conjugate every day, does not mean "to arrange oneself," as newcomers to the country and beginning students of its language may wrongly assume before hearing it said again and again in disparate circumstances—a transport strike, an adulterous affair, money trouble, crowded accommodations, odds and ends from the refrigerator for dinner, and a thousand other challenges large and small. *Arrangiarsi* in its various applications translates accurately as "to make do," or "to find a way out of a predicament," also "to make the best of a lousy situation." The important thing is never to crumple in adversity. The gift for getting out of a tight spot is coupled with uncommon resilience—a national trait that has been cultivated and celebrated since the days of Boccaccio's *Decameron.*

Innumerable are the routine "arrangements" in Italian everyday life. If you want to beat the ubiquitous lines, don't line up at all—pay someone who will do it for you. That is one thing the many messengers, doormen, drivers, and characters with undefined tasks who hang around the lobbies and corridors of most offices can handle. For a pack of cigarettes or the price of a bottle of wine your or somebody else's *usciere* (doorkeeper or office attendant) will pay electricity and phone bills at the post office and cash a check at the bank; he will be glad to run such errands because they give him an excuse for staying away all morning and taking care also of his own affairs. An *usciere* with years of experience and a long-established network of contacts may be able during one of the many bank strikes to make a subarrangement with an employee who will honor a check via the branch office's back door (a favor worth an extra consideration for both).

Instead of lining up with a bunch of others at a municipal office to get one of those birth or residence certificates continually needed in Italy so that one can line up at some other agency, turn to one of the storefront businesses that specialize in dealing with the authorities; they will get that piece of official paper for you. They work like travel agents and are usually combined with driving schools, also selling car insurance and taking care of vehicle registrations.

Every motorist in Italy sooner or later becomes a customer of one or another of the self-appointed car attendants who are "arrangement" personified. They fill a need because parking meters have not been much of a success in the cities that have tried them; the devices were constantly being rifled or vandalized. The Italian Automobile Club runs some parking lots, watched by its uniformed personnel, but these facilities are themselves far from sufficient. However, any few square feet of available space in the streets and piazzas of the crowded inner cities and in the neighborhoods of restaurants, movie houses, theaters, sports stadiums, and beaches will provide a chance for someone to make a living. He will wear an official-looking cap with the word *guardiamacchine* (car watcher) in gold embroidery. He will preside over double and triple parking, will always accommodate a good tipper, and will alone be able to extricate your auto from a jumble of other vehicles. If you don't pay him what he expects for his services or even try to freeload, you may find a scratch on your car's body or a flat tire next time. Of course such a curbside entrepreneur must have made his own arrangements with the traffic police and possibly also with some shadowy power that allots street space in the area.

Speaking of that Italian popular idol, the automobile, watch the mechanic who fixes your car. A spare part is hard to get? He will find it at the flea market, take it from a cannibalized auto, hammer it out himself, or maybe even swipe it from somewhere. If there is no space in his cramped two-man workshop, he will put your car out on the sidewalk and, with his assistant, will be tinkering on it while pedestrians respectfully step into the street, fully aware that important work and an inspiring exercise in "arrangement" are in progress.

Or observe how that famous national institution, Italian opera, works. The great shrines of musical drama elsewhere—the Metropolitan Opera of New York, the San Francisco Opera, Covent Garden in London, the Vienna and Munich state operas—map their programs and sign up casts years ahead (with stars who may have been eclipsed or lost their voices by the time they are to sing the parts assigned to them). Nothing of the kind happens in Italian operatic institutions, from La Scala in Milan to the Teatro Bellini in Catania.

If the performing season is to start in, say, December, it will still be highly uncertain in October whether it can open at all: The promised subsidies from the government in Rome, the regional authorities, and the city have not arrived, the banks are reluctant to grant another loan, the musicians and chorus demand higher pay and threaten to strike, the renowned guest producer insists on expensive new sets and costumes, and the singers miss scheduled rehearsals or show up at the last minute. Managements grope from one "arrangement" to the next. Maybe *Carmen* will have to perform without singing tobacco girls, street urchins, and soldiers, as happened at the Teatro dell'Opera in Rome after the entire chorus walked out; or La Scala will have to postpone a scheduled ballet production until the next season. Once in a while, nevertheless, all the frantic improvisations and make-do end up just right on some magic evening at La Scala or at the San Carlo in Naples or even at the Sferisterio in Macerata (a colonnaded ball-playing court from the early nineteenth century in a remote town near the Adriatic coast, where by dint of "arrangements," occasionally quite brilliant ones, outdoor opera is performed every summer).

The Italian cinema, which has disseminated around the world the imagery of *la dolce vita* and the philosophy of not taking anything too seriously, is all "arrangement." A real-estate tycoon is talked into putting up money for a picture in which his young girlfriend is to get a role; the producer insists that the scriptwriters come up with a scene in a southern village street because a suitable set, a holdover from a Mafia film, still stands in the Cinecittà studios; the director invents an entirely new sequence on the spur of the moment when the *trovarobe* ("things finder," propman) returns from the Porta Portese flea market with what looks like the very first espresso machine ever built, an antique that will yield a couple of gags; and so on, from bright idea to brainstorm to improvisation.

When Ingrid Bergman came to Rome in 1949 to film under the director Roberto Rossellini, then her lover and soon to become her second husband, she was stunned by the absence of any production schedule. In Hollywood the Swedish actress had been used to being told weeks in advance what she was supposed to do on the set almost minute by minute on any given day. On location in Southern Italy, Rossellini seemed to worry much more about the *spaghetti alle vongole* and the right wine for lunch than about the picture he was shooting, and appeared vague as to which scene would come next. A generation later Marcello Mastroianni said he liked working under Federico Fellini: "I show up at the set in the morning, and ask Fellini, 'Hey, Federì, what do you want me to do today?'"

Improvising scenes and dialogues goes back to the commedia dell'arte, in which Harlequin, Columbine, and other stock characters of popular farce quarreled and made up in allusive, topical language to the amusement of sixteenth-century audiences. Today one does not have to be in touch with Italian show business to meet stars of "arrangement." Everyone who has lived in the country for a little while knows a few of them. You haven't seen them for some time, and on meeting them again you ask: "What are you doing these days?" If the answer is, as it often will be, "Oh, *m'arrangio*" (meaning something like "I'm getting along"), don't persist, just change the subject.

Living by arrangements, one may be riding in a chauffeur-driven Mercedes or wearing an expensive designer dress while having only pizza for dinner. The Mercedes may be registered in the name of a company with a mailbox in the Principality of Liechtenstein as its only other tangible asset, and the haute couture number may be a gift from a rich friend. Even the bill for the pizza may be payable in a week under the famed Neapolitan food-on-credit scheme.

Naples especially has long been notorious for cultivating

the art of getting along by "arrangement," the way Cremona is celebrated for its Stradivarius violins and Venice for its gondolas. When Goethe visited Naples in 1787 he was told that in the city, then one of Europe's most populous capitals, 30,000 to 40,000 *lazzaroni* (idlers) could always be found in the streets. The clear-eyed German looked hard but couldn't detect a single one. What he did see he described in his *Italian Journey*: porters for hire looking for customers; seamen smoking their pipes while waiting for an unfavorable wind to abate; small boys picking up horse droppings, which they would sell as manure to farmers in the countryside; children carrying fish from the Santa Lucia waterfront to the markets, or gathering wood chips that the carpenters in the Arsenal were scattering, which they put into baskets and would take home for the kitchen stove; street vendors selling lemonade and cakes; Punchinello in a mock quarrel on a stage set up on a noisy street corner, nearby a quack peddling his nostrums and above them "a balcony on which a quite nice girl was offering her charms." To paint a true portrait of Naples, Goethe remarked, would require lots of talent and years of observation, and one would perhaps come to the conclusion that the so-called *lazzaroni* were not a bit less active than all other classes of people, and were in their own way "working not only to live but also to enjoy."

Two centuries later, thousands of Neapolitans still invent their day and their livelihood every morning, and they seem to enjoy doing so. Maybe the relatives of someone who has just died in a hospital will want to have the body brought home—which is illegal, unless one acquires a fake certificate attesting that the patient is still alive—so that the family and their friends can hold a good, traditional Neapolitan wake. The going tariff for such a macabre service, certificate included, is around $1,200, to be split among four or five people. Another method to get gainfully through the day is to acquire a carton of smuggled American cigarettes on commission and sell packs, or even batches of two or three cigarettes, to smokers in the warren of small streets in the center of the city. Even small boys can do that.

The Neapolitan genius for "arrangement" flowered most memorably in a golden age of finagling that started in the autumn of 1943 and lasted through the late 1940s. It has become an often repeated theme of modern Italian folklore, evoked by Curzio Malaparte in his best-sellers *Kaputt* and *The Skin.* (Malaparte, though no Neapolitan, was a virtuoso in inventing for himself a new persona every time the vicissitudes of his stormy era suggested the need. His real name was Kurt Erich Suckert. He was of German ancestry but, having been born in Prato, considered himself a Tuscan. An earlier follower of Mussolini, he turned anti-Fascist and eventually professed himself an admirer of Mao Zedong. When Malaparte died in 1957, both an Italian Communist party official and a Roman Catholic priest stood at his bedside. He willed his villa on the Isle of Capri to the People's Republic of China, which did not know what to do with it.)

When the Nazis evacuated Naples in 1943 after the Allied landing operations near Salerno, the city's urchins and *lazzaroni* pelted the retreating Wehrmacht troops with stones and bottles, and fired at them with guns long hidden in basements and under floorboards. (The Roman populace did nothing of the kind when the Germans moved out of the capital, undisturbed, in June 1944.)

Under Allied occupation Naples became a major supply base for Southern and Central Europe in an atmosphere anticipating to some extent that of Saigon during the Vietnam War. Italians still tell each other the legendary feats of the Neapolitan shoeshine boys doubling as underage pimps who "sold" blind-drunk American servicemen to prostitutes who would then roll them and strip them to their underpants before dumping them on some street corner where they could sober up. Another classic is the reputed disappearance in the Bay of Naples of an American freighter with many thousands of pairs of footwear for the troops; U.S. quartermaster services thereupon cleverly (they thought) sent to Naples one shipload of all right shoes followed by another of all left shoes, but the thefts continued and a new Neapolitan cottage industry sprang up—workshops specializing in converting stolen left shoes into right ones, and vice versa.

Today the poor neighborhoods of Naples are still honeycombed with poky workshops. Local officials keep repeating that although the city has not one glove factory it produces and exports millions of pairs of gloves every year: They are being stitched together on a piecework basis by women in stuffy one-room apartments in decrepit buildings that open right into the street known as *bassi*; the cutting and sewing machines, on loan from subcontractors, stand close to the kitchen ranges, where the pasta for the entire large family is being cooked, and are moved aside at night to make room for cots and foldout beds. Other Neapolitan *bassi* turn out plaster statuettes to be sold by souvenir vendors outside the Sanctuary of the Virgin of the Rosary at Pompeii or near the Vatican in Rome, as well as plastic handbags, slippers of imitation leather, and a myriad of other cheap items.

Late in autumn every year some shed or dingy apartment in the Naples area will blow up, all too often with people getting killed or wounded. The police don't have to do much investigating; they know at once what caused the explosion—inexpert handling of pyrotechnic material. Like the Chinese, many Italians and particularly Neapolitans are crazy about fireworks and won't pass up a chance for indulging in the mania. The biggest occasion is New Year's Eve when, at midnight, all of Naples erupts in thunder and flames like Mount Vesuvius during one of its historic outbreaks. For months clandestine workshops in and around the city have manufactured and stored pinwheels, flares, Roman candles, and firecrackers that can be as powerful as small bombs. The authorities have issued their ritual warnings against the dangerous industry, raided a few pyrotechnic factories, and arrested dozens of street peddlers caught selling their products. Motorcycle patrols have checked trucks on the highways from Naples to the North and South and have regularly discovered boxes of firecrackers under layers of tomatoes and artichokes. But only a tiny part of the flammable material is ever seized. When the newspapers reappear on January 2 after the New Year's vacation, they carry long casualty lists, as if a battle had been fought—Neapolitans and people elsewhere killed and maimed while setting off their beloved fireworks or when hit by a fun rocket.

The glove industry in the *bassi* of Naples and the clandestine pyrotechnic shops are among the more picturesque of many hundreds of thousands of small enterprises spread over the length and breadth of Italy like the cells of a vigorous organism. Others include furniture and knitwear factories in various parts of the country, each with a few dozen workers; hole-in-the-wall operations in Apulia specializing in fake Louis Vuitton bags ("genuine" fakes that are sold as such and snapped up by Japanese tourists); small hotels and pensions along the coasts and in resorts, run by the owners and their relatives; innumerable dressmakers and leatherware suppliers working for famous-label firms; goldsmiths clustered in Vicenza and Arezzo; some seventy ceramics makers in the majolica town of Faenza alone and many more in other places; manufacturers of fashion accessories and television antennas; and family establishments in the Alpine valleys whose computer-guided machines turn out "hand-carved" wooden sculptures of the Virgin Mary or of Walt Disney characters (unauthorized) that are shipped to distant outlets. Such small industries, immensely varied, account for nearly one-half of all the goods and services produced by Italy. Many self-made entrepreneurs employ relatives and will at peak periods press a teenage cousin or an elderly uncle into service rather than hire costly outside help.

The commonplace opinion that "the Italians don't pay their taxes" must be qualified. Wage earners do (because of automatic withholding mechanisms); all consumers do (through sales taxes and special levies like the one on gasoline, which makes that commodity more expensive than almost anywhere else in Europe). The serried ranks of the tax dodgers are composed of farmers, artisans, handymen, retail merchants, family companies, professional people, and a vast class of shadowy middlemen and fixers. Most of their customers and clients are in collusion with the tax evaders: You pay cash to the plumber and car mechanic, and you don't ask the dentist for a receipt because the fee would go up steeply if you did. If you get a written contract from the landlord (which is by no means sure), it will name a figure for rent far below the real one. Paying anything with a credit card may automatically increase the price by 20 to 25 percent because the transaction results in a record that the fiscal sleuths may get hold of.

Such practices are of course well known in other countries, but in Italy they are the rule. Some time ago the Finance Ministry issued a Red Book listing 200,000 alleged tax dodgers, designed to make them blush with shame. Among them was one Pietro Mazza, said to be thirty years old and a student: He was reported to have made $8 million in a few years without paying a lira in income tax—enough to promote him instantly to the status of folk hero. Press reporters tried to track the "student" with the sensational earning power but failed; they did find his parents, who were living in modest circumstances in a town in Calabria and proved unable or unwilling to provide any information on the younger Mazza's whereabouts and activities. Chances are the evanescent "student" was another *faccendiere*. This term is current Italian idiom for a high-living, publicity-shy individual who seems to have no identifiable job or profession but is a master of "arrangement," with a finger in many pies and interests in many affairs (*faccende*).

Nobody in the world likes to pay taxes, and there are people everywhere who, given a chance, will avoid doing so, but many Italians go to exceptional lengths to evade their fiscal obligations. In 1988 Treasury officials audited 170,000 tax returns and found that in 89 percent of them income had been grossly underreported. Italy's mammoth budget deficits year after year would soon be wiped out if all taxpayers were to become honest overnight, which is as likely as the nation forswearing pasta. Besides, anybody living in Italy knows that there are more ways of circumventing the tax laws than there are ways of preparing spaghetti or pizza. In a nation where the overwhelming majority of the population regards its democratically elected political leaders as a bunch of *ladri* (thieves) and freely says so in public, anyone cheating the government may be sure of general benevolence or at least toleration and can find plenty of accomplices.

Some elegant stores in Rome, Florence, Venice, and Milan employ their own "fiscal hostesses," smartly dressed women who after a sale accompany the customer for a few city blocks; on saying good-bye and thank you, these escorts take the sales slip back: It will be handed to the next client. The reason for this minuet is that agents of the Finance Guard sometimes hang around in the neighborhood of businesses to check on emerging customers and ask for proof that their purchase has been duly recorded by the mandatory cash register and that the sales tax has been paid. By the same token, many grocery stores have trained their staffs to make "mistakes" when they ring up what a customer has to pay: You are told that the milk, vegetables, and olive oil you have bought cost 13,400 lire, and you count out that amount, but if you look at the sales slip it says 1,340 lire, which would indeed be a bargain; few customers protest.

The practice of auto mechanics, plumbers, carpenters, and other craftsmen wanting payment in cash and willing to be prompt and accommodating when told the customer doesn't need a receipt is commonplace in Italy as it is elsewhere. But Italian physicians and dentists too look grim, as if they were themselves going to have a wisdom tooth pulled, whenever a patient insists on a bill. In that case, their secretary will say, the fee goes up by 20 percent. Italy's 150,000 practicing medical doctors report to the tax authorities an average income of $26,000 a year, less than what many middle-echelon white-collar workers earn, although many of them are known to make at least ten times as much. Apart from the medical profession, tax dodging is notorious among lawyers, architects, and hotel managers in tourist areas. Many of these more affluent dodgers, knowing that their expensive imported cars and yachts are likely to attract the attention of the tax office, register them in the names of ghost corporations domiciled in Liechtenstein or the Bahamas.

"Tax evasion is really an unspoken understanding, a contract, among millions of Italians," according to Joseph La Palombara, an American political scientist who has analyzed the Italian democratic system. "There is something fundamentally democratic about tax evasion; one way or the other, the practice is open to a very large proportion of the adult population." Except, that is, wage earners whose taxes are automatically deducted to the full legal extent from their take-home pay and who have no second, black-economy job. Nor can retirees and other economically vulnerable people who are being browbeaten by doctors, merchants, and plumbers into becoming accessories to tax-dodging schemes avoid being squeezed by the revenue-starved state. The entire nation pays stiff levies on consumption, like the gasoline tax, because the fiscal bureaucracy is unable to get enough money out of the rich.

It may be that the cynicism of nearly institutionalized tax evasion appeals to Italians' sense of comedy, with their conspiratorial winking whenever some "arrangement" is being pulled off. The labor unions at any rate keep pressing for fiscal reforms that would at last force big earners to pay adequate taxes, but union leaders know that their own rank and file includes uncounted workers who after hours do all kinds of jobs for cash, no receipt asked or issued. Earnest announcements by the government from time to time that the ultimate sweeping drive against tax dodgers is about to start are taken as a bad joke, like the periodic official promises of an all-out campaign to finish off the Mafia.

Wary of the tax collector, most individuals and quite a few firms in Italy provide incomplete or outright misleading data to officials, or they try to withhold information altogether. The figures published periodically (and belatedly) by the National Institute of Statistics are widely challenged. In 1987 the government conceded that its macroeconomic numbers had been too low all along because they had kept ignoring the country's vast "submerged," or black, economy. Italy revised the estimate of its gross domestic product upward by 15 percent and claimed it had surpassed Britain among the world's foremost industrial powers. Soon afterward the European Community went about reassessing the contributions to its budget that its member states should make, and asked Italy, in view of its increased official wealth, to pay more.

The Rome government protested indignantly, and its foreign minister said, for home consumption, that it had been a big mistake to correct the national statistics—in other words, the "submerged" economy ought to stay submerged and the statistical services should continue "arranging" their numbers.

Actually, Italy's black economy is not just 15 percent of the gross domestic product but, according to some international experts, a whopping 30 percent. (The Organization for Economic Cooperation and Development, the Paris-based group of advanced free-market countries, sets the average share of the black economy in its member states at 4 percent of their gross domestic products, although other experts believe it may be as high as 7 to 10 percent.) Even the most conservative estimates assume that Italy's "submerged" economy is exceptionally flourishing. It is apparently comparable to the black economies in Communist and Third World countries, where illegal trading and deals, institutionalized graft, corruption, and the narcotics traffic are more notoriously rampant.

If outlawed and criminal activities are taken into account, "submerged" Italy may produce as much as one-third of all its residents' income. This would explain such mysteries as why Sicily, statistically among the poorest regions in the nation, can provide so much business for its many bank branches, and why the Naples area and Calabria with their high official unemployment rates are good markets for expensive imported automobiles.

Still, by far the larger part of the black economy is untainted by crime, although it may indeed be illegal to employ undocumented Tunisians as crews on fishing vessels, to have Senegalese peddle cheap print scarves and imitation-leather belts, or to put a wall-to-wall carpet in somebody's living room without signing a receipt for the cash payment. Many small businesses that are listed in the telephone directory and have their own files at the tax office seem to navigate in the legitimate economy but are concealing a bulky submerged operation; they keep two sets of books, one for official use and secret records reflecting real earnings.

The many thousands of independent, resourceful Italians who have created and are running small or medium-size enterprises, all the time making their own "arrangements," are the pioneers of an adventurous trek that within one generation has taken a war-ravaged country with more than half of its active population still on the farms into the forefront of the world's industrial powers. They are the tailors and designers who call themselves couturiers now and are drawing buyers and fashion reporters from New York and Tokyo to their showings; the four Treviso siblings whose mix-and-match knits with their merry colors are today being sold in thousands of Benetton stores around the globe; the owners of the small steel mills in the Brescia region who manufacture structural rods outselling those offered by the state-subsidized steel giants in the European Common Market; the appliance makers who saturated Italian households with refrigerators and vacuum cleaners and conquered foreign markets too; and the managers of 9,000 footwear factories, many of them with fewer than twenty workers, who in the early 1980s marketed 400 million pairs of shoes annually on all continents.

The boom of the Italian footwear industry, however, has proved short-lived. East Asian shoe exporters soon became formidable rivals worldwide and even succeeded in winning customers in Italy. Their sales offensive serves as an example of how vulnerable the Italian system of a multitude of small, independent production units is to competition from Third World countries with low labor costs and modern plants. To keep markets abroad and fend off inroads at home, the small

Italian firms will probably have to band together and adopt more advanced technologies.

At any rate, the small Italian entrepreneurs—many of them former artisans or foremen—have up to now survived and thrived by striking private deals with their labor force, bribing officials, wooing bankers, inventing their own publicity campaigns, mapping strategies to get around laws and regulations, becoming friendly with influential politicians, doing favors left and right to obtain other favors in return, and testing foreign markets with little help from Italian commercial attachés or chambers of commerce (who won't necessarily do for a shoemaker in Monselice near Padua what they do for Fiat or Olivetti). In short, the trailblazers of industrial expansion have had to excel in the old Italian art of fixing things and people.

There is one huge organization that could be chosen as a case study if a textbook on the techniques of "arrangement" were ever written: the National Hydrocarbons Agency (Ente Nazionale Idrocarburi, or ENI). This group, with far more than 100,000 employees, is nominally controlled by the government but for a long time has behaved like a sovereign state within the Italian Republic, with its own laws, loyalties, and foreign policy.

ENI is the creation of one man, Enrico Mattei. Born in a town on the Adriatic coast, son of a carabinieri sergeant, he had a sketchy education and after working for a leather tanning firm had a checkered career as a medium-level manager and marketing specialist in other industries. Toward the end of World War II he joined the anti-Nazi resistance movement and played a minor role in the foundation of the Christian Democratic party. As a reward for his underground activities Mattei received from the new government a modest plum: He was to be the liquidator of the state-owned petroleum agency that Mussolini had set up in the hope it would find oil in fuel-starved Italy or its overseas possessions. Almost all the agency's attempts had failed, and the nation remained dependent on large coal and oil imports. (What Italy never knew was that it was sitting on an underground ocean of oil in Libya, its colony from 1911 until the Allied armies conquered it in World War II.)

Mattei did not close down the petroleum agency, as he was supposed to do, but balanced its budget and stepped up its activities. His men drilled in many places on the peninsula and, while their search for oil remained largely unsuccessful, they did strike vast deposits of natural gas. Methane gas thus became a convenient source of energy for the country's growing industries, and Mattei made the most of it. As manager of a virtual natural gas monopoly, he suddenly had plenty of money at his disposal and was wielding considerable power. His technicians laid a grid of gas pipelines in Northern Italy, ignoring rights-of-way and private properties, and without bothering to secure the prescribed permits. Work crews and earth-moving equipment would appear in an area one day and dig ditches and sink tubings into them the next, leaving it to Mattei's lawyers to sort out protests, claims, and injunctions. Bribing or bullying local officials and real-estate owners into compliance, Mattei usually had his way. His influence mounted as he began subsidizing diverse political parties, factions, and journalists. In 1953 Mattei transformed the old petroleum agency into ENI and became the new concern's president.

ENI thereupon built thousands of modern service stations along the country's highways and, together with Fiat, promoted the expansion of the highway network. Mattei's agency also branched out into engineering, the petrochemical industry, and large-scale contracting. Soon it even had its own daily newspaper, *Il Giorno* of Milan. A black, fire-breathing animal with six legs designed by Mattei's publicity staff—a monstrous wolf? a dog?—became the emblem of the "Italian gasoline," glowering from uncounted signs. Yet Mattei remained an oilman without oil, and as Italy's energy needs rose steeply, ENI had to import ever larger quantities of crude for its refineries and its "Italian gasoline."

Soon Mattei was dickering for prospecting and drilling concessions in petroleum-producing countries, especially in the Middle East. He irked the Western oil companies that had long been entrenched in the area—the "Seven Sisters"—by offering the Iranian and Arab governments a favorable deal: Instead of practicing the then customary 50–50 split of oil profits, ENI would let them keep 75 percent. In Middle Eastern capitals ENI's representatives soon had easier access to the local rulers than did the accredited Italian ambassadors; in Rome, Mattei appeared to have more clout and better information than did the foreign ministers of the weak, quickly changing governments of Italy itself.

Italy had joined the Atlantic Alliance, but Mattei's personal foreign policy, favoring collaboration with Middle Eastern and other Third World states, seemed neutralist if not outspokenly anti-Western. Washington archives contain evidence that the administration of President Eisenhower was viewing Mattei with distrust. Nevertheless, ENI's maneuvering struck sympathetic chords at home. As in domestic politics, "arrangements" have traditionally been a favorite strategy in Italy's international relations. Operating on different levels and through various channels, Rome's diplomacy usually tries to keep in touch with all powers that count. Italy's elasticity in international affairs has often exasperated its allies.

In 1955 ENI money and Mattei's influence helped elect the left-wing Christian Democrat Giovanni Gronchi as president of the Republic. Gronchi confusedly endorsed an Italian drift toward neutrality, but that didn't trouble Mattei. At the same time ENI had been financing a strong faction within the Christian Democratic party, it had been subsidizing other political groups and was bribing a chorus of journalists to sing the praises of the oil-and-gas agency and its chief. (The aged Gronchi was to be portrayed posthumously in lurid colors by Italian newspapers, with dark allegations about his personal integrity.)

The tall, good-looking Mattei was at the height of his power. No *dolce vita* for him: He was working incessantly and traveling often; a few rare hours of trout fishing in Alpine streams were his only relaxation. He was negotiating with the shah of Iran, with Middle Eastern sheikhs, and eventually with the government of newly independent Algeria. He even appeared amenable to making peace, at last, with the Seven Sisters. Mattei died in October 1962, when his personal jet, having taken off from Sicily, crashed near Milan in a thunderstorm. The inescapable theories of a plot variously blamed the Seven Sisters, foreign or domestic secret services, or the Mafia. Investigators found no clues pointing to foul play, but the rumors about Mattei's untimely end linger on.

Today many Italian political experts and sociologists look back on Mattei as a virtuoso of "arrangement" to whom a good deal of the pervasive corruption in the country can be traced. His posthumous admirers concede that he liked cutting corners but contend that Mattei wanted to get things done in order to create jobs and to secure cheap energy for his country. The black, fire-breathing, six-legged wolf or dog has remained the totem of ENI service stations, and the group is still a big employer. Its "Italian gasoline" continues flowing mainly from the Middle East, and ENI must also import natural gas from Algeria, the Netherlands, and the Soviet Union because domestic fields are approaching exhaustion. The roaring Mattei years are no more than a memory.

The remaining enterprises in the broad state sector of the Italian economy are not doing too well either. They include the largest part of the nation's iron and steel industry, big shipyards and shipping lines, major banks, virtually all the country's power plants, the telephone service, the national broadcasting system, the national airline, Alitalia, and a grab bag of manufacturing and other enterprises. Many organizations in this checkered assortment are gobbling taxpayers' money—the steel mills have done so for decades—and all are hampered by political interference and the elephantine bureaucracy.

As for the handful of Italy's large, privately owned industrial concerns, survival often depends on the same techniques of "arrangement" that have kept the nation's small and medium-size firms alive. The big companies have the flexibility and financial resources to substitute their own services for the unreliable infrastructures their country is offering them, so they operate their own electronic mail systems, rely on their own couriers, fly their own corporate jets, train their personnel in in-house schools, and make their money transactions through their foreign subsidiaries and bank connections. If the airports of Milan, Turin, or Genoa are tied up by strikes, the big-company executives dash by car to nearby Switzerland, to fly from there to New York, London, Frankfurt, or Singapore. The leading industrial combines, like semiautonomous principalities within the disjointed Italian Republic, are making "arrangements" commensurate with their size and interests.

To survive and prosper as an entrepreneur, small or big, in the Italian socioeconomic landscape, one not only has to master the art of "arrangement" but also must possess an extra dose of *furbizia* (astuteness). *Furbizia* is a legacy from a long history of political powerlessness, a weapon of the weak. For centuries the people had to humor local princelings and prelates, oligarchs, petty despots, papal legates, Spanish viceroys, French governors, and Austrian generals. To get what one wanted or avoid what one feared, one had to act by indirection, to dissemble, to play a double or triple game. Cunning as a strategy for getting on in life has been cultivated in Italy since time immemorial and is being used today in politics, business and the professions, and everyday existence.

Equally ancient is the Italian delight in the *beffa*, the playing of nasty tricks on someone, usually a powerful or pompous person. Literature since the Tuscan novelists of the thirteenth century, and history itself, are full of celebrated *beffe*, some of them quite cruel, that made everyone—except of course the victim—laugh and applaud. The tradition of the *beffa* is still being observed in smaller cities and towns, often as a by-product of soccer fever. (The Italian idiom indeed likens the excitement caused by spectator sports to the fever produced by typhus, calling it *tifo*; the sports fan is a *tifoso*, a typhus patient.) Friends of a soccer fan band together in an elaborate scheme to make their target believe that while he is in the stadium to cheer on his favorite team his wife or girlfriend is cuckolding him. Eventually everything is ostensibly cleared up, the friends contritely offer their victim a reconciliation dinner, then they get him dead drunk. They load him into a car, drive 200 miles to a town he doesn't know, and dump him on a park bench so that when he at last wakes up with a hangover he is completely disoriented.

Outsmarting the other fellow, making him look dumb (*far fesso*), always wins great admiration in Italy—whether a motorist slips like a tiger into the only free parking slot while a clumsier driver who saw it first is still maneuvering in reverse gear, or a financier with borrowed money takes over a big company in a lightning raid and proceeds to strip it of its assets. Those who have been outwitted by an "arrangement" artist can only voice their disgust at the base tactics of the *solito furbo* (the name for the garden variety of crafty operator). The *furbo* will be envied and get congratulations.

6.

All in the Family?

The true patriotism of the Italians is loyalty to their own families, Luigi Barzini, Jr., used to say. He himself, however, did not have a particularly happy family life, although he rarely talked about it. He and I were "friends," the way the word is often used in Italy: We occasionally had lunch together, got in touch by phone to exchange information or to ask for small favors, and often referred other "friends" to each other. I never called Barzini "Luigi," but always "Onorevole," because as a representative of the Liberal party (a conservative group despite its name) in the Chamber of Deputies he was entitled to be addressed as "Honorable." He remained the Honorable Barzini even after he failed to be reelected to Parliament. His book *The Italians*, a best-seller in the English-language edition, did not make him any friends at home. Yet Barzini was among the foremost Italian journalists of his generation. He was proud to be an Italian, yet he had few illusions about his compatriots.

Until his death in 1984 Barzini always carried the "Jr." with his name to distinguish himself from his late father, who had also been a prominent journalist, and a member of the Italian Senate. Educated in the United States, the younger Barzini was bilingual, and when writing in English he managed to maintain an Italian rhythm that added charm to his style. In 1940 he married Giannalisa Feltrinelli, the widow of one of Italy's richest businessmen. As a foreign and war correspondent, Barzini Jr. hobnobbed with Fascist bigwigs (his father too had supported the Fascist regime) but then became caught in the intrigues that marked the last years of Mussolini's rule, and was disciplined. His punishment consisted of a comfortable exile in Amalfi. After the downfall of Il Duce, Barzini was able to claim he had been persecuted for anti-Fascist activities. He published a new financial daily, *Il Globo*, for some time and later became one of the star writers of *Corriere della Sera* of Milan, the Italian newspaper with the largest circulation and greatest prestige. He also acted as an unofficial consultant to a succession of U.S. ambassadors in Rome.

Barzini's family life was stressful. He had, as he later admitted, cold relations with his stepson Giangiacomo Feltrinelli (whose role in the terrorist underground will be described in chapter 8). Barzini always disapproved of his stepson's restlessness, adventurous life, and political extremism. His marriage to Giangiacomo's mother soon fell apart. I remember her strutting along the Via Condotti in Rome wearing a monocle; she later moved to the United States and generated news by acrimonious inheritance litigation. Barzini remarried. Eventually he separated from his second wife and then lived on and off with women companions. Tall, dark, and good-looking until a mature age, Barzini had always exercised a strong attraction to women. He endured his last illness with stoicism and died like an old Roman.

In *The Italians* he devoted a chapter to the Italian family structure, describing it as a closely knit community held together by emotional attachments and material interests, ever ready to form a common front against all outsiders and to take care of its own. In a nation whose other social institutions are notoriously brittle, the family has indeed long been functioning as the sole unit that, rocklike, withstands hell and high water.

The Italian notion of mutual assistance based on kinship has been termed "amoral familism" by Edward C. Banfield, who analyzed an extreme form of it in his book *The Moral Basis of a Backward Society*. Banfield had spent nine months with his Italian-speaking wife and their two children in a village of 3,400 inhabitants in Basilicata, in the instep of the Italian boot. Interviewing seventy people he found that the place's extreme poverty and underdevelopment were the results of the population's inability "to act together for their common good or, indeed, for any end transcending the immediate, material interest of the nuclear family." The only grouping in the village was a loose club of twenty-five or thirty people who were a little better off than the rest of their fellow citizens; they met to play cards and never discussed any community project. True, this was the Deep South, but Banfield quotes the findings of tests that an Italian researcher, Ivano Rinaldi, had applied to peasants in the province of Rovigo, between Venice and Bologna in Italy's North: There was "a similar, although less marked, tendency to see every situation in terms of family." (The most egregious example of criminal familism is, of course, the Mafia.)

Strong familism, whether conceived as moral or amoral, also characterizes other societies around the Mediterranean. Domineering patriarchs, clinging matriarchs, and relatives who stick together to defend and further the interests of the family or the clan can be found among Spaniards, Greeks, Turks, and Arabs. As for the Italians, there is plenty of evidence that family bonds are loosening. Good times seem less favorable to kinship solidarity than bad ones. Money quarrels, unsavory divorces, and generational conflicts have lately rent several prominent families.

One of them is the Guccis of Florence. For years they

fought messily over control of Guccio Gucci S.p.A., which annually sells hundreds of millions of dollars' worth of fine shoes and other leatherware throughout the world, and over the use of the Gucci name. The family feud was accompanied by fiscal troubles as Italian authorities charged various members of the clan with having accumulated huge funds and other assets abroad in violation of their home country's restrictive financial laws. Despite such unpleasantness the Florentine family name remains a universal byword for a new, elegant, sophisticated Italy; the nation's diplomats are pleased to report to Rome whenever the secretary general of the Soviet Communist party or some other personage among the mighty of the world sports a Gucci product.

Marital and money conflicts also bedeviled the descendants of Angelo Rizzoli, who had built from scratch a publishing and film empire; of Arnoldo Mondadori, founder of the nation's largest publishing house; and of Gaetano Marzotto, under whom the old family spinning mill at Valdagno northwest of Venice developed into one of Europe's largest textile combines.

It was a junior branch of the Marzotto clan that furnished Italy with the ripest society scandal in years. Back when Italy still had a king, the rich Marzotto family was elevated to the nobility; thus, one of Gaetano's sons, Umberto Marzotto, on marrying the pretty daughter of a poor railroad worker in 1954, metamorphosed her into a countess. The new Countess Marta Marzotto bore her husband five children and for many years led the comfortable life of a noble and wealthy provincial matron. Toward the end of the 1960s, she moved to a penthouse apartment overlooking the Spanish Square in Rome and started entertaining the capital's elite. Writers like Alberto Moravia and Pier Paolo Pasolini, film directors like Lina Wertmuller and Bernardo Bertolucci, Communist party leaders, government members, elder statesmen of the Christian Democratic party, and an occasional prelate or two from the Vatican used to drop in to sit on Marta's famous white sofas, eat her rice salad and other snacks, drink the wine from the Marzotto vineyards in Venetia, and engage in the favorite Roman pastime of blandly malicious gossip.

Marta's salon—later transferred to an even more opulent home in a villa below the Pincio—was noteworthy also for its abundance of paintings and frescoes by Renato Guttuso. The Sicilian artist had been an early member of the Communist party, kept pleasing Stalinists with his style of "proletarian realism," and in 1974 received the Soviet Union's Lenin Peace Prize. Because of his political connections—and because most Italian intellectuals and quite a few bourgeois were then fawning on Communists—criticisms of Guttoso's orthodox art were muted. His paintings fetched high prices, his output was prodigious, and he became very rich. When he met Countess Marta Marzotto, the master of "proletarian" art was himself living like a wealthy aristocrat in a medieval tower near the Roman Forum, the Torre del Grillo, with a butler who put on white gloves to serve tea to visitors.

All Rome knew that Marta and the Communist artist were lovers; the countess's husband and Guttuso's wife could not have been unaware of the relationship. Guttuso portrayed his mistress in innumerable paintings—dressed, naked, in her bathroom, in fantastic or allegorical poses—and quite a few of these works were hung in her salon. The affair took a comedic twist when Marta started a parallel liaison with a handsome, gray-haired politician of the extreme left wing, Lucio Magri. Guttuso made frequent scenes and vented his jealousy by painting unflattering portraits of his rival. A sad denouement came late in 1986, when Guttuso succumbed to cancer at age seventy-four, a few months after his wife,

Mimise, had died. While he was lying sick in his tower home, Marta had—inexplicably to her—been denied access, so she mobilized her friends in the police department and in the Vatican to get messages through to her lover. High-ranking Communists and Christian Democrats attended Guttuso's funeral, and right afterward a welter of investigations, lawsuits, contentious interviews, public recriminations, and denials shed a lurid light on what had all those years been going on in Countess Marzotto's salon and in the Communist painter-prince's tower.

It turned out that Guttuso before his death had adopted a young Sicilian, who, since the painter had been childless, appeared to be the sole heir to his fortune, which consisted of, among other assets, real estate in Rome and Sicily and many paintings. A young Roman came forward, claiming to be an illegitimate son of Guttuso, and relatives of the artist's dead wife also staked claims to the inheritance. Marta Marzotto did not ask for any part of Guttuso's fortune but kept maintaining publicly that the painter had during his last illness been illegally prevented from seeing her. Eventually Marta's husband started divorce proceedings, and she requested the court to order Count Marzotto to pay her a lavish alimony. By then in her midfifties, Marta Marzotto resumed her brilliant role in Italian society, gracing many celebrations and top parties, acting as moderator on television talk shows, and clearly savoring her succès de scandale.

While the family affairs of business tycoons and aristocrats provided object lessons illustrating the decadence of kinship loyalty among the rich, the House of Savoy, Italy's ruling family until 1946, also supplied piquant morsels for the gossip magazines over many years. Umberto II, the nation's last king, separated from his queen, the Belgian-born Maria José, soon after they arrived in exile in Portugal, and she took up residence near Geneva. The split-up royal couple's three daughters went through widely publicized marriages and divorces, and their only son, Prince Victor Emmanuel, married an Italian commoner. The French police arrested Victor Emmanuel on a charge of manslaughter—he appeared to have shot and killed a young yachting-set German off the small island of Cavallo, south of Corsica—but the prince was soon free again, and the case against him languished. Following ex-King Umberto's death, his four children bickered over the rich inheritance. Victor Emmanuel's claim to the throne of Rome was challenged by a cousin, Prince Amedeo of Savoy-Aosta, but then the two pretenders made up. Most Italians followed such royal mischief with amusement rather than emotional involvement. Although King Umberto was voted out by only a slight margin in the 1946 plebiscite that led to the birth of the Italian Republic, a few Italians today profess themselves monarchists. A Savoy restoration seems about as likely as a French king reigning again in Versailles or the Tuileries.

Discord among close relatives and disruption of kinship bonds that appear to contradict the stereotype of the unassailable Italian family are not confined to the prominent and the rich. I know scores of ordinary Italian families with sons and daughters estranged from their parents, siblings locked in bitter lawsuits and no longer on speaking terms, and aged widows and widowers abandoned by their children or relegated to old-people's homes with perfunctory visits or telephone calls every now and then. The chronic-disease wards of Italian hospitals fill up every summer with elderly patients whom their relatives park there for months so they can enjoy their vacations unencumbered by an ailing grandmother or uncle. Prosperity, birth control, freer sexual mores, feminism, and the introduction of divorce (much later than in neighboring countries) all have contributed to weakening family structures that once were at least proverbially solid.

Barzini asserted in 1964 that divorce would "never" be legalized in Italy. He himself, like many thousands of his compatriots, had ended his marriages by juridical stratagems: One could take up pro forma residence in the tiny Republic of San Marino, in Switzerland, in Mexico, or in some other country with easy divorce laws, or one could obtain a Roman Catholic church annulment with the costly guidance of specialized lawyers. But divorce legislation in Italy long seemed out of the question because the church and the dominant Christian Democratic party were adamantly opposed to any reform of the laws regulating marriage.

Yet divorce was introduced in Italy in 1970, when the left-wing parties and the small anticlerical center groups in Parliament surprisingly mustered enough votes. True, the new rules called for a five-year waiting period from the moment a married couple had formally separated. Nevertheless, the old principle that an Italian marriage was indissoluble—save through annulment by a state or church court—had been scrapped. The Christian Democrats remained nearly isolated in the Chamber of Deputies and the Senate in their defense of the old, rigid legislation. They were backed only by the neo-Fascists.

The Vatican was outraged. Militant Roman Catholics collected enough signatures to request a referendum aimed at repealing the divorce statute. Urged on by Pope Paul VI, the church hierarchy pulled out all the stops in an effort to bring out a massive repeal vote, and the Christian Democratic party dutifully went along, staging a nationwide antidivorce crusade. A peak of silliness was reached when the veteran Christian Democratic leader Amintore Fanfani, a onetime and future premier, warned at a rally in the Sicilian city of Caltanissetta that the divorce legislation would enable disgruntled wives to run off with their maids to set up lesbian households. The referendum took place in 1974, and two-thirds of the electorate upheld divorce—a humiliating blow to the clerical forces. Many Italians who went to mass every Sunday had voted for divorce, proving that they, like Roman Catholics in other countries, were selective in obeying the teachings of their church.

Many couples who had long been living apart, maybe with new partners by whom they had children, were at last able to have their collapsed marriages lawfully ended and to remarry. But the large, general rush into divorce that adversaries of the reform had predicted did not occur. In 1987 the legal waiting period between separation and divorce was reduced to three years. By then it was assumed that one out of every fifteen new marriages would end in divorce—a far smaller divorce rate than in France, Britain, or the United States. And, not surprisingly, divorce is much more frequent in the industrial North than it is in the underdeveloped South of Italy.

An increasing number of Italians are now cohabiting without having bothered to go through a wedding rite in a church or city hall, and the numbers of single-person households, especially in Rome and the big cities of the North, are on the rise too. It is commonplace to run into someone who will introduce a live-in partner as "my companion." (*Compagno* and *compagna*, the masculine and feminine forms of the Italian word for "companion," also happen to be used in Communist party parlance for "comrade," a coincidence that occasionally causes misunderstandings.)

The introduction of divorce meant an uncomfortable moment of truth for uncounted Italians, particularly for married men who had, more or less clandestinely, been conducting adulterous affairs. For years they had been telling their mistresses that if there were only a way to end their unhappy marriages they would of course become man and wife and live openly and happily together. Now that this solution was possible, many men and quite a few women who had been maintaining triangular relationships began stalling. Some said they preferred to wait for divorce until their children had grown; others who had always claimed their spouses did not understand them showed no inclination at all to shed them. Long before divorce became legal, Guglielmo Giannini, a playwright who was then publishing a mass-circulation weekly and was on his way to becoming a political force for a few years, told me, "If one wants to get rid of the wife with whom one has been married for a number of years to live with a younger woman one loves, there are many ways to do it, even without divorce—but who has the heart to do it?" Giannini did not, nor did numberless other Italians, before or after divorce legislation.

Some Italians seem to need the thrills and stress of adultery. Luigi Pirandello remained creative while caught in the enduring predicament of marriage to a high-strung, possibly insane wife who kept him fearful, all the while maintaining a love affair with an adoring actress, Marta Abba. Mussolini, in those same years, would rip off the shirts of female admirers who had been admitted to his monumental office in the Palazzo Venezia and throw them on a couch without—as some of those visitors later confided—taking off his boots. Later Il Duce, then in his fifties, settled into a permanent liaison with Clara ("Claretta") Petacci, the daughter of a well-to-do Roman physician who held a job in the Vatican health department.

Mussolini had a villa for Claretta and her family built on Mount Mario, a hill in the north of Rome, and saw her almost daily in his office. When the wartime fuel shortage led to a general ban on private cars, he placed a fake taxicab with a police driver in plain clothes at the disposal of his mistress so that she could shuttle unobtrusively between her new home and his Palazzo Venezia. All the time the dictator kept up the appearance of his marriage to Rachele, who had been his hometown sweetheart, sleeping every night in the Villa Torlonia, their residence on the eastern outskirts of the capital.

After a carabinieri detail arrested Mussolini in a palace coup in July 1943 and a Nazi commando freed him, he sent for Claretta to rejoin him at his new refuge on Lake Garda and saw her again daily while he was going through the motions of ruling over his Nazi-satellite "Social Republic" in that northern part of Italy the Allied forces had still to occupy. There was a long-delayed confrontation between Rachele and Claretta, almost in the way Italian wives who at last learn of their husbands' unfaithfulness vent their rage in a hair-pulling fight with their rivals. When Communist partisans captured Mussolini and Claretta in April 1945 and put them up against a garden fence on Lake Como, she tried to shield him with her body; they died together, and their corpses were strung up, heads downward, at a service station in the Piazzale Loreto in nearby Milan.

After the ultimate collapse of the Fascist dictatorship and the end of World War II, researchers found proof in the government files that Mussolini had all those years been spying on his own lieutenants, Italy's military leaders and other prominent personages of his regime. His secret police had been opening letters, tapping hundreds of telephones, and shadowing many people. Every day Il Duce had set aside ample time for perusing the police reports about the peccadilloes, greed, and secret vices of his ministers, generals, and Fascist party officials. He must have thought that through such surveillance he'd be sure to remain in absolute control, but he may also have derived cynical pleasure from the evidence of how rotten his underlings were.

While the newly free Italian press was reveling in disclosures about the turbulent love lives of Il Duce and his henchmen, there were soon other spicy affairs to talk about. Palmiro

Togliatti, leader of the Italian Communist party when it re-emerged from long obscurity to develop quickly into the strongest Marxist machine in the West, became the protagonist in a fascinating triangle. The cold, intellectual Communist kept living with his wife of many years, Rita Montagnana, when, in his early fifties, he started an intimate relationship with a young party comrade who had just been elected to Parliament, Leonilde ("Nilde") Iotti. Togliatti's wife was an old Communist who had shared exile in Moscow with him, and veteran party activists were shocked when they learned of their leader's fling with young Nilde. For some time the two lovers were able to steal some privacy only in a spartan office suite at Communist party headquarters in Rome's Via delle Botteghe Oscure.

Eventually Togliatti publicly repudiated his wife, obtained a divorce in the Soviet Union, and married Nilde there. His late-blooming romance did not diminish his prestige among the rank and file, nor the respect he commanded among many non-Communist Italians. After his death in 1964, Nilde Iotti was co-opted into the inner councils of the Communist party apparatus and in 1979 was elected president (speaker) of the Italian Chamber of Deputies.

Adultery and unfaithfulness have always been major themes in Italian life and art. A famous episode in Dante's *Divine Comedy* (*Inferno*, canto 5) recalls how the beautiful Francesca da Rimini and her brother-in-law and lover were put to death by her husband, Giovanni ("the Lame") Malatesta, after he had discovered their affair. Another Malatesta, the young and passionate Parisina, was beheaded with her stepson after her husband, Duke Niccolò III of Ferrara, had surprised them as lovers. In a murky Renaissance tragedy in 1576, Isabella de' Medici, who was widely renowned for her beauty and learning, was strangled by her own husband, Prince Paolo Giordano Orsini, who posthumously slandered her as a nymphomaniac while he himself married his mistress after conveniently having her husband stabbed to death. Yet despite such celebrated family tragedies, erotic and adulterous entanglements have mostly been farcical in the eyes of Italians, ever since Boccaccio in his *Decameron* and Machiavelli in *La Mandragola* made fun of cuckolds.

In our time the great actor and film director Vittorio De Sica lived for years in a bigamous situation that might have made an excellent plot for one of his hilarious movies. He was the father figure in two households—one with his actress wife, Giuditta Rissone, by whom he had a daughter, the other with the Spanish actress Maria Mercader and their two sons. He eventually divorced his wife in Mexico, apparently without her knowledge, and married Maria there, but in Italy he remained legally married to Giuditta. Shuttling between his two homes in Rome—whenever he was not on one of his frequent and ruinous gambling trips to Monte Carlo—De Sica imperturbably enjoyed two Christmas and two New Year dinners every year, and would separately take his daughter, Emi, and his sons, Manuel and Christian, to the circus. Giuditta and Maria soon found out about De Sica's double life, and their children, at Emi's initiative, eventually met in a Roman park, but the actor-director carried on the charade almost to his death in 1974.

The other master of Italy's neorealist film school, Roberto Rossellini, instead managed, like a biblical patriarch, to establish outward harmony between his Roman ex-wife; his second wife, Ingrid Bergman; the Indian divorcée Sonali Das Gupta, with whom he set up housekeeping in Rome; and the various children the three had borne him. His real nemesis for some time was Anna Magnani, the volcanic Roman actress who had given an unforgettable performance in his classic *Open City*. Rossellini was living with Anna in a suite at the Excelsior Hotel on the Via Veneto in Rome when he received Bergman's invitation to Hollywood. He told Magnani he was going to walk the dog, left the pet with the hall porter, and rushed to Ciampino Airport to catch a flight to the United States. By the time Bergman arrived in Rome to star in a Rossellini picture, Magnani had vacated the Excelsior suite, and the Swedish actress moved in. For months, however, Rossellini was persecuted by his former lover—who herself had long been separated from another film director—and he remained deathly afraid of her ambushes and real-life scenes.

After Rossellini had escorted Bergman from the airport to the Excelsior, I rode with them up to their suite. With us was a young free-lance photographer who had squeezed into the elevator and brazenly penetrated into the Rossellini suite to take pictures there too, flash after flash, until the film director with the help of a hotel security man threw him out. I had stopped at the entrance to the suite, glimpsing a lavish flower arrangement inside; the arrival of the world-famous movie star in Rome also warranted coverage by *The New York Times*, for which I was reporting.

A few months later the American media would get even more excited, and Bergman's conduct would be brought up in the U.S. Congress, after she had given birth to Rossellini's son in a Roman clinic while still being legally the wife of Dr. Peter Lindstrom of Los Angeles. The Bergman-Rossellini romance, denounced as scandalous by puritanical Americans at the time, helped spread the myth of the Latin lover—in the shape of the mature and well-fed Rossellini, as it was—and of his wicked charm all over the world.

The impudent young man who would not be shaken off by Rossellini and Bergman was a new character on the Roman scene, and he soon had plenty of local competition. Federico

Fellini included the archetypal, aggressive free-lance photographer among the characters of *La Dolce Vita*, and called him Paparazzo. The movie director may have picked this fairly common name from the telephone directory (Fellini himself gave different versions later of how he chose the name). *Paparazzo* sounds close to the Italian word *papataceo*, denoting a kind of big mosquito, and to a Roman dialect term for cockroach, *bacarozzo*.

Rome was then "Hollywood on the Tiber." American moviemakers, attracted by its low production costs and by the Californialike climate, had started using the Cinecittà (Cinema City) studios on the capital's southeastern outskirts, which had been built under Mussolini. For supporting roles at the side of Hollywood stars local actors were hired, and all the extras were Italians too. In an American remake of *Quo Vadis?* one girl in ancient Rome's surging populace was a bosomy fifteen-year-old from Pozzuoli near Naples whom her actress mother was pushing into a movie career: Sophia Loren. For some years in the 1950s famous producers, world-class stars, directors, cameramen, and scriptwriters shuttled between California and the Italian capital. Then production expenses in Italy rose, local talent demanded higher pay and union contracts, and American filmmakers started looking for other, cheaper locations in Europe. One was Spain. In 1964 an entire Russian village with wooden houses rose near Madrid for the movie version of Pasternak's *Doctor Zhivago*.

Hollywood on the Tiber, while it lasted, not only taught plenty of know-how to local film people but also helped launch the nascent Italian fashion industry on its path to international success. Three seamstresses from the village of Traversetolo near Parma—Zoe, Micol, and Giovanna Fontana—who in 1957 had moved to Rome and opened a workshop off the Spanish Square, now won Ava Gardner,

Elizabeth Taylor, and Audrey Hepburn as clients. The Fontana sisters were among the first Italian designers to seek out prospective American customers in their own country. Micol Fontana told me later that when she was making her first business trip to the United States, the customs inspector at what was then Idlewild Airport asked her routinely: "Do you carry any salami or any other food with you?" He must have thought that anyone with an Italian passport was bringing goodies from the old country to cousins in Brooklyn or New Jersey. The dressmaker, already well known in Italy, opened her bags and showed the inspectors the samples of her and her sisters' haute couture designs, which she was going to offer to department store buyers.

The intrusive craft of the paparazzi was another Italian industry born in Hollywood on the Tiber. Today practitioners with telephoto equipment waylay and besiege prominent individuals at home and abroad to take pictures in unguarded moments or embarrassing situations, and a slew of gossip magazines, largely for middle-class family consumption, are their eager customers. Favorite targets are royalty and ex-royalty, aristocrats, café-society figures, entertainers, and sports stars. The paparazzi, however, are selective in their invasions of other people's privacy. Obeying an unwritten code, they leave Italy's top politicians, industrial tycoons, Mafia godfathers, and Roman Catholic prelates alone—these are powerful personages who might cause them serious trouble. *Eva Express, Novella 2000*, and similar publications regale their many readers in every issue with photos showing a rock idol with a finger in his nose, topless beauties frolicking with princely playboys, or an aging actor pawing his new teenage girlfriend, but never a government member at a discreet dinner with his mistress or a racketeer paying off high officials.

The paparazzi and the print media for which they work have accustomed the Italian public to a class of high-living people who change their spouses and lovers the way avid readers discard paperbacks, are seen in fashionable resorts, drive luxury cars, and launch new fashions. Much of this is fictional, arranged by publicity agents or by the paparazzi themselves, and all of it is remote from the nation's everyday family life. For uncounted Italians the world as projected by the paparazzi has nevertheless become real.

Mention of the salaciousness and frequent vulgarity in Italian information media is in order here. The country's newsmagazines offer soft-core pornography and articles about sexual themes—usually presented tongue-in-cheek as sociological or psychological research—much more often than do comparable publications in other Western countries. The daily newspapers, even the most reputable ones, feature incest and rape cases at great length and seem always to welcome titillating material. Columnists deem it necessary to enliven their prose with earthy references to cuckoldry or erotic prowess.

Corriere della Sera of Milan printed a front-page editorial about "glandular exhibitionism" in the nation's public life, explaining that Italian politicians, business executives, and other leading personages were being evaluated "according to those parts of the body where virile power is expressed or presumed to reside." Such "glandular culture," the editorial declared, was an annoying expression of "vulgarity." It would be difficult to find similar topics on the front page of a major American, British, French, or West German newspaper.

As for the "glandular exhibitionism" of Italian leaders, one is reminded of Count Galeazzo Ciano, Mussolini's son-in-law and foreign minister, who was a redoubtable womanizer. Like many Italian men of the upper class, Ciano had an uninhibited way of scratching his crotch in public, a habit that unnerved British Foreign Secretary Anthony Eden when he met his Italian opposite number in Rome shortly before

World War II broke out, and later also irritated Hitler's foreign minister, Joachim von Ribbentrop, who had to confer often with Ciano.

Today, Italian films produced for home consumption are often replete with obscenities; coarse words (which in Italian usually come in more than four letters) long ago seeped into video programs too. Sexually explicit material is routinely shown on Italian state television and on the private networks in prime time, when, presumably, children are watching with their elders. Anyone familiar with the Italian vernacular who has a chance to overhear youngsters just let out of school will be struck by the grossness of their language. Although I have not seen any comparative survey, I would venture to say that the inscriptions on Italian school buildings and house walls are far more likely to contain obscene words and symbols than do graffiti in America. (The urge to write on walls, especially when they are freshly painted, seems irresistible to many Italians, as it must have been to the ancient Romans. The houses of Pompeii were covered with electoral slogans and private messages.)

Quite a few Italian women brought up in the traditional way before entering the job market have told me how shocked they initially were by the vulgarities they continually heard in the conversation of their male colleagues, and of some female ones too. Coarse expressions that were formerly confined to barracks and bordellos have become colloquialisms since the late 1950s. "It is sufficient to ride on public transport, enter an espresso bar, line up in front of an office window, etc., to hear crude speech dominate unopposed, involving—and this is new—also elderly persons," wrote a woman observer of Italian society in *Panorama* magazine of Milan. "We are today one of the most vulgar peoples in the world."

A hitherto unfamiliar level of public licentiousness was

reached when a performer in hard-core pornographic films and shows was elected to the Italian Chamber of Deputies in 1987. Having officially become "honorable," she enjoyed parliamentary immunity—at least until her colleagues lifted it—from the many obscenity charges in which she was embroiled almost from the day of her arrival in Italy. Her name was Ilona Anna Staller, but she was much better known by her stage name, Cicciolina (the Cuddly One). A native of Budapest, Ilona started a career as a photo model in a Hungarian state agency at the age of thirteen and became an Italian citizen on marrying an immigrant from Calabria when she was twenty-one. She soon moved to Italy, separated from her husband, and picked the Roman talent agent Riccardo Schichi as her porno Pygmalion.

The blond Cuddly One posed for men's magazines and performed in live "adult" shows—sometimes with a python, sometimes urinating on the stage in front of her audiences—and for publicity would from time to time strip in public places. The paparazzi loved her. In preparation for the 1987 parliamentary elections, leaders of the Radical party had the idea of including Cicciolina on their roster of candidates. The intention was to increase interest in the group, which is pledged to fight for human rights, including the rights of homosexuals and prostitutes. To general surprise, nearly 20,000 voters of the Rome-Viterbo-Latina-Frosinone constituency chose the Cuddly One from among the candidates, and she became a legislator. As *onorevole*, Cicciolina attended few Chamber sessions and rarely showed up at meetings of the Armed Forces, Transportation, or Posts and Telecommunications committees to which her colleagues had successively assigned her. Instead she traveled widely in Italy and abroad, continuing her hard-core shows and appearing topless from Lisbon to Jerusalem while other lawmakers, and a good many other citizens worried about the prestige of the Republic's institutions, were gnashing their teeth.

Centuries before the Cuddly One was prancing in porno shows and state television was featuring nudity and scurrilous language, the Italians, despite strictures by the Vatican and the priesthood, already had a reputation for sexual permissiveness. In the Renaissance and afterward the courtesans of Venice and Rome were famous all over Europe for their charms, sophistication, and greed. When Goethe at the age of thirty-seven, in 1786, escaped the stuffiness of the court in Weimar to visit Italy for the first time, he at once started an affair in Rome with a "Faustina"; he would later tell her in hexameter that she should not feel sorry "that you yielded to me so fast." Stendhal learned much about the country from his Italian loves and praised the passionate nature of its women. English lords found the highlights of their grand tours in the ambisextrous amours of Italy. Byron had a notorious liaison with Countess Teresa Guiccioli of Ravenna and occasionally sought bisexual adventures in nearby Venice. Schopenhauer, who despite his philosophical misogyny consumed women as regularly as he read *The Times* of London, conducted something like a steady relationship in Padua for some time. The German lyricist August Graf von Platen and many other famous and obscure homosexuals from various countries found fulfillment in their *voyages en Italie*. Tolstoy in *Anna Karenina* had Count Vronsky and Anna flee to Italy, where nobody would care whether they were married or not. (They got bored eventually and made the mistake of returning to St. Petersburg.) And Gabriele D'Annunzio celebrated sensual gratification in an emblematic novel, *Il Piacere* (Pleasure).

D'Annunzio, with his narcissism, his harem of beautiful and noteworthy women (including the actress Eleonora Duse), his chronic debts, and his kiss-and-tell urges, was an exemplary ancestor of the Latin lover. But times change. Today's stereotypical Italian erotic athlete is usually far less literate though better looking than was the short and bald poet of fin-de-siècle decadence. The Latin lover, a movie cliché since Rudolph Valentino (né Rodolfo d'Antonguolla in Apulia), may by now have become caricatural, but he is still an unadvertised asset of the Italian tourist business. Hotel lobbies, discotheques, beaches, and resorts are his habitat. Deeply tanned, his hair tenderly groomed, in summer his fine shirt wide open to display the gold chain over his virile chest, he is always ready to minister to love-starved foreign women. Don't call him gigolo, because most of the time he wants no money for his services. It is rather pride in achievement that motivates him. A lifeguard on the Adriatic Sea boasted in a television interview that in one bathing season he had bagged more than one hundred female quarries.

A number of women visitors to Italy seem to look forward to instant masculine attention. Crossing the Italian frontiers by rail, I have more than once observed female tourists in the coach start flirting right there with the young and often good-looking policemen who check passports and luggage. An Italian customs guard who had for months been on duty at the border point on the Brenner Pass told me that an alley behind the police barracks had become a veritable Latin lovers' lane: German, Swedish, Dutch, and other women travelers would get there an initiation into Italian ardor.

The notion that a lot of foreign women are coming to Italy in search of erotic adventure is widespread in the country and often leads to molestation of tourists—and not just quick feels in crowded buses. Every Italian summer brings a crop of rape cases with young travelers as victims; a girl tourist who accepts the invitation of a couple of nice-looking, smiling youths in a car who offer to show her the sights of the town may be in for a nasty experience, and she may also end up being robbed of her purse. If she complains to the police, there may be some unpleasant questioning, and the newspapers will write that another *inglesina* or *americanina* (a little English or American girl) has claimed to have been assaulted. The diminutive carries condescending overtones and faintly suggests that the victim of the alleged rape had really been asking for it.

What is known as *caccia alle straniere* (hunt for foreign women) is a pastime of young Italians—often off-duty soldiers—in tourist centers, even in St. Peter's Square in Rome. The chase is an expression of some Italian males' urge to prove their virility and seductiveness, a trait the Sicilian writer Vitaliano Brancati castigated as the national male vice of *gallismo* (roosterism).

Cases of sexual violence, particularly gang rapes, involving Italian women have lately become so numerous that feminist groups speak of a "social emergency." It may, however, be assumed that a good deal of this increase is just statistical, the result of assault victims' greater readiness to turn to the police. Women's organizations concede that the police investigators and magistrates are showing greater respect for victims of sexual violence than they did only a few years ago, but complain that rapists often still receive lenient sentences, which may be even further reduced on appeal. In the past a man facing assault charges got away scot-free if his victim was unwed and he then married her in what was known as a "reparative marriage." A legal reform in 1981 abolished that semibarbarous institution. Another archaic usage—elopement to force reluctant parents to give their consent to an undesired marriage—still survives in the Deep South.

What survives too is violence caused by outrage over real or presumed sexual looseness: fathers or brothers chastising the seducers of girls, husbands killing their wayward wives and their lovers, betrayed wives taking revenge on their rivals. Such "crimes of honor" have traditionally been frequent in Southern Italy, especially in Sicily, and more recently have occurred among southerners who have moved to the country's North. Italian courts have long conceded extenuating circumstances to perpetrators of violence presumed to have acted to defend their or their family's reputation. The judicial recognition of the "crime of honor" lingers on. In one typical case a jury of six women and two men in Trapani, on the western tip of Sicily, in 1987 found that a young fisherman who had beaten his thirteen-year-old sister to death because she had come home late at night had been motivated by reasons "of particular moral and social value." The slayer was sentenced to six years in prison with a chance of being pardoned for good behavior after four years. During the trial the court heard a postmortem report stating that it had not been possible to ascertain whether the victim had ever experienced "complete sexual relations." The girl's virginity, or earlier loss of it, was clearly considered relevant to the case, though evidently not to its judgment.

Virginity in unmarried women is still highly prized by many Italians despite the recent changes in sexual mores. When a nationwide sample of 1,000 people of both sexes was polled in 1987, 57.1 percent were found to attribute prime importance to female virginity before marriage. Predictably, the strongest vote against premarital sex for women came from the Deep South. There, according to Giovanni Raffaele of Messina University, virginity has long been an economic rather than an ethical value: "a capital, an asset, to be used in the marriage market," often a girl's only dowry.

The other principal matter of male preoccupation, especially in the South, is the faithfulness of women. There is no worse insult to a man than calling him *cornuto* (cuckold), or just making horns at him by stretching out the forefinger and pinkie of one's hand. This gesture is often made by angry motorists, and on occasion leads to mayhem, even murder, when the recipient reacts to the affront by chasing the offender, getting out of his car, and starting a fight.

Nearly every Italian man is horrified by the idea of being cuckolded, even though, as sociological research and anecdotal evidence show, adultery is quite common. The many private investigators who thrive not only in Italy's South but all over the country say that about four-fifths of their assignments are connected with suspected premarital or marital infidelity. (Private eyes in Italy are often retired police officers or carabinieri sergeants.)

Apart from the lingering insistence on the purity of women and faithfulness in marriage, what else has remained of the traditional Italian family ethos? Above all, there are the strong mother-son bonds, a characteristic shared with other Mediterranean cultures. The classic Italian *mamma* pampers her boy, keeps telling him he is unique, defends him like a lioness, condones his failures and vices, schemes to get him ahead in school and in life, wants him to stay always close to her if not in her home, and when he gets married is jealous of her daughter-in-law. An astonishing number of Italian men in their thirties and forties live with their parents; their fathers may not be so happy with the arrangement, but their mothers are glad to press their mature boys' shirts, cook their favorite dishes, and sympathetically listen to the tales of their erotic conquests and troubles.

The self-admiring Latin lover is to some extent a product of such momism. Some years ago I observed a doting Roman matron escorting her teenage son to an outdoor date with a local girl during their summer vacation in the Italian Alps. The boy and the girl strolled into a forest while his mother stood guard outside. After about half an hour the mother called into the thicket: *"Hai fatto, Marcello?"* (Are you through, Marcello?); the boy's instant reply: "Just a minute,

Mamma!" Marcello later probably gave his *mamma* a play-by-play account of what had happened.

In the dynamics of Italian family life, father-daughter relations also are close, sometimes too close. Judging by reports in Italian newspapers, rape of girls by their fathers is no rarity, especially considering that only a fraction of such occurrences ever become public. All too often the press alleges that the incestuous situation had gone on for months or years, and that the victim's mother had been aware of it but had acquiesced. If there are cases of sibling incest, they get much less publicity. A Sicilian artist friend once explained her lesbianism to me with the disclosure that as an adolescent she had been raped by her brother. In a 1988 court case in Naples a young man was sentenced to three years and seven months in prison for having raped his two sisters, aged nine and twelve. Why such mild punishment? "We never grant extenuating circumstances to fathers who have raped daughters," presiding judge Massimo Amodio explained to reporters. "Between brothers and sisters the mechanics are more complex: there is some sort of affection."

The number of Italian families in which large groups of brothers and sisters grow up together is at any rate rapidly diminishing. Italy now has one of the lowest birthrates in Europe, 10.2 per 1,000 population, against 29.4 per 1,000 half a century ago. (The 1987 birthrate in the United States was 15.6.) Naples today produces proportionally fewer infants than Stockholm. The Italian nation is close to zero population growth and may shrink after the year 2000. Legal and clandestine abortions appear to be the most widespread form of birth control—more than 360 abortions per 1,000 live births. A 1987 report on a three-year study project undertaken by the Italian Association for Demographic Education, a pro-birth-control group, showed that only 2.8 percent of 52,079 women questioned said they were taking oral contraceptives. Most Italian women seem convinced that the pill has harmful side effects.

Despite the recent changes in Italian kinship structures, millions of families throughout the country keep functioning in the traditional way, providing warmth, security, moral and economic support, and assistance in crises. Hundreds of thousands of such self-supportive families have also become successful businesses.

The family-run pension is found in thousands of versions, above all around the upper Adriatic Sea, from the beaches east of Venice to the forty sandy miles from Ravenna to Pesaro that are known as the Romagna Riviera. One summer in the early 1980s I had occasion to watch brilliant teamwork by a family that owned a small hotel near Rimini. This is Fellini country: The film director was born in Rimini in 1920 and as a youth witnessed the takeoff of what was to develop into the formidable Adriatic vacation machine.

A boy, not yet twelve years old, grabbed my suitcase after I had pulled up at this seaside *albergo*, which had been recommended to me. Later I noticed that he also ran to the railroad station to meet every train on which prospective guests might arrive. His father, Franco, a man in his forties, was serving in the dining room and at night would do a little clowning to entertain the patrons, mostly Swiss and Germans, and maybe get them to order another bottle of his Sangiovese, Albana, and Lambrusco wines.

Franco's wife and mother both worked in the kitchen, seven days a week, preparing lasagne and other glories of the Emilia-Romagna cuisine. They and a sixteen-year-old daughter made up the twenty rooms, and the girl, who spoke a little French and German, fielded telephone calls from Zurich, Dortmund, and Brussels. An older son served as life-guard on the beach outside the hotel, rented deck chairs and umbrellas, procured rowboats, sold gelato, and played the Felliniesque role of seaside Casanova for the benefit of women guests from the cold North. Busy though he was, he would always find time for taking departing customers to the railroad station in the family Fiat, which would usually earn him an extra tip, and more than rarely a hug and a whispered "Come and see me in Frankfurt [or Amsterdam, or St. Gall]!" Many of the guests during my stay at the hotel had been there in earlier years, and quite a few would during the winter write postcards and letters to Franco, his family, and, especially, the older son.

Italy's big hotels were at that time—the height of the vacation season—hit by a nationwide strike of 800,000 workers in the tourist industry, and their bemused guests had to make their own beds and seek out some espresso bar for breakfast. The little *albergo* near Rimini kept functioning as regularly as the tides of the sea outside. The work force was all family; there were no salaries to pay, no social security deductions to be calculated and withheld, no contracts to be renegotiated. I also had an inkling that Franco, who did the bookkeeping with the help of his daughter, went easy on taxes, underreporting the number of guests to the fiscal authorities. I paid about twenty dollars a day for a spartan but clean room with a shower and three simple, filling meals.

Owing to inflation, Rimini rates have gone up every year, but the Romagna Riviera was for a long time one of the best buys around the Mediterranean if you paid in German marks, Dutch guilders, or Swiss francs. At the height of its fortunes, around the time of my stay, the myriad of *pensioni* and a few bigger hotels in the area netted hundreds of millions of dollars every season and, directly or indirectly, provided work for 200,000 people. However, competition from even cheaper beaches in Spain, Yugoslavia, and Greece began to divert northern vacationers from Italy. The labor unions and the government eventually forced Franco to register his older son and his daughter as employees, pay them at least minimum wages, and deduct income tax and social security contributions from their nominal earnings. Alarming reports about the increasing pollution of the upper Adriatic and its infestation with decayed, gelatinous algae contributed bad publicity. The Romagna Riviera countered by building vast beachside saltwater swimming pools and aquatic amusement parks in addition to the many discotheques that had sprung up earlier. But despite the new fiscal constraints, the latticework of small, family-operated hotels and pensions from the Bay of Trieste to the beaches near Ancona have managed to keep their prices low and the upper Adriatic competitive in the Mediterranean scramble for thrifty vacationers.

The "arrangements" that are continually required to keep Italy running are comparatively easy when the partners or accomplices in a deal are relatives. Accordingly, countless small or medium-size businesses that have boosted the Italian economy are family enterprises, or started as such.

The outstanding case history is that of Luciano, Giuliana, Gilberto, and Carlo Benetton. When their father, the owner of a car-rental business in the small town of Ponzano Veneto, near Treviso on the Venetian mainland, died soon after World War II, all four had to think about earning money quickly. The firstborn, Luciano, started at fourteen, making himself useful in a Treviso clothing store. He soon proved he knew how to sell. Giuliana, who had for years been knitting pretty sweaters and cardigans for herself and her brothers, entered a knitwear workshop and learned to handle its machines. In 1954, the nineteen-year-old Luciano talked his sister into jointly buying a knitting machine on credit and turning out their own sweaters.

The growth of the brother-sister operation in less than

twenty-five years into the world's largest knitwear producer, an international holding company with a chain of specialty stores around the globe and several hundred million dollars in annual sales, is a business-school legend: how the sales wizard Luciano in one initial swoop marketed 700 sweaters produced by his sister; how he traveled to Rome to watch rowing and basketball events in the 1960 Olympic Games and was struck by the way foreign visitors were snapping up knitwear in the capital's stores; how he found those same stores interested when he returned to Rome with samples of Giuliana's sweaters in thirty-six merry colors; how brother and sister opened their first small factory in their hometown; how Luciano studied wool-working techniques during a 1962 trip to Scotland; how the younger brothers joined the family enterprise, taking over the mechanical and financial sides while Giuliana stuck to design and Luciano focused on sales; how the Benettons made shrewd use of subcontractors and franchisees; how all their sweaters came in neutral gray wool and only at the last moment were dyed shocking pink, pastel turquoise, or whatever other color was the season's craze; how their lavish publicity pictured young people of all races sporting their coordinated jeans and sweaters in the "United Colors of Benetton"; how professional managers and a second generation of Benettons were brought into the firm; and how the company in 1986 went public, with its shares quoted on the Milan stock exchange, while the family kept the controlling interest. In 1989 Benetton stock certificates were traded on the New York Stock Exchange. There are still hundreds of families in Italy who dream that their entrepreneurial ventures may one day take off the way the Benettons' did. Yet as Italian capitalism is maturing, and with fewer brothers, sisters, and children of business clans around or willing to pitch in, outside managers, financiers, and corporate raiders are more likely to get into the act. The decline of the large, close-knit business family is also likely to transform the country's economic landscape.

At the same time, it remains true that most of Italy's privately owned, large industrial companies have retained some features of a family enterprise. Outside the hefty state sector, Italy has many fewer corporate giants than do the other leading industrial nations; the largest is Fiat, and it is still in effect the family holding of the Agnellis of Turin.

A proud industrial-financial principality, Fiat rolls out around 2 million cars annually, accounting for more than one-eighth of Europe's total automotive production. It also builds trucks, railroad and earth-moving equipment, and aircraft; takes on large contracting projects; is active in telecommunications, insurance, and financial services; and controls newspapers and magazines. While the Turin-based group has more international ramifications than any other Italian combine, Fiat's muscle at home as an employer of more than 280,000 workers (in 1989), as an important contributor to Italy's gross domestic product and foreign-trade earnings, and as a power center dominating a substantial segment of the information media is formidable.

Many Italians think Fiat's power is excessive and ought to be curbed by antitrust legislation. It is widely believed, for instance, that pressures from the Turin automaker have for decades induced the national government to neglect modernization of the state railroads in favor of highway construction. The Agnellis, for their part, appear convinced that what's good for Fiat is good for Italy.

Giovanni (Gianni) Agnelli, the elegant grandson and namesake of the company's turn-of-the-century founder, has for many years been regarded as the uncrowned king of Italy. He was in fact repeatedly mentioned as a possible president of the Republic and might have been nominated and even elected by Parliament if he had seriously wanted the figure-head job. As it was, his power as head of the Fiat realm was much greater than that of Italy's head of state.

To his countrymen he was *l'avvocato* (the attorney) because he had, as a young man, won a law degree from Turin University (he has never practiced that profession). In his early years, after military service during World War II, he acquired a reputation as an international playboy; meanwhile, a shrewd manager from outside the Agnelli clan, the short, brisk Vittorio Valletta, was presiding as chief executive officer over the company's reconversion from wartime to civilian production. Instead of building small—and ineffectual—tanks and army trucks, Fiat started filling Italian roads with midget cars of the Topolino (Mickey Mouse) model. The new models that the Turin plants were building during the 1950s gradually became larger.

Perhaps inspired by the example of Henry Ford II, the third-generation scion of another automotive dynasty who had asserted himself in Detroit, Gianni Agnelli started taking over control of Fiat when he was in his early forties. He became the corporation's president in 1966 and before long was recognized at home and abroad as one of Italy's very few world-class entrepreneurs and financiers. He brought panache and sophistication to the part and was fortunate in his choice of executives. Fluent in English and French, with a Neapolitan-descended princess as his wife, shuttling between homes in Turin, Rome, St. Moritz, Paris, and New York, and surrounded by beautiful women, *l'avvocato* always found time for skiing in the Swiss Engadine or for yachting in the Mediterranean between business trips in his private jet.

Tall, appearing more interesting than handsome with his deeply lined, faintly Asian ("Etruscan") face under hair that had early turned an attractive gray, Agnelli knew how to generate charm when he chose. On other occasions he could be haughty, condescending, and a snobbish name-dropper. He did not mind being considered an arbiter of male fashions at home: When he let his necktie hang out over his pullover or wore his wristwatch over his shirt cuff, thousands of men from Trieste to Trapani copied him. Affecting brown survival shoes in combination with conservative business suits, he started a rage for thick-soled, stout, brown footwear that, to be acceptable, had to carry an American label like Timberland and had to be imported (into Italy, one of the world's foremost shoe manufacturers and exporters!). At times Agnelli seemed to have given priority over any other Fiat business to the purchase of some high-priced center half for the company-owned first-division soccer team, Juventus. From the bleachers of the Turin stadium, the Juventus fans—many of them Fiat workers who had emigrated from the Deep South—could glimpse *l'avvocato* sitting next to the head coach during championship matches.

For some years the Libyan strongman Colonel Muammar al-Qaddafi was Gianni Agnelli's partner in the auto business: Fiat had needed an injection of fresh capital and had let Libya acquire a sizable block of its shares. The United States reacted with displeasure at Libyan part ownership of a major European industry with a proven defense potential, and Qaddafi was eventually bought out again, with a considerable profit for the dictator and some problems for the banks that handled the transaction.

Fiat's management style of hard-nosed efficiency—with competent, dedicated, and well-paid engineering and administrative staffs and highly automated workshops—had by then come to be regarded as the very opposite of Italy's wheezing state bureaucracy. Fiat seemed another culture, almost another country. To make sure the eventual transition to a fourth Agnelli generation with dozens of family stockholders would not jolt the automotive empire, *l'avvocato* in 1987, when he was sixty-six years old, vested supreme control of the concern in a small directorate, including his younger brother Umberto and top managers from outside the clan.

If an "attorney" was outstanding among Italy's few big-time entrepreneurs, he had a counterpart and rival in an "engineer" who appeared intent on building a new family dukedom. Carlo De Benedetti, thirteen years Agnelli's junior, indeed had a Turin engineering degree, and everybody called him *l'ingegnere*. He was a descendant of a Sephardic family that had settled in Piedmont generations earlier. De Benedetti's father owned a metal-hosing factory in Turin and was doing well until the Nazis occupied the city along with most of Italy following the royal government's armistice with the Allied powers in 1943. The De Benedetti family fled to Switzerland, and the future *ingegnere* attended school in Lucerne, where he learned German; like *l'avvocato*, he also picked up French and English. (The polyglot skills of Italy's two top business leaders would become much noted in contrast to the linguistic parochialism of almost all Italian premiers and government ministers, officials who might be able to spout well-worn Latin sayings and quotations but spoke no modern language other than their own.)

Home again from temporary exile, the older De Benedetti after the war rebuilt the Turin family business. *L'ingegnere* took over at age thirty-three and parlayed his father's metal-hosing plant into an auto-parts factory with 1,600 workers. In 1976 *l'avvocato*, impressed by De Benedetti's managerial success, offered him the job of chief executive officer at Fiat. The Turin automaker was then facing new labor trouble, mounting competition from West Germany, and financial difficulties. When *l'ingegnere* accepted, his new employers took over his share in the De Benedetti auto-parts enterprise in exchange for 6 percent of Fiat stock. Despite this cross-investment, De Benedetti's stint with Fiat lasted only one hundred days; he said later he didn't get along with members of the Agnelli family, and he soon resigned.

De Benedetti bought into a near-bankrupt tanning company and used it as a basis for corporate engineering through the acquisition of small manufacturing enterprises. Soon another old family corporation, Olivetti, beckoned. Founded as a business machines manufacturer by an earlier Piedmontese *ingegnere*, Camillo Olivetti, the company had become internationally renowned through the handsome design of its products; an Olivetti typewriter remains among the exhibits of New York's Museum of Modern Art.

The second-generation chief of the enterprise, Adriano Olivetti, was a utopian dreamer who appeared much more interested in urban planning and social experimentation than in selling typewriters and calculating machines. He gathered a group of social scientists, architects, and designers around himself and founded a political movement, Comunità (Community). Described by critics as technocratic, "Calvinistic," and "Swiss," Comunità competed in some elections with the established parties, but few Italians voted for its candidates. Olivetti died in his sleeper compartment during a rail trip. When in 1987 De Benedetti started out at Olivetti's modern corporate headquarters in Ivrea, some 30 miles north of Turin, the company was stagnant, far behind its competitors in electronics and office automation, and deep in debt. De Benedetti turned it around in a few years.

Working fourteen to sixteen hours a day, Olivetti's new chief shook up its management, streamlined its work force, and dragged the company into the computer age. By the middle of the 1980s Olivetti was the leading Europe-based manufacturer of automatic office equipment, and since 1983 the company has been allied with the American Telephone & Telegraph Company to produce personal computers (AT&T had become a major stockholder of Olivetti).

A driven man and a work addict without any hobbies

and apparently, unlike Gianni Agnelli, without any ambitions to play a role in high society, De Benedetti was not content with his success at Olivetti. With a keen eye on acquisition prospects, he kept expanding his personal interests in various directions. At home and in other European countries, particularly France, he assembled a conglomerate that included stakes in newspapers and magazines, insurance and other financial services companies, the Buitoni pasta firm in Italy, and the Yves Saint Laurent fashion house in Paris.

Early in 1988 De Benedetti acquired a block of shares in the Société Générale de Belgique, the Brussels-based holding company that for generations had been regarded as a national institution in Belgium, and made a bid to control it. The Italian entrepreneur's explanation for his raid on the powerhouse of the Belgian economy was that the time had come for building Europe-wide corporate groupings. Belgians who until then had thought of Italians mainly as immigrant workers in their mines and waiters in their restaurants were stunned. René Lamy, chairman of the Société Générale, told reporters in a press conference: "We don't want Belgium to be colonized." An Italian television camera focused on a portrait of the bearded King Leopold II of Belgium, the ruthless colonizer of the Congo, on the wall behind the chairman. It was an adroit visual comment: The Société Générale had helped the king in the exploitation of the onetime "heart of darkness," the Belgian Congo (now independent Zaire). De Benedetti eventually failed in his bid to gain full control of the Belgian business giant and had to content himself with a seat on its board of directors. He nevertheless continued to expand his interests in Italy and abroad, showing up only rarely at Olivetti headquarters. By involving his sons in his deal making, De Benedetti seemed determined to found another Italian industrial dynasty.

Family bonds were essential also to the fortunes of the

Ferruzzi agrobusiness empire. When Serafino Ferruzzi died in a crash of his corporate jet in 1979, at age seventy-one, few Italians were aware that he had been controlling a sizable chunk of the world cereal market. Born into a family of small farmers in the Ravenna area, Ferruzzi had studied agriculture at Bologna University and, after graduation, had developed a farming enterprise that, without much ado, branched out internationally. In the process he had also acquired cement works and other industrial plants. After his death the husband of his daughter Ida, Raul Gardini, took over leadership of the Ferruzzi Group and emerged as one of the chief players in Italian business when he assumed control of Montedison, one of Italy's largest conglomerates, based on chemical production. In 1989 the Agnelli, De Benedetti, and Ferruzzi families controlled 45 percent of all the shares quoted on the Milan stock exchange.

Most of the other major groupings in the private sector of Italian industry are, like Fiat and Ferruzzi, dominated by dynasties of capitalists—the sons and grandsons of company founders; their brothers, sisters, cousins, and sons-in-law. Outstanding examples are the Pirelli rubber and tire company, which for a few years in the 1970s was in partnership with Dunlop of Britain and in 1988 made an unsuccessful bid to take over the Firestone Tire & Rubber Company of Akron, Ohio; the Marzotto textile firm and hotel chain; and the Mondadori publishing house, before it came to be controlled by De Benedetti.

Small investors, to be sure, can buy shares of the big family corporations, but they are kept in the dark about what is going on in the boardrooms and have no role in the backstage maneuvers, feuds, and deals. The Milan Bourse, the nation's leading stock exchange and the only one that counts, is virtually an insiders' club. On Italy's business-financial scene, it's still largely all in the family.

7.
Mafia,
Inc.

On any given day at least a couple of people, often more, are languishing in mountain caves, farm sheds, or suburban apartments, being held for ransom. Some days the police are looking for half a dozen people who are known to be separately in the hands of kidnappers. The chances that the lawmen can free the prisoners are always dauntingly slim. Relatives of abduction victims usually entreat the investigators not to interfere with their own efforts to make a deal with the criminals and buy the liberty of their loved ones at a price they cannot afford without going into debt. While these families are negotiating with the kidnappers through secret channels, they will appeal to the information media to observe a voluntary news blackout in their cases, a request that is always heeded. The missing person may be children, grandfathers, business executives, or young daughters of wealthy parents. If everything goes according to script, the prisoners will turn up in a remote corner of the country after several months, maybe more than a year, stagger to the nearest farmhouse or carabinieri station, and make a phone call home.

That night television will show the exhausted-looking victim of a long ordeal. A man will have grown a beard and may tell of endless days and nights chained to a post in a drafty grotto with little food and never a chance to wash. A girl set at liberty by her abductors will stonily say, "They treated me well, they didn't touch me." If she has been sexually abused, as is more than likely, she keeps it to herself, or at most tells her mother. She knows by instinct that nothing will be gained by broadcasting the fact that she has been "dishonored." Only a foreigner, Rolf Schild of Britain, has denounced the sexual violence that occurred during the seven months he, his wife, and their deaf-mute daughter were in the hands of Sardinian bandits.

Many Italians seem to regard people-snatching for gain as a fact of life, an inevitable transfer of wealth from the rich to the poor with, yes, some hardship. They do not appear to realize that their nation has long held the European record for kidnappings, as if it were trying to compete with Lebanon in that shameful field. In some years the official number of cases in Italy may be as high as 150 to 170. Then there are people, especially in Sicily, who simply disappear; presumably they become the victims of Mafia abductors who don't care for ransom payments but want to torture and kill them in vendettas and executions of which the authorities learn only years later, if at all.

The Italian media each time speak routinely of an Anonima Sequestri (Kidnapping, Inc.), as if these abductions for ransom were all the work of one shadowy, nationwide organization. Kidnapping, it is true, is a criminal enterprise requiring a number of people acting in concert: Prospective victims are to be carefully chosen, meaning that the financial resources of their families must be explored and their personal habits observed; the places of work and the homes of the targeted must be cased; a secret prison has to be readied; getaway cars have to be stolen; two or three men at least are needed for the actual abduction (with an extra woman useful if the intended victim is a child); personnel for guarding the prisoner around the clock, possibly for many months, are needed; sometimes the victim is transferred from one prison to another to minimize the chances of discovery, requiring additional logistics; meanwhile, contact with the victim's family is to be established, negotiations must be conducted, and the ransom has to be collected, often by installments; and the funds must eventually be laundered to avoid detection through the serial numbers of the 50,000- or 100,000-lire bills.

Kidnapping is essentially a Sardinian-Calabrian cottage industry, the business of a cluster of gangs formed by professional criminals who have the know-how for pulling off abductions for ransom successfully, and often have Mafia connections. Occasionally an outsider thinks it might be a good idea to have a rich uncle or the daughter of a factory owner in the neighborhood abducted and is prepared to split the ransom with the bandits who do the actual job; it does not seem difficult to find and hire professionals who know how to go about the job on the basis of information supplied to them. Quite often a gang sells its prisoner to another group, most likely Calabrians, who will take care of the rest.

Sardinian bandits operate not only on their own island, especially in the backward province of Nuoro, but also on the mainland. Sardinian shepherds have long been tending flocks in Tuscany, and whenever someone is abducted in that well-to-do region the local newspapers automatically suggest that the Anonima Sarda (Sardinia, Inc.) has been at work. The Sardinian kidnappers are particularly dreaded because of their ferocity; even if ransom is paid to them, it is by no means certain that they will release their prisoner, who may in fact already be dead. The police suspect that their Sardinian captors fed the cut-up bodies of some missing persons to the swine. Nothing has ever been heard of forty-two victims who disappeared in Italy between 1978 and 1986.

Every summer many thousands of visitors from the Italian mainland and from abroad spend vacations on the scenic shores of Sardinia. The Costa Smeralda (Emerald Coast) in the northeast of the island is today an enclave of luxury hotels, fancy condominiums, and exclusive country clubs created by the business acumen of the Aga Khan and populated during the warm months by members of the international yachting set and other wealthy people from Turin to Düsseldorf. They, like most mainland Italians, know little about Sardinia's lonely interior, with its sullen mountain ranges and the *nuraghi*, the stone mounds that are the remains of the fortress homes of prehistoric chieftains. Even the ancient Romans never completely controlled the island's wild interior and apparently did not care to do so. Their contempt for the supposedly perfidious Sardinian "barbarians" is echoed to this day by the name *Barbagia*, denoting the brooding hillside southwest of the provincial capital Nuoro.

Banditry has been endemic in the interior of Sardinia since time immemorial, and cattle rustling has remained a feature of country life on the island almost to this day. Sardinian criminals have long found, however, that it is easier and more lucrative to kidnap rich people and hold them for ransom than to steal flocks: A few threats or blows will make a prisoner shut up; it is harder to prevent sheep from bleating or cows from mooing. Present-day Sardinian bandits are no Robin Hood characters; they have adopted modern guerrilla tactics. Four long-wanted members of a kidnapping band who were killed in a shoot-out with the police, reinforced by a local posse, in a gully of the Sopramonte massif southeast of Nuoro in 1985, were clad in uniformlike camouflage outfits and armed with submachine guns and hand grenades.

After his election in 1985, President Francesco Cossiga, a Sardinian, appealed to the bandits among his fellow islanders "in the name of the law, of humanity, of the pride that is the heritage of this land, of Sardinian honor," to release all the prisoners they were then holding. The plea fell on deaf ears. Cossiga was the second Sardinian to serve as head of state; President Antonio Segni (1962–1964) too was a native of the island, and his successor, Giuseppe Saragat, was of Sardinian ancestry, born in Turin. (It should be noted too that Sardinia has produced a Nobel laureate in literature, the novelist Grazia Deledda [1926], and several outstanding scholars, scientists, and political leaders. Nevertheless, many Italians think first of banditry when they hear "Sardinia.")

While the Sopramonte range is providing hideouts for Sardinian criminals and prison caves for their victims, the outlaws of Calabria find similar inaccessible corners on an even larger scale in the Aspromonte (Harsh Mountain) massif, in the toe of the Italian boot. Sardinian kidnappers operating on the mainland and other local gangs in Northern and Central Italy often turn over their prisoners to Calabrians, who will hold them in some Aspromonte grotto or shack until ransom is collected. One victim, Marco Fiora, was seven years old when armed men tore him from his parents as he was being taken to school in Turin in 1987. The boy reappeared seventeen months later in the same clothes he had worn at the time of the kidnapping, but 900 miles to the south, near an Aspromonte village. The police said the gangsters had released little Marco because they had been afraid of being discovered when they saw a helicopter fly over the hillside just as they were moving the boy from one secret prison to another. Few people believed the story. Marco's father, a businessman, was known to have been in touch with the kidnappers through priests and other middlemen, and he had apparently paid up. The gang had at first asked for $3.6 million but probably had eventually scaled down their demands.

The Aspromonte, northwest of Reggio di Calabria, rises to an altitude of nearly 6,450 feet and extends over nearly 200 square miles—about the area of the New York boroughs of Brooklyn and Queens combined. With pine and chestnut forests over wide areas, and honeycombed with ravines and caves, the massif has for hundreds of years been the realm of brigands and fugitives from justice. Some criminals on the police's Most Wanted list are believed to have been hiding on the Aspromonte for years.

Calabria—like the Abruzzi, Corsica, Albania, and other mountainous regions around the Mediterranean—has a tradition of brigandage going back to the fall of the Roman Empire. Jakob Burckhardt records the story of the herdsman who contritely told a priest in the confessional in a remote part of the Kingdom of Naples (Calabria) during the fifteenth century that he had unwittingly broken the rule of Lent by allowing a few drops of milk to find their way to his mouth while he was making cheese; the confessor, "familiar with the customs of the country, discovered through questioning that the penitent and his friends often robbed and murdered travelers" without any twinges of conscience. The French historian Fernand Braudel notes that in Calabria in the sixteenth century "outlaws flourished, aided by circumstances and the terrain; their crimes were more frequent and more horrifying than elsewhere, and their audacity knew no bounds." Brigandage in the Mezzogiorno flared up again after the area had been annexed to unified Italy in 1860. It took several years and 120,000 men of the regular army to "pacify" the South in what was a veritable civil war.

The Calabrian bandits won prime newspaper space and television time all over the world in 1973 when they sent an amputated ear and a shock of hair of J. Paul Getty III, a grandson of the late oil billionaire, to the Rome newspaper *Il Messaggero* as proof that they were holding the American and that they meant business. Young Getty had been abducted by unknown men in the central Piazza Farnese in

Rome and had been handed over to a gang of Calabrian professionals. Initial contacts between them and the Getty family led nowhere, and the bandits took persuasive action. They severed their prisoner's right ear and mailed it to the newspaper by special delivery. Postal service at the time happened to be in even worse disarray than usual, and the envelope with its grisly and by then shriveled contents was received in Rome weeks later.

The Gettys, impressed by the evidence (reinforced by a series of photos of the prisoner minus one ear that were mailed to another Rome daily), paid a ransom variously reported as amounting to between $2.8 and $3.4 million. Young Getty was released near a service station on the Salerno–Reggio di Calabria highway five months after he had disappeared. His grandfather, whose parsimony was legendary, is said to have vowed he would get even with the extortionists, and he may have enlisted some Mafia family to do the job; it is doubtful, though, that he ever got his money back.

In 1988 Sardinian gangsters who kidnapped a contractor, Giulio de Angelis, mailed a bloody piece of one of his ears to his relatives with the warning that unless they paid $2.9 million "without any discount" the prisoner would die. The family complied, and the contractor was freed five months after his abduction. He reported that his jailers had clipped off the upper part of his right ear with an ordinary pair of shears. In July 1989 a Sardinian-Calabrian gang clipped both ears of a kidnapped coffee importer, Dante Bernardinelli, and mailed the bits of tissue, along with a photo of the bleeding prisoner, to his family. Supplying a piece of a victim's body—an ear, a finger—to relatives is a part of the kidnapping ritual that has developed through the ages. The gangsters usually make it clear that they are not in a hurry and can keep their prisoners for months or even years, sending out one body piece after another, before either freeing or killing their victims. Following an abduction, weeks may pass during which the anguished family receives no word from the criminals, and the police seem helpless. After the relatives are deemed sufficiently softened up, they will be relieved, even grateful, when a middleman makes the first vague approach, if only to mention an exorbitant price for the missing person's return. Then a frustrating haggle usually ensues, with long intervals between progressively reduced ransom demands and increased counteroffers. Often the kidnappers are much better informed about a family's financial possibilities than is the tax office. Properties and valuables will have to be sold and debts incurred to scrape together the requested sum.

Modern technology provides new twists in the grim kidnapping game. A Polaroid picture of a prisoner holding a newspaper with a recent date and headlines well visible may be forwarded to relatives as proof that the victim is (or was) still alive. The family may receive a recording of the prisoner's voice pleading that they meet all the captors' demands quickly. The police, without telling the family of an abducted person, monitor their telephones, but the gangsters, aware of this procedure, establish contact in roundabout ways. Relatives will be warned at every stage of the long-drawn-out negotiations not to cooperate with the law unless they want the prisoner's death. Often the families of missing persons publicly inform the kidnappers that their victim is suffering from severe heart trouble or some other critical condition and needs continual medication. Most of the time these statements are untrue; they are simply meant to impress on the gangsters that their prisoner may die on them and also to induce them to buy the suggested drugs in some pharmacy (many drugs are sold in Italy over the counter without medical prescription).

Antikidnapping laws permit the authorities to freeze the bank accounts and other assets of a victim's family to make sure no ransom is paid. But since the police are only rarely able to free anyone from the hands of gangsters, relatives do everything to raise cash, appealing to friends or turning to loansharks while bargaining with the kidnappers.

From time to time, usually after yet another particularly shocking abduction, the interior minister, who is in charge of maintaining law and order, will fly from Rome to Reggio di Calabria or Nuoro to preside over what the information media describe as a "security summit." Prefects of the Calabrian or Sardinian provinces, who are the local representatives of the central government, as well as the regional police chiefs, carabinieri commanders, high magistrates, and other top officials will attend. Carabinieri details will comb the Aspromonte or Sopramonte slopes and gullies, and helicopters will scan the mountains and hills.

In 1988 the government sent an entire mountain brigade of the Italian army, with field artillery, from the North to the Aspromonte to hold maneuvers with the avowed intention of rounding up Calabrian gangsters, or at least frightening them. The transfer of the Alpine soldiers to the Deep South by truck and boat yielded good television footage, but the bandits simply lay low awhile, and the army brigade was withdrawn after a few weeks, leaving the local carabinieri to hunt for the outlaws as they had done before.

In the summer of 1989 the armed forces staged another Aspromonte invasion on an even larger scale. Navy and air force units backed crack detachments of the army and police. Newspaper and broadcast reports sounded like accounts of the Allied landing in Normandy in 1944. The outcome of the spectacular military effort involving thousands of men was nil.

Search parties usually discover an unlicensed rifle or two hidden in some barn, but little more. The inhabitants of the villages on the slopes will stolidly explain that years ago sheep were killed by wolves, or chicken devoured by foxes, and that is why they need the weapons. Of course nobody has ever heard of or seen any bandits or kidnap victims.

Such periodic sweeps by lawmen are also a very old custom. The chronicles report that in 1578 the Spanish viceroy of Naples, the duke of Mondéjar, ordered an all-out drive against the brigands of Calabria, who were assassinating travelers and holding people for ransom. More than four hundred years later the collection of huge sums for the release of abducted Calabrians—pharmacists are a favorite target—or people in the distant North is still a major source of income. The funds are usually recycled through Mafia conduits.

"Kidnapping, Inc.," despite the modernization of its techniques, has retained an artisan character; it remains part of the folklore, like poaching or cattle rustling. Truly big money today is being made on the Italian crime scene by the drug barons, by Mafia contractors who win every bid for public works projects, and by racketeers who impose their "protection" on industrial plants and on smaller businesses, down to neighborhood shoe stores and market stalls.

At the end of 1988 the latest of the high commissioners for the Fight against the Mafia, Domenico Sica, told the national Parliament in a written report that "in some areas in Sicily, Calabria, and Campania the control of the territory by criminal organizations is total." Implicit was the admission that a twenty-five-year government drive to smash the Sicilian Mafia, the Calabrian 'Ndrangheta, and the Neapolitan Camorra had been futile. Gianni Agnelli, president of Fiat, observed that the situation in the crime-infested regions of the Mezzogiorno was approaching the lawlessness in Colombia.

The Italian state had by the early 1960s come around to acknowledging officially that the Mezzogiorno was the base of organized crime. The national Parliament set up a commission to investigate "the phenomenon of the Mafia in Sicily," and the body has become a permanent group, like the Foreign Affairs committees of the Chamber of Deputies and the Senate. And Italian lawmakers, politicians, and sociologists have for generations referred to the Mafia as a "phenomenon." The word seems to suggest that the Sicilian subculture of crime might be regarded in the same way as the periodic eruptions of Mount Etna or the droughts that parch the island—a force of nature about which little or nothing can be done.

To cope with the "phenomenon," the Parliament in Rome passed new laws aimed at curbing activities *di stampo mafioso* (Mafia type). In 1982 the government appointed Carabinieri General Carlo Alberto Dalla Chiesa as its anti-Mafia high commissioner. Dalla Chiesa was a Piedmontese who had been engaged in anti-Mafia police work in Sicily for ten years earlier in his career, before winning national renown as a frontline operative in the government's offensive against political terrorism in the 1970s. He knew what he was up against when he started his new assignment in Palermo. Soon he complained to intimates that he was feeling isolated there, that he was receiving scanty support from the central government in Rome and almost none from the local authorities.

Fifty-seven days after his arrival in the island capital, Dalla Chiesa and his young wife were assassinated as they were driving home from his office at night. All efforts to track the gunman who had ambushed them failed. Which shadowy power had given the order to kill them? The question has never been answered.

Dalla Chiesa's murder, like no other event in a long time, brought home to a stunned nation the fact that the Mafia had remained among its most serious problems. It is in fact a prime reason why the Mezzogiorno seems to be drifting away from the rest of the country instead of getting closer.

The criminal groups in Southern Italy can be regarded as a fateful inheritance from the Kingdom of the Two Sicilies. Gladstone denounced the bizarre realm that Spanish-descended Bourbon sovereigns were autocratically ruling from Naples as a "negation of God." In the Mezzogiorno it has lately become fashionable to depict the reign of the Bourbon King Ferdinand II (1830–1859) as an idyll under a populist monarch who spoke the dialect of the Neapolitan slums, was adored by the little people, and loved pizza. In truth, that ruler had his warships savagely bombard Messina and Palermo in 1848 to suppress uprisings—which earned him the nickname King Bomba—and had many thousands of his subjects kept in irons in his fetid prisons and galleys because they were suspected of liberalism. Banditry was rampant throughout his realm, as it had been over the centuries, and Ferdinand was said to be in cahoots with the Neapolitan Camorra. Contempt for the decrepit Bourbon state in Southern Italy and its inept, greedy, and corrupt officials inevitably fostered lawlessness.

The roots of such antistate feeling, however, go back to the successive waves of invasions that the South has endured through history. In Sicily the foreign masters, unable to control the populace, usually made deals with the local landowning barons and other chiefs. These, in turn, hired peasant stalwarts and maybe brigands to guard their estates in exchange for protection from higher authorities. Thus from the Middle Ages a boss system had developed, and with it widespread disregard among the islanders for the laws of foreign rulers. During the same centuries, Northern Italians had been under the domination of the French, the Spanish, or the Austrians, but opposition to foreigners in that region was long confined to the city intelligentsia while the rural population remained docile.

By the early nineteenth century a well-developed Mafia structure had emerged in Sicily, and similar groupings outside the law were powerful in the mainland regions of the southern kingdom. In 1838 an official of Ferdinand II, Pietro Calà Ulloa (a Spanish name), reported from Trapani in Sicily's west that many puzzling "unions and brotherhoods" were active in various other cities and towns of the area. He described them as "sects . . . without any political color or purpose, holding no meetings, having no other tie than dependence on a chief who may be a landowner here, an archpriest there." An archpriest is the dean of the clergy in a cluster of Roman Catholic parishes; today too one hears now and then of "Mafia priests." Trapani has remained a seemingly impregnable Mafia stronghold. Calà Ulloa, the unusually perspicacious Bourbon official, described the brotherhoods as illegal "little governments" operating their own systems of justice. He pointed out, for instance, how they would approach someone who had suffered a theft and offer to have the stolen goods returned for a consideration.

Until quite recently, whenever a foreigner's pocket was picked or a purse snatched in Palermo, the advice offered was not to turn to the police but to get in touch with some personage—maybe a lawyer or an architect—with reputed Mafia ties. Sometimes the stolen wallet or bag would be returned, eventually. There were also stories of some distinguished visitor to the island capital who, shortly after complaining about having been robbed, was led into a room where all the articles stolen or snatched during the preceding forty-eight hours were neatly laid out so that the guest might identify the missing property—a proud demonstration of how tightly the Mafia controlled petty crime.

The word *Mafia*—possibly derived from an Arabic root—has in the Sicilian dialect long had the meaning of beauty, attractiveness, and pride tinged with arrogance, audacity, and the refusal to submit to any authority. The term was first used in print to denote an association of criminals in 1862, when the popular Sicilian playwright Giuseppe Rizzotto brought out a drama, *The Mafiosi of the Vicaria District in Palermo*. (The Vicaria neighborhood near the island capital's waterfront still has a bad name today.) By then Sicily, with the rest of the Mezzogiorno, had become part of the unified kingdom of Italy. In the South, Garibaldi had been adulated as a liberator in 1860–61, but soon people there were wondering whether they had not simply been subjected by a new kind of invader—Northern Italian soldiers and carpetbaggers. The Mafia and its mainland counterparts fed on such malaise.

Camorra is Spanish for "quarrel," a continued hostility against the authorities. *'Ndrangheta* is said to derive from Greek dialects that were long spoken in Mezzogiorno and to contain a corruption of the Greek root *andr-* (male); therefore it would mean something like "manliness." Another crucial word of the Mafia vocabulary, *omertà*, from the Latin *homo* or the Italian *uomo* (man), expresses the same notion. *Omertà* is usually translated as "conspiracy of silence." It is the unwritten iron code in all of Sicily and much of the Mezzogiorno: Never supply information to the police or any other official authority, even if you yourself have been the target of insolence or the victim of a crime.

A Sicilian woman who is present when her father or brother is shot down by gunmen will maintain she has not seen anything. The wife of a reputed carabinieri informer took her dying husband to the hospital telling the nurse he was "not feeling so good." The postmortem found ninety bullets in his body. When police questioned the widow about who had attacked her husband, she seemed astonished: "Did they shoot him? I didn't notice anything." Even children will not talk. Distaste for the police has until today remained widespread throughout the Mezzogiorno. In the Sicilian dictionary, *sbirro*, which means not only "cop" but also "informer," is as terrible an insult as *cornuto* (cuckold). The two epithets are often spat out in tandem.

The word *Mafia* is never used by mafiosi. They would

and will refer to themselves and one another as "men of respect" or "men of honor." Hence the nickname the Honorable Society (*società onorata*). What is the honor of the mafioso? First of all, to "make oneself respected" by being able to impose one's will on others and leaving no real or imaginary slight unpunished. Also high in the Mafia value system is a Mediterranean perception of sexual honor: virility, virginity in unmarried women, and the faithfulness of wives. For many centuries a betrayed husband had to kill his wife's lover, and maybe her as well, to regain a minimum of respect; that honor code lingers on today.

In Sicily's "rural Mafia," as it existed in vast areas until after World War II and is still present in some places in the island's interior, local bosses more powerful than the mayor, the parish priest, and the carabinieri commander together called the tune. They would, through middlemen, extort protection money from landowners who did not want their orange groves cut down or their sheep stolen; they would also control the precious water allotments from the aqueduct, and mediate between cattle rustlers, kidnappers, and other criminals and their victims. If a village lothario needed persuasion to marry the girl he had seduced, the Mafia chief would see to it.

Each Mafia boss had and still has a cluster of henchmen and "soldiers" doing the dirty work for him. Blood ties have always played an important part in the Mafia structures; many local units of the Honorable Society used to be nothing but a grouping of all or most of the male members of a clan or extended family. However, a kind of pseudoadoption has often been practiced by mafiosi to select and groom young talent: A boss will become the sponsor at baptism or confirmation of a relative, or even of someone born outside the clan, who will then owe particular fealty to his godfather. The godson may even eventually claw his way to the top of the *cosca*, the general name for a Mafia gang.

Hidden backers are essential to the success of the *cosca*. They may be lawyers who act as advisers and go-betweens, and as defense counsel if there is trouble with the police or the courts; government officials, judges, bankers—"citizens above suspicion," in the Italian phrase—may be secret Mafia supporters too. The Honorable Society can do many favors in return. There is documentary proof that Vittorio Emanuele Orlando, the Sicilian statesman who was Italy's premier from 1917 to 1919, and who acted as one of the Big Four at the Paris peace negotiations after World War I, was throughout his political career in touch with mafiosi. Every legislature of the Italian Republic since World War II has included senators and deputies who were said to owe their election in some Sicilian district to the Mafia.

Contrary to the Mafia lore of popular fiction, there is no hard evidence that the Honorable Society in Sicily ever had a rigid and executive hierarchy. The ingrained individualism and factionalism of the Sicilians prevented permanent, islandwide organization. However, when émigré mafiosi in the United States and Canada found themselves in an industrial society with corporations, trusts, and holding companies, and with board chairmen and chief executive officers assisted by secretaries and legal departments, they built criminal replicas of such institutions and bodies—Cosa Nostra (Our Thing).

From time to time some "chief of all chiefs" has emerged in Italy. He usually has been a "man of respect" of paramount prestige who would mediate between the various *cosche* (gangs) rather than act as the supreme ruler of an underground organization spread across the island. The most famous "chief of all chiefs" was Calogero (Don Calò) Vizzini of Villalba, a small town near Caltanissetta in the interior. Like a proconsul of ancient Rome or an Oriental potentate, he used for many years to hold court in the town square every day, accepting the homage of his *clientela* and listening to favor seekers. At the end of World War II, the Allied Military Government named him mayor of Villalba. Don Calò died in 1954; his headstone in the town cemetery carries the inscription "Defender of the Weak, and Enemy of Injustice."

Ever since the national unification the central governments of Italy have periodically announced all-out drives to suppress the Honorable Society. Soldiers from the mainland would surround entire villages and conduct house-to-house searches. In 1871 Rome trumpeted that Sicily had been "liberated from its Mafia." Similar claims have been heard again and again during the following decades, and they have always turned out to be hollow.

Alleged mafiosi were regularly acquitted by the courts. One notorious boss, Vito Cascio Ferro, was tried inconclusively sixty-nine times before he was at last sentenced to a prison term in 1926. In that year Mussolini vowed to smash the Honorable Society once and for all. The dictator chose a northern official, Cesare Mori, as commander of his anti-Mafia offensive and gave him strong police forces and sweeping powers. Mori had thousands of suspects rounded up and interned or exiled without trial. Il Duce too proclaimed he had rooted out the Sicilian Mafia; actually it would only lie low for a few years.

The Honorable Society made a comeback during the last phase of World War II. In fact it rendered services to the Allied forces, infiltrating and gathering intelligence in Sicily. In Catania a shoeshine man who had for some time had his stand outside the building of the Fascist Federation, a local power center, turned up after the Allied invasion of the island in the uniform of a United States Army major.

In the United States the gangster Lucky Luciano (his real name was Salvatore Lucania) had supplied information on his Sicilian contacts and as a reward was released from prison. Luciano was deported to Italy. On his arrival I asked him at

Rome's railroad terminal what he had done to regain liberty. His pockmarked face went blank, and he turned to his body-guards: "Let's go!" Lucky Luciano was to live for years in Italy as a man of means; he ostensibly dabbled in legitimate business, acquired a blond Milanese girlfriend, and died peacefully in his bed.

By then the "rural Mafia" had become a quaint relic. Hundreds of thousands of Sicilians were abandoning the countryside to crowd into the cities, many "men of honor" among them. By 1955 the Mafia had moved into Palermo in force and selected the city's wholesale produce market as its first takeover target. To this day Palermo householders pay tribute to some *cosca* whenever they buy a dozen eggs or a kilogram of lemons. The building boom in the rapidly growing southern cities offered other pickings for the new "urban Mafia," as did control of cigarette smuggling—then a flourishing industry—and of street crime.

The new transatlantic air services facilitated alliances and frequent exchanges between the Sicilian *cosche* and American Cosa Nostra families. Until then the island Mafia and Cosa Nostra in the United States and Canada had been distinct criminal societies, linked only by the ethnic background of their members, by the use of the Sicilian dialect as their operative language, and by the similarity of their methods—intimidation, extortion, torture, and murder.

A quantum leap in Sicilian crime occurred in the late 1950s, when several *cosche* joined the rapidly expanding international drug business. A formal decision to that effect was taken, Italian officials assume today, when Sicilian and U.S. mafiosi held a meeting in the Grand Hotel et des Palmes in Palermo in October 1957. That once posh establishment in the center of the island capital had long enjoyed the favor and patronage of ranking "men of respect." The local authorities were aware of the Mafia conclave but did nothing to break it up. The participants included a nephew of the late Don Calò, Giuseppe Genco Russo, whom many *cosche* then acknowledged as "chief of all chiefs"; Lucky Luciano; the Sicilian-American gangsters Joe Bonanno and Frank Garofalo; and other notorious criminals. That meeting was followed a few weeks later by the famous conference of mafiosi from the Eastern Seaboard of the United States in the mansion of the gangster Joseph Barbara at Apalachia, New York, which had been called to agree on a successor to the underworld chief Albert Anastasia and to sort out feuds between various Cosa Nostra families. New York State police and federal agents raided the meeting and arrested sixty-five hoodlums.

Soon Sicily became an important link in the East-West narcotics traffic. From Turkey, Lebanon, Afghanistan, and other eastern countries the Mafia took over large quantities of heroin—or of base morphine to be processed into heroin in clandestine refineries on the island—and reexported the product to the United States. According to the Italian expert Pino Arlacchi, at one time "just four Sicilian Mafia groups held a market share amounting to 30 percent of all heroin introduced annually into the U.S.A." Some *cosche* also handled opium, hashish, and eventually cocaine brought by smugglers from Latin America. The mafiosi increasingly sought the help of the Neapolitan Camorra and the Calabrian 'Ndrangheta in the growing drug traffic and were savagely competing with gangsters from Corsica and Marseilles.

Italy itself, especially Rome and such wealthy northern cities as Trieste, Verona, Milan, and Turin, also became a lucrative end market for hard drugs. In 1988 no fewer than 758 people in Italy died of drug overdoses, almost three times as many as in 1986. The easy availability of heroin from the Mafia networks was viewed as a major reason for the Italian narcotics epidemic, which appeared to be more virulent than in most other European countries.

The enormous profits in successful drug deals—up to 2,000 percent of invested capital in some phases of the heroin or cocaine chains—provided the Sicilian mafiosi and their allies with huge funds and tremendous clout. "All of Italy is at risk," premier Bettino Craxi warned. "In entire provinces the authority of the state seems lost." The Mafia drug tycoons used their money in part to buy flashy, steel-plated cars and build sumptuous villas secured by electronic defenses. After paying off their own henchmen, purchasing police acquiescence, and bribing magistrates and other officials, the mafiosi still had plenty of funds left to be plowed into ostensibly legal businesses and industries. Many credit institutions in Italy and Switzerland and offshore fiscal havens appeared only too happy to handle all that cash, thereby becoming instrumental in money-laundering schemes.

"Narcolire" and "narcodollars"—money from drug deals as well as kidnapping ransoms and other Mafia profits—were invested in small and medium-size contracting firms and manufacturing companies, jewelry stores, fashion boutiques, restaurants, and hotels. In Milan alone scores of businesses were investigated on suspicion of financial backing by racketeers. *L'Espresso* magazine of Rome wrote that the Mafia "is one of our biggest multinational corporations," comparable in cash flow to Fiat or Pirelli.

At the same time, the sums at stake and the greed of the mafiosi brought about a new level of violence. In the old times a local "man of respect" did not very often have to order one of his hitmen to fire the *lupara* at some landowner who would not pay protection money, or to eliminate some errant members of his *cosca* who had started carrying out robberies on their own. (The *lupara* is the short or sawed-off double-barreled shotgun used for hunting wolves; it has remained a favorite murder weapon, although the Mafia has for years been importing submachine guns from the Middle East.

When a Sicilian disappears, and is presumed to have been assassinated by some *cosca* and the body is never found, the populace whispers that he has fallen victim to the *lupara bianca*, the "white" wolf gun that leaves no trace. The missing body may rest in a block of concrete, the bottom of a well, or some remote grotto that has become a secret Mafia cemetery.)

Until a few decades ago the Mafia could secure compliance with its orders through a simple warning by a go-between or a more tangible form of intimidation, like slaughtering a few head of cattle or blowing up someone's car. The Honorable Society traditionally preferred to get on well with local officials, or maybe buy them, rather than oppose them openly or have them killed. Dalla Chiesa, who would be murdered in Palermo in 1982, was a colonel commanding the carabinieri forces in the island capital when he reported to Rome nine years earlier that the "new Mafia" was departing from its old show of respect for the authorities. Its "use of increasingly more audacious and unscrupulous methods tends to impose on the citizenry the insolence of, and oppression by, an asocial minority," Dalla Chiesa warned.

As rival gangs in their drug-related turf wars in Sicily, Calabria, and the Naples area started an unending series of murders, they also kept decimating the ranks of the police and judiciary in Sicilian cities. After each spectacular assassination the president of the Republic, the premier, and other government members, politicians, and high officials flew to Sicily to attend the victim's funeral, took part in another law enforcement "summit meeting," and reiterated the customary public pledge that the fight against the Mafia would be stepped up. As they filed out of the church after the requiem the worthies from Rome would sometimes be booed by outraged local people.

In the late 1970s some Sicilian intellectuals, politicians, civic leaders, and educators at last started speaking out publicly against Mafia domination. Salvatore Cardinal Pappalardo, the son of a Sicilian carabinieri sergeant who became archbishop of Palermo in 1970, denounced the Mafia as an organization "of seemingly blameless persons and groups who impose the law of the shotgun to protect their dirty interests." Other Sicilian notables also dared to pronounce the *M* word that had been taboo on the island for so long.

The U.S. Drug Enforcement Administration and the Federal Bureau of Investigation deployed undercover operatives in Sicily and elsewhere in Italy, and prodded the local authorities into anti-Mafia action. For the first time leads were supplied. Italian and U.S. investigators and magistrates met and agreed on coordinated strategies. Courageous prosecutors and judges—who had to travel in bulletproof cars from their heavily guarded homes to fortresslike offices in Palermo and other Sicilian cities—brought hundreds of mafiosi to book.

Monster trials were held in a bunker-style structure hastily built as an annex to the archaic Ucciardone jail on Palermo's waterfront, which had been under virtual Mafia control since Bourbon times. In one such proceeding 457 accused mafiosi, held in iron cages, faced their judges. Damning evidence was presented by a notorious gangster, Tommaso Buscetta, who had been extradited by Brazil and turned state witness. He was a sensation: Up to then no ranking mafioso had ever broken the code of *omertà* in a Sicilian courtroom.

The fifty-nine-year-old Buscetta, however, had been a loser in a savage gang war, and he desperately needed a refuge. As a protected witness he had earlier testified in the "Pizza Connection" trial of Cosa Nostra heroin dealers in New York who had been using a pizza parlor as their front. The information Buscetta provided had also led to hundreds of arrests in Italy. The Palermo magistrates appeared to believe his story of a Mafia "cupola" in Sicily, a secret twelve-man commission that, he said, decreed all murders. If such a Mafia tribunal actually existed, it must have been set up on the pattern of the Cosa Nostra conferences in the United States. When the Palermo trial ended after twenty-two months of hearings, 119 defendants were acquitted and the others received prison sentences totaling 2,665 years, including nineteen life sentences. (In Italy a sentence for life in prison is reckoned to last thirty years.)

But Sicilian violence did not subside. A new chain of assassinations started, and during a mere two weeks in the fall of 1988, eighteen people, including a judge, were murdered by Mafia gunmen. Sicilian magistrates started quarreling among themselves, ostensibly about judicial methods in dealing with the Honorable Society, and Italy's head of state publicly admonished them not to favor lawlessness by their squabbles. Meanwhile, in Calabria and in the Naples area no week went by without gang killings.

Mafia crimes, often described by the police as "settlements of accounts" between competing gangs, were also committed in other parts of Italy with increasing frequency. In their efforts to control new drug markets and search for opportunities to invest surplus cash, factions of mafiosi had been branching out all over the nation and beyond. In addition, the spread of southern crime patterns was furthered by a policy of exiling reputed gangsters to towns in Central and Northern Italy whenever there was insufficient evidence to bring specific charges against them.

The police and the judiciary in Sicily had relegated hundreds of such suspects to faraway places in the peninsula on the theory that they would become innocuous once they were removed from their island habitat. Often just the opposite happened: The deportees infected and corrupted their new surroundings, kept in touch with their Sicilian accomplices from pay telephones and through couriers, found new associates among the southern immigrants in nearby big cities, and with them started functioning as new Mafia colonies. In the early 1980s many a town in Italy's Center and North rebelled when it learned it had been designated as the new place of mandatory residence for some alleged mafioso from Sicily or Calabria. A legal reform eventually ended the practice of exiling suspects.

The ferocity of the crimes continually committed by the Mafia, the 'Ndrangheta, the Camorra, and the Sardinian-Calabrian "Kidnapping, Inc.," clouds the international image of Italians as hot-blooded, yes, but also easygoing, soft, and humane. Mafiosi kill their rivals and other victims, sometimes after torture, and they do so in cold blood rather than in fits of passion. Most Italians regard themselves as a live-and-let-live people and therefore are truly horrified whenever television and the newspapers report the latest savagery in gory detail. The Mafia crimes inevitably feed North-South ethnic prejudice. Underlying all this is the contention—most often unspoken, but sometimes expressed privately in so many words—that those lawless southerners are not genuine Italians at all, and that their cruelty is the result of the admixture of foreign blood—maybe Arabic, maybe Spanish—in earlier generations.

8.

On Many Sides
of the Law

Whenever a person has been murdered or kidnapped or some other crime has been reported, the information media announce that "carabinieri and police are investigating." Sometimes it is the other way around, but it is always the two that rush to the scene, carabinieri in black uniforms (in winter) or blue ones (in summer) with broad red stripes along their trousers, and state police in two-tone blue outfits. Carabinieri vehicles are painted black, whereas state police cars are blue.

In most of Italy's urban areas anyone seeking quick police intervention has a choice of two emergency telephone numbers—112 for the carabinieri and 113 for the state police. Patrol cars of the two competing forces crisscross the cities, and separate contingents of carabinieri and state police, usually equal in number, keep order at public rallies or parades. Distinct details of the two forces guard the approaches to St. Peter's and to the State of Vatican City in Rome. Each group of lawmen will make its own arrests, question its own suspects and witnesses, and occasionally withhold evidence from the rival corps.

Tensions between competing police organizations occur also in other countries, but in Italy they are institutionalized; the lack of coordination and the undisguised rivalry between the nation's two major law enforcement agencies have long hampered the fight against the Mafia and against crime in general. The carabinieri and the state police monitor each other's communications and have been known to detain plainclothes operatives and informers of the rival force. Whenever an alleged assassin is captured or a kidnapping victim is freed, state police and carabinieri vie in claiming success and protest to media executives if their asserted role does not receive the credit they think it is due. During the first years after World War II, the state police—then called Public Security Police—and the carabinieri in turn made secret deals with one or the other Mafia *cosca* in Sicily.

The Carabinieri Corps, like a number of other Italian institutions, was created in imitation of a French model, in this case the Gendarmerie. Founded in the Kingdom of Sardinia-Piedmont in 1814, the body was taken over and greatly expanded by unified Italy. The Carabinieri Corps is to this day considered a service branch of the Italian army and is often referred to simply as the Service *(L'Arma)* without any further qualification. It acts as military police, watching over the discipline of the soldiers of all services and rounding up deserters in peace and war. But this is only a small portion of the many duties of the carabinieri.

The force also serves as rural police throughout the nation, with permanent detachments in 5,000 of Italy's 8,000 towns and villages; at the same time it maintains an increasingly strong presence in the major cities. The carabinieri depend on the armed forces hierarchy in matters of personnel, equipment, training, and military-police work, but in their role of civilian law enforcement they are supposed to take orders from the judiciary as well as from the minister of the interior. Actually, the carabinieri often seem a law to themselves.

They pride themselves on their esprit de corps, and (at

least until recently) they have screened their recruits carefully and trained them more thoroughly than do other uniformed government services. A young man who is admitted into the corps will undergo intensive indoctrination and may, twenty years later, by then a *maresciallo* (master sergeant), find himself representing the majesty of the law in some village in Sardinia or Friuli. If he is honorably discharged he will have little trouble landing a job as a security guard with some bank or private firm. The carabinieri code stresses obedience to superiors, and it insists on spit and polish.

On ceremonial occasions the carabinieri turn out in early nineteenth-century uniforms with high tufts on their bicornes, their old-fashioned ammunition boxes on broad white straps slung over their tailcoats. As an operative force, the corps has modern armament, its own tank brigade and helicopter fleet, paratrooper and antiterrorism units, and frogmen. Specialized sections conduct sting operations to catch drug peddlers, track looted works of art, and nab those responsible for doctored wine, adulterated olive oil, and river pollution from industrial waste. The corps operates its own intelligence network and provides many agents for the government's undercover services.

The carabinieri motto is "Faithful through the centuries." Faithful to whom, or to what? Until the early years of World War II, carabinieri loyalty to the sovereign was unquestioned. When King Victor Emmanuel III, faced with the national catastrophe of a military defeat, in a palace cabal in 1943 decided to get rid of Mussolini, whom he had unflinchingly been backing for two decades, he ordered the carabinieri to provide a detail that would arrest the dictator. The carabinieri obeyed. When the Nazis later occupied a large part of Italy, they deported thousands of carabinieri to Germany.

Today the leadership of the Carabinieri Corps emphasizes its loyalty to the Republic and its democratic institutions on all suitable occasions, and indeed obedience to the laws and the government remains an important part of the carabinieri mystique. The top officers of the corps do not seem to mind, may even be secretly pleased, that newspaper cartoons, films, television programs, and a plethora of jokes depict the rank-and-file carabiniere as a dense yokel in uniform who will carry out to the letter any order received from a superior. Carabinieri foot patrols usually consist of two men, ponderously walking side by side—"one can read, the other write," the popular saying goes.

Politically, almost all carabinieri officers are known to be conservatives. At various times some of them, "borrowed" by the nation's secret services, allegedly became implicated in right-wing plots. However, the Carabinieri Corps as a whole, comprising around 110,000 men in 1989, has remained an irreplaceable instrument for keeping the country together. Italy is not a nation with a bent for coups d'état, but if any conspiratorial group ever tried to seize power it would first of all have to seek carabinieri backing. The carabinieri were standing by benignly when Mussolini's Blackshirts staged their "March on Rome" in 1922. The event was no putsch but a choreographic exercise—a junket of right-wingers from Perugia to the national capital, a parade and a picnic—after King Victor Emmanuel had requested Mussolini to form a new government and Il Duce had arrived from Milan in a railway sleeper coach.

Whenever Italians today discuss the hypothetical overthrow of the democratic regime by a band of plotters, they borrow a term from Spanish and Latin American military lore, *golpe*, as if to underline the fact that the very idea of a coup d'état (*colpo di stato* in Italian) is alien to their thinking. Implied in any talk of an Italian *golpe*, a very remote possibility, is the suggestion that carabinieri officers would somehow be involved.

The traditional rivals of the carabinieri, the state police, are a civilian force of uniformed and plainclothes men and women, today numbering more than 100,000. It grew out of the police organizations of the various Italian states that were merged into the unified Italian kingdom in the second half of the nineteenth century. Mussolini, who never fully trusted the carabinieri (rightly, as it turned out), favored and expanded the national police force; he considered it prudent to have two different countrywide law enforcement bodies that would watch each other. Today the state police operate mainly in the cities and major towns as well as along the principal routes of communication. They employ more detectives than the carabinieri, and in many places appear to know more about the underworld than do their rivals.

But that is not all of it in law enforcement. A third national organization, the Finance Guard, with more than 60,000 men, is often engaged in investigative work parallel to and in competition with that of the two main police forces. On orders from the Treasury, the Finance Guard is supposed to track tax dodgers, catch smugglers, and probe the money affairs of corporations and wealthy private citizens. Its cadre wear gray uniforms with yellow facings but may also be on duty in plain clothes. They can make arrests, and the intelligence arm of the Finance Guard bugs telephones.

This police body has of late also been playing an important part in the fight against the drug trade, and occasionally the government and local magistrates entrust the Finance Guard with confidential assignments when carabinieri or state police units seem unreliable, or must themselves be investigated. Or, sometimes, it is the other way around: A former commander in chief of the Finance Guard ended up in prison for having connived with oil companies that had been defrauding the state of gasoline tax.

Then there are, at least officially, two national secret services—one engaged in espionage and counterintelligence work, the other focusing on domestic subversion. The armed services also each have their own intelligence branch, and the major political parties and party factions too are gathering secret information. On any given day several thousand spies and agents are snooping and, above all, monitoring telephones all over the country. The Vatican, for example, knows that any one of its incoming or outgoing wire communications will be monitored or taped by one or more of the several secret agencies busy in Rome.

The government's spy organizations are widely distrusted: Parliament has repeatedly investigated allegations of their "deviating" from their legitimate tasks by playing confidential information into the hands of politicians, manipulating subversive groups, or making deals with criminal organizations. One such transaction with a Camorra gang was said to have resulted in the liberation of a kidnapped Naples politician, Ciro Cirillo.

Throughout Italy's vast and checkered security forces, the southern element has during the last few decades steadily advanced. It is preponderant today in all services, even in the Carabinieri Corps, whose cradle was in the country's Northwest. With the industrial economy in Italy's North and in vast patches of its center booming, creating new well-paying jobs, the number of young people prepared to make a career of tedious and possibly dangerous police work and to live for years in military barracks kept diminishing. At the same time the prospect of a steady government salary and of wielding a fraction, however tiny, of state power appealed to poor southerners. (Since people in the Mezzogiorno are on average shorter than Northern Italians, the statutory minimum height for carabinieri and state police was reduced in the same way it was for police departments in the United States to enable them to enroll more recruits with Latin American and Asian backgrounds.)

The gradual transformation of the Italian law enforcement apparatus into a predominantly southern force may not be a bad thing. A well-trained and thoroughly indoctrinated police officer from the Mezzogiorno is apt to have a better understanding of how a mafioso's mind functions than would his colleague from the North. And since most organized crime in Italy is based in the South, it makes sense that most lawmen have their roots there too.

As has happened in other nations, the Italian police organizations have also had their scandals lately, even the image-conscious Carabinieri Corps. In 1987 three men of a carabinieri station at Monza near Milan were convicted of raping a young Englishwoman whom they were holding for interrogation. Carabinieri and state police operatives have been implicated in robberies, drug trafficking, and other sundry crimes. On one occasion, members of the two main rival bodies even cooperated against a gang in the Trieste area that, among other enterprises, hijacked a mail truck, taking off with $400,000. On the other hand, in a 1989 shoot-out near Vercelli in Piedmont, two off-duty carabinieri who had joined a robbers' band killed a colleague trying to capture them at a roadblock.

Newcomers to Italy are struck by the variety of uniforms they see everywhere—carabinieri and state police on foot, on motorcycles, in squad cars with flashing lights and screaming sirens, or on horseback; customs guards at frontier points and in airports; white-helmeted traffic cops; and other municipal patrolmen and patrolwomen. Three-man patrols composed of one member each of the army, navy, and air force strut around railroad terminals and the piazzas of garrison cities. Even the Vatican has two separate police forces: the blue-uniformed Security Service, made up in large part of former carabinieri and state policemen, and the Pontifical Swiss Guard, recruited from the Roman Catholic cantons of

Switzerland, in resplendent blue, red, and yellow Renaissance garb that was designed, it is claimed (probably wrongly), by either Michelangelo or Raphael. The Switzers and the Italian security guards not only separately protect the pope's safety, they also watch over sensitive areas inside Vatican City and compete with each other the way the carabinieri and state police do outside.

With one member of some law enforcement organization for about every 160 citizens, Italy should be a well-policed nation. Yet murders, thefts, and other lawlessness are on the increase, as ranking magistrates tell the nation at the beginning of every year. Italy's chief prosecutor, Vittorio Sgroi, stated in his 1989 report that the perpetrators of seven out of every ten crimes are never identified, and that about one-half of the persons allegedly implicated in the remaining three cases are acquitted in court. The chief prosecutor warned above all against what he described as the surge of petty crime—burglaries, muggings, purse snatchings, harassment— that remained unpunished and were being accepted as inevitable, a fact of life. All too many denizens of what Sgroi called the "subterranean geography of crime" regard anyone who is caught by the police to be either stupid or dogged by exceptional bad luck.

Crime is bigger business in Italy today than tourism, but its profits were ignored when the government tried to quantify the earnings of the nation's "submerged" economy (see chapter 5). Magistrates and sociologists estimate that between 500,000 and 1 million Italians—out of a population of 57 million—have earnings in violation of the penal code, not just income from the "submerged" economy. According to the CENSIS data, in 1988 unlawful activities in the country were generating $73 billion, or 12 percent of the nation's total output of goods and services. The research institution very conservatively figured that the annual amount of ransom money actually collected was $3.6 billion, a figure dwarfed by the estimates for the profits of the drug trade ($22.0 billion a year); extortion rackets ($8.7 billion); graft, bribes, and kickbacks ($8.0 billion); robberies, frauds, arms trafficking, and clandestine gambling ($18.0 billion); and other crimes (about $12.3 billion).

Under current Italian legislation it is not punishable to make a living as a prostitute (a business estimated by CENSIS to produce a yearly volume of $4 billion), but exploiting prostitution is illegal. Accordingly, the courts tend to define pimping broadly: A night concierge of the Cavalieri Hilton Hotel in Rome was sentenced to a year and four months in prison because he had allowed alleged call girls to visit hotel guests in their rooms, charging double occupancy. Landlords who rent apartments to prostitutes may also be prosecuted. At the same time, leading newspapers list the addresses or telephone numbers of "masseuses," "astrologers," "chiromancers," and "escorts" in their classified columns every day, and nobody has any doubt about what the advertisements mean.

Prostitution has flourished in Rome since antiquity and was tacitly tolerated even during the many centuries when the popes were temporal rulers of the city. Venice, Bologna, Florence, and Naples were, from the Middle Ages, also notorious for their bevies of courtesans. Until 1958 the Italian police licensed "houses of tolerance," the legal term for brothels, but reform legislation enacted in that year closed all bordellos. Since then streetwalkers and call-girl rings have proliferated, with organized crime often in control. Attempts to organize prostitutes in a kind of trade union were made by some veterans of the profession in the Friuli region in Italy's Northeast, the area where no less than one-third of the nation's army forces are permanently stationed.

How much protection money is being paid to racketeers, and how much cash changes hands in graft arrangements is anybody's guess. Many such crimes never become known because there is no complaint. In 1987 a Catania political scientist, Franco Cazzola, published a study of corruption cases implicating politicians and officials that had come to national attention during the preceding one hundred years. According to the study, only one out of every two such affairs investigated by the judiciary in Northern Italy actually resulted in a court sentence punishing the culprits; in the Mezzogiorno the proportion was one guilty verdict in every four cases. "In Sicily, the state is lenient with the corrupt and the corrupters," Cazzola concluded.

Yet the cash flow from criminal activities in the North is huge too—it "has to be estimated at around 15 percent of the entire region's gross product" in Lombardy, according to the president of the Milan Chamber of Commerce, Piero Bassetti. At one time in the mid-1980s, the Milan motor vehicles bureau was paralyzed because almost its entire staff had been arrested on charges of having sold thousands of driver's licenses to motorists who had never bothered to take the driving test.

Corruption and mismanagement in the Mezzogiorno started worrying the European Community when it found that 20 to 30 percent of its subsidies for Southern Italy's embattled agriculture were being skimmed off illegally. Farmers belonging to Mafia-backed syndicates produced fake documents to collect Community funds for olive oil that was never pressed and for tomato fields that did not exist. An official of European Community headquarters in Brussels who visited Sicily to investigate suspected rackets was run over by a motorcycle and suffered fractures of both legs. In 1989 British Prime Minister Margaret Thatcher, commenting on a report by the European Commission in Brussels that the Community was being defrauded of more than $10 million every year, asserted bluntly that much of that money was being channeled to the Sicilian Mafia and to the outlawed Irish Republican Army.

The alarming increase in Mafia crime started just as Italy's police forces were facing a tremendous test—the threat to the nation's democratic institutions by political terrorism. Shaky though the police machinery of the Italian state might look, it did eventually succeed in smashing the murderous conspiracies of right-wing and left-wing extremists without essentially curtailing the civil liberties guaranteed by the Constitution. The peak period of terroristic violence lasted from the late 1960s to the early 1980s; Italians call it "the leaden years" (a translation of *Die Bleierne Zeit*, the title of a film by the director Margarethe von Trotta that depicted the plumbeous atmosphere in West Germany during the 1970s). The ultraradicals of the Baader-Meinhof gang, who called themselves the Red Army Faction, were then fighting the despised capitalist system, the North Atlantic Treaty Organization, and the West German state with sabotage and assassination, and had become role models for Italian extremists. One maverick among the Italian ultraleftists, the rich publisher Giangiacomo Feltrinelli, knew and admired Ulrike Meinhof, the *pasionaria* of the Red Army Faction.

Soon after the end of World War II, small neo-Fascist groups in Italy had started to create alarm with bomb plots and arson. As the violence increased, a few government officials warned that not all attacks were being carried out by rightists but that an underground network of leftist terrorists was also developing. The established left-wing parties, the Socialists and Communists, scoffed at the suggestion.

Italy's "leaden years" are today dated from the bombing

in a Milan bank in 1969 that caused the deaths of sixteen
people. The police at first blamed the crime on a group of
anarchists and made few arrests. (One of the detainees fell,
jumped, or was pushed out of a window at police headquarters and died; another alleged anarchist plotter was put
through a series of trials and eventually was cleared.) Meanwhile, a new theory had gained credence—that the bombing
had been engineered by neo-Fascists at the instigation of a
secret-service faction in order to increase political tension.
Undercover agents and right-wing extremists had conspired,
it was alleged, to make leftist radicals appear as the authors
of the Milan massacre, thereby provoking popular demand
for stern measures against Communists. As I mentioned in
chapter 3, the tortuous judicial proceedings to clear up the
mystery of the Milan bomb plot were to drag on inconclusively for two decades.

The left-wing parties and a broad sector of the Italian
press continued for some time to blame the rash of bombings
and other outrages on rightist conspirators, on the Italian
secret services, and—who else?—on the U.S. Central Intelligence Agency. But the evidence mounted that clandestine
ultraleftist factions were indeed engaged in subversion and
terrorism. Communist partisans who in the mountains of
Central and Northern Italy had fought the Fascists and the
Nazis during the last years of World War II, and younger
people who had been radicalized during the student revolt that swept European universities in 1968 had been
forming bands for urban guerrilla warfare and revolutionary
activities.

Feltrinelli himself went underground, and the millionaire publisher's descent into the shades deserves to be retraced
in some detail.

Giangiacomo Feltrinelli was heir to one of the largest
fortunes in Italy, comprising forests in Italy and Austria,

much real estate in Italy, banks, and shares in many corporations. Feltrinelli's grandfather had laid the foundations for this economic empire, and his uncle and father had greatly expanded it. When Giangiacomo was nine years old, he lost his father. Educated by governesses and tutors, the shy, lonely boy spent much time on the family estates in Austria and learned to speak German fluently. Back in Italy again, he was converted to Communism by a gardener at one of the family's villas. He never got on well with his stepfather, Luigi Barzini, Jr., and at age eighteen he enlisted in an Italian army unit attached to the United States forces and served in it until the end of World War II. The young millionaire thereupon joined first the Socialist party and then the Communists, and financed a Milan research center specializing in the history of workers' movements as well as, for some time, a Communist publishing operation. In 1955 Feltrinelli founded his own publishing house and soon attracted international attention by two literary coups: He brought out Giuseppe Tomasi di Lampedusa's *The Leopard* and Boris Pasternak's *Doctor Zhivago*.

Tomasi di Lampedusa's book had been rejected by Italy's leading publisher, Mondadori, among other houses; the novel, set in Sicily at the time of the island's conquest by Garibaldi, was soon hailed as a masterpiece and sold more than a million copies worldwide. The Pasternak work, brought by Feltrinelli to the West, was a sensation. The young Italian publisher had learned of the manuscript through friends and had middlemen smuggle it out of the Soviet Union. He acquired the world rights from the author and, despite pressures from Moscow and the Italian Communist party aimed at preventing publication, went ahead with it, having it printed in both Russian and Italian translation.

Doctor Zhivago earned at least $3 million in royalties, but the author saw little, if any, of the money. I asked Feltrinelli in a 1958 interview how he was handling the royalty funds, and he replied that he was holding them "on my books" for Pasternak. After the Russian writer died in 1960, Pasternak's heirs, mainly his sons Evgheni and Leonid, were to receive the royalty money. It is suspected that the Soviet government withheld a large portion of it.

The *Doctor Zhivago* affair contributed to Feltrinelli's break with the Communist party. He announced that "Communism does not have an answer for everything; the Italian Communist party has disappointed me." In 1965 the publisher visited Cuba for the first time and became an ardent admirer of Fidel Castro and Che Guevara. He also signed up the Cuban dictator for a volume of memoirs, but Castro never delivered a manuscript. Feltrinelli, Giangi to his friends, made other trips to Cuba, and in 1967 he traveled to Bolivia to attend the trial of another Che Guevara fan, the French writer Régis Debray, who had run afoul of the local authorities. Feltrinelli was arrested with his traveling companion—who was to become his fourth wife—and expelled from the country. More than three years later a Bolivian army officer who had been instrumental in the capture and death of Guevara, and possibly also in the arrest of Feltrinelli, was shot to death in Hamburg, where he'd been serving the Bolivian consul. The assassin was the German-Bolivian radical Monica Ertl, a friend of Feltrinelli, and the murder weapon, a Colt revolver, was found to have been bought and registered in Milan in the publisher's name.

All this time—while he was getting increasingly absorbed in extremist movements in Italy and was making frequent trips to Latin American countries, Algeria, and the Middle East—Feltrinelli was becoming a popular figure in the international radical-chic set. He appeared on the cover of *Vogue* magazine, modeling a "Zhivago" maxi fur coat for men. He sailed two yachts and played the generous host to left-wing intellectuals, members of the Italian establishment, and visiting radicals from abroad in glittering parties in his sumptuous villa on Lake Garda (where Mussolini had resided during the last eighteen months of his life) or in his castle at Villadeati in Piedmont. Ulrike Meinhof and her husband were among his house guests.

From 1965 on Feltrinelli drifted into a conspiratorial twilight. For some time he focused on Sardinia as a potential Cuba in the Mediterranean, and tried to win over local separatists and even common brigands for revolutionary action. When the Sardinian project failed, he attempted to latch onto the youth rebellion of 1968, but student audiences in Rome, Paris, and West Berlin jeered at the millionaire who was urging them to smash capitalism and NATO.

In 1968 Feltrinelli decided to go more fully underground, leaving his publishing business in the hands of his German-born third wife, Inge Schoental (they had married in Mexico). Under the assumed name Osvaldo, he led a curious semiclandestine life, slipping in and out of Italy with a false passport and minus his mustache, but surfacing in Austria, Switzerland, and France to give interviews in which he warned against a rightist coup d'état that, he said, was imminent in his native country. Ultraleftists with more authentic credentials ridiculed Feltrinelli as a "checkbook guerrilla" and as self-appointed CEO of "Revolution, Inc.," but they accepted money from him, a "cow to be milked" for their own purposes.

Feltrinelli did manage to stitch together a flimsy underground network of "Proletarian Action Groups" (GAP), paying salaries to his operatives and taking some of them to Czechoslovakia for training in a school for saboteurs near Prague. He also established contacts with Palestinian factions in Beirut and with urban guerrillas in Uruguay. In Italy, Feltrinelli's GAP carried out some bombings and made clandestine broadcasts calling for revolutionary violence, and eventually the millionaire radical connected with leaders of a nascent underground movement of violence-prone ultra-leftists, the Red Brigades. But the movement did not trust him and his GAP.

Apparently seeking to prove his own revolutionary mettle and the military capabilities of his network, Feltrinelli plotted to blow up the pylon of a high-voltage power line that rose on a tract of his land in the Milan suburb of Segrate. The action was aimed at plunging a large part of Milan into darkness, possibly to facilitate a series of terrorist attacks mounted by the GAP. Feltrinelli bungled the bombing, was gravely wounded in a premature explosion, and was abandoned by his own sabotage commandos. Maybe they even helped him die; the postmortem attributed his death to loss of blood.

When Feltrinelli's mangled body was found beneath the pylon on March 15, 1972, it was carrying forged identity papers in the name of Vincenzo Maggioni; the police, who for years had been shadowing the millionaire revolutionary despite all his disguises, quickly identified the corpse. Leftists in Italy and abroad asserted that Feltrinelli had been assassinated by secret services or had walked into a trap prepared by them. Years later, even the Red Brigades leaders who had been contacted by Osvaldo accepted the official version that he had died because of his inexperience in handling explosives. Whatever the truth, Feltrinelli's violent death seemed a fitting end to an ambiguous life during which he had yearned for personal commitment and had striven to be taken seriously as a revolutionary, despite his wealth.

The Red Brigades, which had spurned Feltrinelli's offer of collaboration, were of a different sort. The ultraleftist underground sect was founded by a handful of students of the new School of Sociology in the Alpine city of Trent and quickly spread to other colleges and universities. Many of the original members had had a Roman Catholic upbringing and had been influenced by the anticapitalist currents that had been gaining strength within the church since the late nineteenth century. Along with similar clandestine radical groups, the Red Brigades considered themselves units of an "armed party" pledged to destroy by military methods the capitalist system and the Italian state that they claimed was its servant. They murdered police officers, magistrates, high officials, journalists, and other presumed representatives of the "system," and carried out kidnappings for ransom and robberies as revolutionary methods of "self-financing."

The Red Brigades and the other clandestine factions disseminated leaflets in which they expounded their program: They were fighting, they explained verbosely, against the monopolies of the multinational corporations that had enslaved Italy, and for a communistic society. Many members of the nation's leftist intelligentsia, including university teachers, appeared sympathetic to the "armed party." Other respected writers like Leonardo Sciascia and Alberto Moravia professed their equidistance from both the "armed party" and the embattled state. It took some time before Italy's Communist party apparatus came around to acknowledging that ultraleftist terrorism existed, and at last to disavowing and condemning it.

In some cases over the "leaden years" it was doubtful whether a specific act of violence was the handiwork of rightist or leftist plotters. Between 1969 and 1987, neo-Fascist and leftist terrorists killed 419 people, including many members of the police forces, and injured several thousand. Whenever the gunmen or gunwomen of the Red Brigades wanted to administer nonlethal punishment, they fired at people's legs. The Italian idiom was enriched by the new term *gambizzare* (roughly, "kneecapping"). The practice of such brutal "warnings" before outright murder had long been a Mafia ritual. The political terrorists adopted the old techniques of the Mafia also in abducting wealthy people and dealing with their families to collect ransom.

In turn, Mafia gangs in Sicily and on the mainland, impressed by the firepower of the Red Brigades, abandoned the traditional *lupara* and started using some of the efficient weapons with which the political terrorists were amply equipped—especially Soviet-made Kalashnikov and Czech Skorpion submachine guns. A large part of the Red Brigades' arsenal was shipped to Italy from the Middle East along heroin-smuggling routes that led to some remote cove on the country's extended coastline.

In the nation's penitentiaries, captured political terrorists were in theory to be segregated from common criminals, yet the separation was far from total. The imprisoned ultraleftists were able to recruit and indoctrinate new followers from among other inmates, and neo-Fascists established contacts with mafiosi. Jailbirds taught the terrorists their tricks for staying in touch with the outside world even from the new maximum-security prisons that Italy had hastily built in various parts of the peninsula and on the islands.

The darkest months of the "leaden years" came early in 1978, when a commando of the Red Brigades kidnapped Aldo Moro, a former premier who was then president of the Christian Democratic party and was generally expected to become Italy's next head of state. Three of Moro's police bodyguard were killed in the attack in a residential district in Rome. The terrorists had prepared a soundproof secret prison in an apartment they had previously rented in a middle-class neighborhood, and they kept Moro there for fifty-five days, subjecting him to many hours of questioning about what had been going on behind the scenes of Italian politics and taking pictures of him for release to the press. The jailers also allowed the former government chief to write many agonized letters to relatives and political associates.

During those fifty-five days, Italy's vast security apparatus tried frantically, and futilely, to locate where Moro was being held. Thousands of policemen and secret agents tried to follow up purported clues that might lead them to his prison, and there was much bungling. The Red Brigades continually teased the authorities with false leads. Frogmen dived into an icy lake in the Apennine Mountains following one report that the abducted politician's body had been dumped there. A motorized carabinieri detail, acting on a tip, actually closed in on the building in which the former premier was being detained, only to drive right on when they noticed a patrol car of the state police parked outside; the rival force too had received information pointing to the apartment house but failed to search it thoroughly.

Eventually the terrorists killed Moro with a Skorpion gun in the garage of their hideout, put his body in the luggage compartment of a stolen Renault, and abandoned the car in the heart of Rome, near the Christian Democratic and the Communist party national headquarters. Moro had for years been maneuvering to bring about some sort of collaboration between those two groups, the nation's main political parties, and the terrorists' leaving his body to be discovered in the vicinity of their bureaucratic centers was like thumbing their noses at both. The shock of the Moro kidnapping and assassination spurred Parliament to give the police and the judiciary broader powers in their fight against terrorism.

During the "leaden years" several hundred Italians went underground; others led split lives, doing quiet and competent work as teachers, nurses, or office workers while spying on potential targets for attack or providing "safe houses" for armed terrorists. The fanaticism of a few was combined with the thirst for adventure of many Italians, men and women attracted to conspiratorial activity and political violence as a means of acting out juvenile or romantic fantasies.

In another sense, these young people were like those of the preceding generation who had gone into hiding in the cities to avoid being pressed into Mussolini's last-ditch army, or had taken to the hills to fight the occupying Nazi forces. The partisans during the last part of World War II, it is true, faced hardship and, if caught, probable torture and death, whereas the terrorists who escaped arrest in the 1970s were realizing not leaden but excitingly glamorous years. They had plenty of money from "self-financing"—robberies and kidnappings for ransom—and were able to afford comfortable hiding places and gourmet meals. During the summer months, political violence would subside because so many neo-Fascist and ultraleftist plotters were vacationing on the beaches of the Adriatic Sea, Sardinia, or, preferably, the French Riviera. And even in peak periods of attacks on banks, abductions, the planning and execution of murders, clandestine strategy sessions, and the writing of doctrinaire manifestos, there was plenty of time and opportunity for radical *dolce vita*. Underground love affairs blossomed, and continued into the prisons. A few female conspirators managed to have babies in jail years after they had been arrested.

After many aborted attempts, investigators at last succeeded in infiltrating the underground networks—one of their informers was a spurious Franciscan who feigned enthusiasm for violent action to right society's wrongs and became known as Friar Submachine Gun (*Frate Mitra*)—and several members of clandestine groups took advantage of new legislation that offered leniency as a reward for collaboration with the authorities. Such plotters who had turned state witnesses were labeled "repenters" by the information media, a word with ethical and even religious overtones, although expediency rather than genuine contrition seemed the more likely motive for their change of mind. One way or another, police in time rounded up most of the terrorists. On being picked up they usually declared, "I am a political prisoner," and refused to answer questions.

Hard-core terrorists who were still underground condemned the "repenters" as traitors and in some instances killed members of their families in Mafia-style "lateral" vendettas. Mass trials were held with alleged terrorists kept in three different dock cages: one for the unrepentant, the second for defendants who had declared themselves "disassociated" from clandestine groups but were unwilling to collaborate with the authorities, and the third for "repenters." Invectives often flew back and forth between the cages. Whenever the unrepentant among the Red Brigades members were given the chance to expound their ideology in court, they spouted a hodgepodge of undigested Marxist and anarchist doctrine and paranoid rhetoric to denounce Western capitalism and imperialism.

Defendants who went along with prosecutors, and former plotters who had become state witnesses—perhaps after having themselves taken part in terrorist murders—received short prison sentences and were soon free again. They included Marco Donat-Cattin, the son of a Christian Democratic leader and government minister.

The overwhelming majority of Italians, Communists included, eventually appeared to approve of the way the state had coped with the deadly emergency of terrorism. But even as the "leaden years" seemed to have ended, thousands of policemen in bulletproof vests remained assigned as bodyguards to government members, high officials, and magistrates. Tiny bands of ultrarightists and left-wing radicals were still at large, able from time to time to pull off some small act of aggression, and to have one's own round-the-clock antiterrorist guard had become a status symbol, cherished above all by politicians.

On the other side of the law, in the land where Etruscan vases and Lacoste shirts are being faked industrially, it came as no surprise that genuine terrorists too found their imitators. Occasionally common criminals carrying out some robbery would announce, "We are from the Red Brigades!" to frighten their victims and mislead the police. Wags suggested that the bona fide revolutionaries should carry credentials.

9.

The Question of Being Serious

In January 1875, more than four years after the soldiers of King Victor Emmanuel II had penetrated into papal Rome and declared it the capital of Italy, the national hero Giuseppe Garibaldi left his home on the windswept island of Caprera off Sardinia's north coast and paid his first visit to the city in a quarter of a century. Thousands of Romans cheered him when he arrived by rail from the seaport of Civitavecchia, and enthusiastic young patriots unhitched the horses from his carriage to pull and push it to the Hotel Costanzi, where he was to stay.

At age sixty-eight Garibaldi was crippled by arthritis and needed crutches to walk. Over his red shirt he was wearing the poncho he had affected since his early days as a guerrilla leader in the civil wars of Brazil and Uruguay, and he had his customary gold-embroidered velvet beret on his head. At the hotel he addressed the vast crowd gathered outside. *"Romani!"* Garibaldi exclaimed. *"Siate seri!"* (Romans! Be serious!)

His admonition seemed aimed at the entire newly unified nation. As for the Romans, they erected an equestrian monument to Garibaldi on the Janiculum, the hill on the right bank of the Tiber where in 1849 he had unsuccessfully defended the city from the French troops that were about to conquer it for the pope. On horseback, over a pedestal always covered with graffiti, the Hero of the Two Worlds (Latin America and Europe) frowns on Rome spreading out below. Almost every other major city in Italy and many small towns have their own Garibaldi monument, and their Piazza Garibaldi or Via Garibaldi too, or perhaps, like Rome, all three. Yet it may be argued whether Romans or Italians in general have heeded the hero's exhortation to be serious. It may be Italy's strength, indeed, that so few of its people ever have.

"Facite 'a faccia feroce!" (Make a ferocious face!) Thus the king of Naples, speaking in the local dialect, would order his ragged troops on parade, trying to make them seem more credible as a military force. Evidently they could not maintain the prescribed belligerent expression for any length of time, and before long must have reassumed the characteristic sardonic grin of the Neapolitans. Just so, whenever Italy has pulled a "ferocious face," the outside world has sooner or later detected a wink, a smirk, a gesture of clowning exaggeration, or a deprecatory signal. By not being earnest for too long a time the Italians as a nation have gotten away with a lot of things—diplomatic fickleness, military disasters, colonial atrocities in Libya and Ethiopia, Fascism, and the catastrophic alliance with Nazi Germany.

With all his patriotism, courage, and generosity, Garibaldi seemed un-Italian in that he totally lacked a sense of humor, taking himself and everything else very seriously indeed. Un-Italian too was Garibaldi's disinterestedness, which made him live in near poverty even when he was world famous, likewise his idealism to the point of naïveté in matters of politics and diplomacy. There was something quixotic in this national hero who wanted to fight oppressors anywhere—in the pampas of South America, in Sicily, in the Alps, on the Rhine, or in the Balkans.

On the other hand, he did strike his contemporaries as very Italian in his continual entanglements with women, almost to his death, and in his love of rhetoric. The way he started and conducted his military enterprises, taking awesome chances, struck Italians as familiar too, and attracted thousands of volunteers to his banner. To this day the Italian phrase *alla garibaldina* (Garibaldi style) describes an undertaking that is begun with cheerful audacity, little advance planning, and plenty of gambling—let's hope for the best. Many things in Italy are launched *alla garibaldina*: operatic performances after a few rehearsals or none at all, vacations without an itinerary or hotel reservations, college examinations for which the student has only scantily prepared, business ventures with insufficient funds and a lot of promissory notes, and political or military campaigns without well-thought-out strategies. Sometimes they succeed beyond reasonable expectations, sometimes they end in shameful failures. An egregious example is the way Mussolini plunged his country into war in 1940, confident that his ally Hitler would win the blitzkrieg and that Italy, with just a few thousand casualties, might pick up rich spoils—Corsica, Tunis, and Dalmatia, in addition to Nice, Garibaldi's birthplace.

Following Garibaldi's death on his island in 1882, the orators in Parliament commemorated him as a "shining star" and a "blinding meteor" in the history of the nation. The eulogies sounded as if the defunct hero had been as extraneous to everyday Italians as a heavenly body is to earth.

Italy may not have followed Garibaldi's admonition to "be serious," but it has kept striving to be taken seriously by others. Such efforts at burnishing the nation's image continue today as Italy keeps claiming membership in the club of big powers, and as the Rome government, its generals, and its diplomats abroad react with pique whenever they feel bypassed in international relations and decisions. Thus the Big Five of free-market economies—the United States, Japan, West Germany, Britain, and France—had to become the Big Seven by inclusion of Italy and Canada, mainly to mitigate Roman sensibilities. Important decisions nevertheless continued to be taken by the original Big Five. And in the European Community, the Italian representatives forever suspect that an unofficial "directorate," made up of West Germany, France, and Britain, or just the governments of Bonn and Paris, is really running the show.

"We are not yet feeling secure in the world of the big powers," observes Treasury Minister Giuliano Amato, a thoughtful university professor from Turin. "We are worrying more about being present when they meet than about what's on the agenda." Italian newspaper correspondents at the Brussels headquarters of the European Community keep warning their readers that their nation is being viewed by the other members of the group as, in the words of *Corriere della Sera* of Milan, "bizarre, extravagant despite its enormous deficits, confused, meddlesome: in short, very 'Mediterranean.'" According to the correspondents, delegates from the other European governments are puzzled and scandalized to see Italian cabinet ministers turning up in Brussels or at conferences elsewhere not only with their interpreters—because Italian politicians notoriously speak no language other than their own—but also with dozens of secretaries and mysterious flunkies.

All too often the Italian representatives at international meetings appear badly briefed, have hazy or no instructions from their home government, betray scant familiarity with the issues to be discussed, and in debates or press conferences baffle their listeners with Roman gobbledygook hard to understand let alone translate. Even the Spaniards, "Mediterraneans" too, seem to have trouble taking Italian government officials seriously. "There are a lot of things we should learn from Italy," Miguel Angel Ordóñez, a Spanish undersecretary for commerce, declared. "The Italians have incredible innovation and management. But our public administration is more serious, better, and more qualified." In the councils of the European Community and at home, Italian government spokesmen and politicians always enthusiastically advocate further European integration; all the while, Italy stands in default on more Community regulations than any other member.

A vague feeling that Italians, for all their charm, are untrustworthy seems to reflect also on the things Italians try to sell. Presenting the findings of an international consumer survey at an industrial symposium in Milan in 1988, Vittorio Ghidella, then chief of the automotive division of Fiat, said that other Europeans liked the Italians because of their jovial behavior, their food, and their women, but in general did not trust their products: The design and elegance of Italian apparel and other manufactured goods were widely appreciated abroad, but the lingering stereotype was that things made in Italy were unreliable and of poor quality.

Which image of Italy do foreigners really have? an interviewer asked the late historian Rosario Romeo in 1985. "A very bad one," the scholar replied. "Not in the sense that Italy might be hated the way Germany still is, but because it is regarded as a messy, inefficient, undereducated country, incapable of consequently rising to any challenge." Romero added, "Foreigners are often hypocritically polite when they talk to us. What they usually say is that the Italians have a great talent for survival. However, considering that the Soviet Union and Germany have both recovered from World War II after losing 10 to 12 percent of their population, I am asking myself whether Italy could survive a similar ordeal."

It might be objected that the Italians survived World War II precisely because they did not fight as stubbornly as the more "serious" Russians and Germans did, because they eventually changed sides when they knew who was winning, and because they surrendered instead of holding out and thus suffered few casualties. By not being all too serious about World War II, Italy got out better than did its erstwhile allies, Germany and Japan, even though those two "serious" nations eventually caught up with the Italians on the road to recovery and became economic superpowers. A 1988 poll in Japan ranked the Italians as the "most stupid" among major nations because of their perceived lack of seriousness. The poll was received with incredulity and mirth in Italy. The popular reaction was Doesn't everybody know we are smart? The stupid ones are the Japanese because they work too hard and never have a good time.

Most other people throughout the world do not reproach the Italians for lacking seriousness but rather seem to envy them: Maybe one should imitate them, and not look too earnestly at life and its vicissitudes. A survey of information media around the globe over an extended period would in all likelihood show that when news from Italy is printed or broadcast it has usually been chosen for its entertainment value—a Roman society scandal with a cast of tycoons, aristocrats, and movie starlets; a spaghetti-eating contest in Naples; Vatican prelates implicated in the shenanigans of shady financiers. Even such lethal matters as the Mafia are often given a humorous slant by newspapers and television networks abroad. It appears that the world, numbed by bad news from every quarter, is looking to Italy for comic relief.

Although many Italians will, when they are in the company of foreigners, obligingly indulge in a bit of buffoonery, Italian officials and diplomats resent the fact that their nation is depicted as the clown of Europe. Foreign media correspondents in Rome and Milan quite often find themselves under pressure to tone down what Italian critics denounce as their "unfavorable" reporting; when these journalists point out that the facts about which they wrote or broadcast are indisputable, they are told that, yes, this may be the case, but they should also have chosen positive aspects to balance the negative ones.

Efforts to persuade the world to take Italians seriously started even before national unification. When Cavour was chief of King Victor Emmanuel II's government in Turin in 1855, he talked his sovereign into sending 15,000 Piedmontese-Sardinian soldiers to the Black Sea to join the British, French, and Turkish troops in the Crimean War against Russia. Little Piedmont had no business in the Black Sea, but Cavour contended that "the glory that our soldiers will bring back from the Orient will be more useful to Italy than all beautiful speeches." As it turned out, there was little glory for anybody in the butchery at Sevastopol.

In the first few decades after Italy had at last been united, nationalistic bombast erupted, helping to push the still fragile country into a colonial adventure that ended in military disaster in Ethiopia in 1896. Undeterred, poets like Giosuè Carducci (who won the Nobel Prize for literature in 1906) and Gabriele D'Annunzio insisted that Italy, rather than loved, should be respected in the world by doing great deeds. Filippo Tommaso Marinetti, the writer who founded the school of futurism in literature and art, praised danger, power, militarism, the machine age, and war, and called for a drive to wean Italians from spaghetti in order to harden the national character. A broad nationalist current in politics helped bring about Italy's intervention in World War I. (When the archives were opened much later, it appeared that the nation would have been able to obtain most of the territories it was to gain in 1919 without going to war and suffering the loss of 600,000 men. In 1915, however, the nationalists wanted belligerence for reasons of prestige.)

The strongest and longest effort to have Italy taken seriously was made by Mussolini from 1922 to 1945, and for the first decade or so he seemed to have succeeded in convincing people and governments in other countries that he had forged a "new Italy."

To pick up an old chestnut, didn't he manage to make the trains run on time? The achievement, which for a number of years was genuine and won the applause of old Italian hands, should not be dismissed lightly. (During the Fascist regime, Italians joked that it would have been enough if Mussolini had become a stationmaster rather than master of the nation. Others suspected in jest that Il Duce had a special agent posted in each railroad station, charged with resetting the clocks so that trains seemed to arrive on time even if they happened to be late.) Sticking to rail schedules had been a problem in Italy ever since the first steam engine started puffing between Naples and Castellammare in 1839. In the Mediterranean world, time all too often seems to be a creamy substance that can be spread out rather than a measurable dimension. Sundials, a sunny country's original way of determining how late it is, permit some leeway. Today the Italian state railroads with all their chronometers and electronic equipment appear unable to observe their own timetables; even such a crack train as the Milan-Rome *rapido*, which was supposed to link the nation's two largest cities nonstop in three hours and fifty-eight minutes when it was introduced in 1988, is usually fifteen to thirty minutes late.

During the 1920s Il Duce was widely admired by statesmen and writers abroad. Winston Churchill paid eloquent tribute to him in print, and Oswald Spengler, author of *The Decline of the West*, extolled him as a new Caesar, "his steely hand at the rudder." Mussolini was then credited with having defeated the Sicilian Mafia, and he did eradicate the age-old scourge of malaria from the Roman Campagna by reclaiming the Pontine Marshes. But then, instead of further channeling the nation's energies and resources into the Mezzogiorno, he sought to conquer an African empire.

Several of Mussolini's aides later quoted him in their

memoirs as repeatedly saying he would prefer Italy to be hated in the world than liked or ignored. The dictator, who was self-taught and loved to display his questionable erudition, often committing silly boners, may have been thinking of Lucius Accius's *oderint dum metuant* (let them hate as long as they fear). The Fascist regime, which loved to cite Latin maxims, adopted *Roma doma!* (Rome, conquer!) as an official motto, and Mussolini himself told his countrymen in speeches that they were the most intelligent and warlike people on earth. Eventually, when defeat followed upon defeat and hundreds of thousands of Italian soldiers had been captured in Africa, in the Soviet Union, in the Balkans, and on their own soil, Il Duce in many bitter remarks disparaged the people who for twenty years had been cheering him. He called them unserious, immature, lying, and unintelligent; even Michelangelo had needed first-rate marble to create his works, Mussolini muttered, giving his listeners to understand that in his eyes the Italians were mere clay.

The nation by which Mussolini felt let down indeed had an old reputation for lacking martial virtues; still today many Italians are convinced they belong to an unwarlike race, too civilized to excel in the military arts. "The Italians were never good soldiers," said Giorgio Bocca, a leading journalist, during a 1988 television debate. Bocca, who had fought in the anti-Nazi resistance movement during World War II, elaborated in a magazine column: "During the centuries of foreign domination, under foreign protectorates, we have become used to regarding civil—urban—war as the only kind of fighting within our capabilities, leaving 'big' wars to powerful foreigners and seeking to get through 'big' wars with as little damage as possible. In 'big' wars, let's face it, we have always cut a mediocre figure, and the mediocre esteem that the Italian armed forces are enjoying in the world today is rather well deserved."

Long before the era of massive intervention in Italian affairs by the big European powers—the Spaniards, French, and Austrians from the fifteenth to the nineteenth century—local rulers showed little inclination to bar foreign armies from the peninsula or throw them out when they invaded. Such enterprises would have required a concerted military effort that almost never could be achieved. For centuries the Holy Roman emperors used to descend into Italy to be crowned by the pope, their progress usually unimpeded by local forces (robbers, it is true, might waylay and massacre stragglers of the imperial expeditions in wooded gorges or on steep mountain passes, and urban mobs in Rome or other cities might harass the barbarians and eventually force them to an ignominiously quick return home once the sacred crowning rite had been performed).

In the late Middle Ages and during the Renaissance, the rich Republic of Venice, Florence, the papacy, and the dukedoms and city-states of Italy all employed condottieri—soldiers of fortune who hired out to whoever would pay most and who often changed employers or struck secret deals with adversaries, sometimes rising, like the Sforzas of Milan, to become in their turn independent rulers and employers of other condottieri. Some of these condottieri were foreigners. The outstanding example is Sir John Hawkwood, the son of an Essex tanner who in the employ of Florence (but actually at the behest of Pope Gregory XI) fought against Milan. After Hawkwood had saved Bologna for the papacy in 1374, the grateful Gregory, a Frenchman, made him lord of the fertile little fiefs of Bagnacavallo and Cotignola near Ravenna.

The private armies that the condottieri hired, trained, and led were to a large extent made up of non-Italians—Swiss, Germans, and Dalmatians. The popes had their own Swiss Guard from the beginning of the sixteenth century, and during the Sack of Rome in 1527 the Vatican's foreign legion died almost to a man, saving the life of the Medici Pope Clement VII as Emperor Charles V's Spanish and German soldiery were running wild in the city. Some one hundred years later the Protestant reformer Ulrich Zwingli would still thunder from his pulpit in Zurich against his countrymen's propensity to serve as mercenaries in foreign lands. The practice nevertheless continued until the nineteenth century, and the papal Swiss Guard is still on duty in the Vatican.

The system whereby Italian rulers and governments had their wars fought by paid professionals and foreigners introduced elements of alienation, cruelty, and treachery into the Italian image of military affairs that may linger to this day and help explain what has been described as the nation's innate pacifism. Jakob Burckhardt described the relationship between the governments and their condottieri as "thoroughly immoral." The condottiere had to fear nobody as much as his employer, and vice versa. Sometimes the condottiere had to give his wife and children as hostages, who might suffer if he was unsuccessful or, as happened none too rarely, suddenly changed sides. Even if a condottiere won one victory after another, he was considered dangerous to the power that had hired him, and the more dangerous he was deemed, the more likely that he had to be eliminated. (Italy's national soccer championship today presents a caricature of the condottieri age: First-division teams pay millions of dollars to hire star players and coaches from Latin America, Sweden, and other European countries, even the Soviet Union; after each lost game there is talk of firing the foreign trainer or trading the foreign stars.)

The centuries of foreign domination that are supposed to have caused the Italian distaste for "big" wars started with the peninsula's invasion by the French under King Charles VIII in 1495. Called in by the ruler of Milan in an intrigue that was characteristic of the country and that epoch, the French occupied Florence, Rome, and Naples without encountering any resistance. "The French came into Italy with wooden spurs, carrying in their hands chalk to mark their quarters," observed Pope Alexander VI, the utterly rotten but sharp-witted Spaniard. The French king's horsemen, noticing the docility of the Italians, had indeed put their iron battle spurs into their saddlebags and every evening would jauntily move into billets that their advance men had designated with chalk crosses.

While the French soldiery were savoring the easy life of Naples (many of them caught the virulent new Neapolitan sickness that a few decades later would be called the Gallic disease, or syphilis), the Borgia pope, with a few Italian princes, Spain, and the Republic of Venice, at last cobbled together an alliance against Charles VIII and his barbarians. The French king, fearing that he might get bottled up with his troops in the treacherous peninsula, started the long march home. The new Holy League gathered its forces and put them under the command of Francesco Gonzaga, the marquess of Mantua, who had a reputation as an accomplished military leader and was assisted by the crack condottiere Bernardino Fortebraccio (Strongarm).

The league's plan was to ambush the retreating French in the hills between the Tyrrhenian coast and Parma, to envelop and massacre them there. The Italians had fresh troops, a three-to-one numerical superiority, and familiarity with the terrain. Yet they lost the battle, fought near the Apennine village of Fornovo in 1495, and the French and their king were able to return safely to their country.

The Battle of Fornovo "is the turning point in Italian history," according to Luigi Barzini, Jr. "The distant consequences of the defeat are still felt today. If the Italians had won . . . Italy would have emerged as a reasonably respectable nation." Barzini even ventured to suggest that the Italian national character would have developed along different lines if the marquess of Gonzaga (whose condottiere died in the battle) had carried the day at Fornovo.

The French, far from home and weakened by disease, fought for their lives and won by their discipline. The Italians did not lose because the Taro River was swollen by recent rains—a circumstance that might easily have been reconnoitered—but because of their proclivity for individual maneuvering rather than concerted action, and because of their lack of contingency planning, their disorganization, and their tendency to panic when things seemed to go badly. Fornovo was "one of these decisive moments when the soul of a nation, being tested, fails," Vincent Cronin wrote. "Abroad pulses quickened. It was obvious now that any power that wished could invade Italy and get away with it."

Francesco Gonzaga nevertheless kept maintaining he had won the Battle of Fornovo and had forced the French king to flee. The marquess commissioned his court painter Andrea Mantegna to portray him in full armor in a fresco honoring Our Lady of Victory in a new church he had built in Mantua to celebrate his self-claimed triumph.

It was not the last time that rhetoric and myth embroidered some Italian disaster to make it seem a success. Grandiloquence re-formed also the Italians' sense of what had happened during the Risorgimento, the period of Italy's unification in the nineteenth century. The official rhetoric surrounding the Risorgimento has been translated into gleaming white Brescian marble and gilded bronze in the colossal monument to Victor Emmanuel II that Italy erected on the north slope of the Capitol in Rome between 1885 and 1911. To foreign tourists it is known as the Wedding Cake. From the Piazza Venezia a staircase leads up several flights to an "altar of the fatherland" at the foot of a statue of Rome in mock-antique style with processions of personages paying tribute approaching from either side. An equestrian statue of King Victor Emmanuel II is surrounded by martial symbols and allegorical sculptures representing Self-Sacrifice, Justice, Strength, Freedom, Unity, and Italian cities and provinces. The entire monument is surmounted by forty-nine-foot columns creating the effect of a giant old-style typewriter in a kind of white stone that will, by its mineralogical nature, never mellow. Understatement was never an Italian trait, and the hideous composition was meant to celebrate the heroism of the Risorgimento and relate it to the virtues of the ancient Romans (symbolized by the hallowed Capitol behind it). From time to time some Italian architect or writer suggests that the embarrassing marble heap should be razed altogether, but the chances that this will ever happen and that the Capitol will again be visible from the north remain almost nil.

Revisionist historians have by now succeeded in freeing the saga of the Risorgimento from such turgid emblazonment. True, the revolutionary fervor of the students and intellectuals who were plotting in the patriotic secret societies and the astonishing successes of Garibaldi's guerrilla bands did capture the imagination of the contemporary world. And Garibaldi himself was admired everywhere, and was lionized during a visit to England. Yet the achievements of the regular Italian armed forces were anything but heroic, and the peasantry proved apathetic or even fought against the Garibaldians.

King Carlo Alberto of Sardinia-Piedmont resigned in 1849 after his troops were defeated by the Austrians at Novara. Ten years later the Piedmontese army won its victories over the Austrians at Magenta and Solferino, but only with the support of French troops. At the ensuing peace talks at Villafranca near Verona between Emperors Napoleon III of France and Franz Joseph of Austria, Sardinia-Piedmont was not even represented. It was given Milan anyway.

In 1866 the forces of King Victor Emmanuel II were

beaten by the Austrians at Custoza near Verona on land and off the island of Lissa (now Vis in Yugoslavia) at sea. Italy won Venice and its hinterland all the same because its ally Prussia had crushed the Austrians at Sadowa. And in 1870 Victor Emmanuel's *bersaglieri* were able to enter Rome because France had withdrawn its garrison from the city.

When the young Italian kingdom felt bold enough for African enterprises and, in 1895, invaded Ethiopia, it took Emperor Menelik II only a year to raise enough troops to rout the Italians at Adwa, forcing the Rome government to recognize the independence of his empire. The historian Denis Mack Smith has pointed out that at Adwa, "in one single day, as many Italians lost their lives as in all the wars of the Risorgimento put together." (The national unification had been bought with a relatively low price in blood; between 1848 and 1870 no more than 6,000 Italians died while fighting for unity.)

In 1915 Italy broke its old Triple Alliance with Germany and Austria-Hungary, and after secret negotiations with both camps entered World War I on the side of the Allies. After more than two years of attrition in Alpine warfare in the Dolomite Mountains, the Austro-Hungarians, reinforced by seven German divisions, broke through the Italian front lines at Caporetto (now Kobarid in Yugoslavia) and poured into the Venetian plains as far as the Piave River. Ernest Hemingway, who served as a volunteer ambulance driver on the Italian front and was wounded, described the "gigantic" retreat in *A Farewell to Arms*. His narration culminates in the scene at the Tagliamento Bridge, where Italian "battle police" order officers who have abandoned their units and fled to be shot on the spot by a carabinieri detail; the "battle police" are acting with "all the efficiency, coldness and command of themselves of Italians who are firing and are not being fired on."

To this day Caporetto has remained an Italian byword for disgrace. When the Italian national skiing team won no medal during the world championship contest in Colorado in 1989, newspapers at home wrote about "our winter sports Caporetto." Yet the aftermath of the 1917 disaster was one of Italy's finest hours: The nation pulled itself together, determined not to capitulate, and the armed forces were reorganized. A British army and several French divisions beefed up the new front line and helped the Italians defeat the enemy at Vittorio Veneto, three weeks after Germany and Austria-Hungary had requested an armistice. The Allied victory gained Italy the Trentino, South Tyrol, and Trieste.

Mussolini conquered his short-lived African empire by means of atrocities that are also acknowledged by Italian historians. Control over most of Libya (first occupied in 1911) was established by mass executions of tribesmen. When Italian forces again invaded Ethiopia in 1935, they ran into stubborn resistance; they conquered Addis Ababa only after Il Duce had given the order to use poison gas. After the Italian viceroy, Marshal Rodolfo Graziani, was wounded in a bomb plot in the Ethiopian capital, thousands of inhabitants were indiscriminately killed in reprisals.

In the Spanish Civil War, Italian Blackshirt militia troops, described by Rome as "volunteers," were beaten by Republican forces at Guadalajara in 1937. When Mussolini pushed his country into World War II in June 1940, Churchill commented sardonically that it served the Nazis right to get the Italians as allies—"we had them last time."

Episodes of individual heroism have been recorded in all the wars in which Italians were embroiled. Alpine engineers daringly tunneled under enemy positions at 6,000 feet in the Dolomites during World War I. An Italian speedboat penetrated into the Austro-Hungarian military harbor of Pola and sank the battleship *Viribus Unitis*, a celebrated *beffa* (nasty trick). During World War II, a handful of Italians held out in the Oasis of Jarabub in the Libyan Desert against overwhelming enemy forces for weeks, and Italian midget submarines sneaked into the British naval bases of Gibraltar and Alexandria to carry out successful sabotage missions. Such feats, however, were overshadowed by humiliating defeats that even Mussolini's oratory and propaganda machine could not transform into victories.

On the other hand, myth has overgrown the honorable reality of the anti-Nazi resistance movement in Italy toward the end of World War II. Today Italian schoolchildren can read in their textbooks that their country's North was liberated from the Nazi soldiers and their Fascist auxiliaries by an Italian "people's army" that was fighting from house to house. It would seem there had been no United States Fifth Army, British Eighth Army, or French, Polish, and other Allied contingents—the forces that actually compelled the German divisions to surrender. Italian anti-Nazi partisan bands, made up of courageous men and a few women, did exist, and their members did defy battle-hardened German soldiers, but their contribution to the country's liberation was marginal. The role of the partisans in Northern Italy has above all been exaggerated by Italian Communists and other left-wing groups. However, according to the British political scientist P. A. Allum, a Marxist, the Italians who had enrolled in resistance formations in 1945 were "an exiguous minority" of the population.

In any case, the resistance movement during the last stage of World War II proved again that irregular formations in the tradition of the Garibaldians as well as guerrilla actions are the type of fighting that Italians are especially good at. They require great individual daring and little drill and discipline, although in them a person's skills and intelligence can come into full play. The wave of political terrorism in the "leaden years" (see chapter 8), to some extent directly inspired by the World War II partisan movement, demonstrated once more Italians' taste and talent for conspiracy. The "armed party" too showed a liking for martial rhetoric: The Red Brigades were no brigades but, at most, platoons or squads; they spoke of their "military arm," and a parallel terrorist group wanted to be known as Front Line; captured plotters solemnly asked to be treated like prisoners of war—as if the Geneva Convention applied to assassins.

The regular armed forces have never attained in Italy the prestige they have traditionally enjoyed in France, Germany, Spain, or Latin America. Yet neither has there ever been serious danger of a military coup in Italy, although Giangiacomo Feltrinelli fantasized for years about an imminent rightist *golpe*.

Today Italy maintains an armed establishment of nearly 400,000 men, two-thirds of them draftees counting the days until they will be able to go home again. The strategic planners of NATO, to which Italy has belonged since its creation in 1949, know—but never say so publicly—that in an emergency they could count on only a limited number of fully trained, adequately equipped, and operational Italian army brigades, naval units, and air force squadrons. More important to NATO is Italian real estate—the naval, air, and missile bases that the country keeps readily providing when other nations around the Mediterranean appear increasingly reluctant to grant facilities for the Western Alliance, let alone for U.S. forces.

The Constitution of the Italian Republic declares that the nation "rejects war as an instrument of offense against the freedom of other peoples and as a means of resolving international controversies." The charter, however, also proclaims that "the defense of the fatherland is the sacred duty of the citizens" and calls for compulsory military service. Most Italians consider the obligation for young men to spend twelve months in the army or air force, or eighteen months in the navy, useless and wasteful. *Naia*, a word from the Friulan dialect with distinctly unpleasant overtones, originally meaning "race" or "tribe," is now commonly used to denote military service. Draft dodging is considered smart. The easy way is to have oneself found unfit for military service because of poor health; sons of rich or influential parents are, unsurprisingly, more likely to be certified as infirm than those of poor ones.

A recruit who hasn't managed to avoid *la naia* will, after the initial shock of a few weeks' basic training, mobilize relatives and acquaintances to have himself transferred to his home province or city. For the well-connected defender of the fatherland, furloughs will be frequent and extended. Precocious masters of "arrangement" will become orderlies to colonels or in officers' messes, or secure soft jobs in some office of the military bureaucracy.

For the less adroit or fortunate soldiers, who have to stay in the barracks during their draft term, *la naia* provides survival training. Veterans advise recruits to put the legs of their iron bedsteads into their shoes at night so that the shoes cannot easily be stolen. Hazing by old-timers, nicknamed *nonni* (grandfathers), is common. The anonymous A.F. from Lecce in the Deep South, identifying himself only as a soldier of the crack Folgore (Lightning) Division, wrote in a letter to *L'Espresso* magazine of Rome that he had experienced "Dante's Inferno" in his company: The corporals "continually insulted us [recruits] because we were all from Mezzogiorno (they called us 'Africans'), whereas almost all of them were northerners." *Nonnismo*, harassment by draftees with seniority, is given as the main reason for soldiers' suicides, which occur on average once a month. Boredom in military installations engenders drug use and prostitution, and cruising homosexuals in Italian cities and near armed forces bases know they can easily pick up off-duty servicemen in civilian clothes during the evening hours.

In ancient Rome the discipline in the valorous legions produced, in Gibbon's words, "a degree of firmness and docility unattainable by the impetuous and irregular passions of barbarians." And so Mussolini gave his army eagles and standards the way the caesars had and conferred on the officers of his Blackshirt militia the titles Centurion and Consul. But twentieth-century Italians are as remote from the Romans of antiquity as are today's Greeks from the Athenians of Miltiades or modern Egyptians from the era of the pharaohs. Two millennia after the legions were marching on the consular roads radiating from Rome, and after innumerable wars, the Italians maintain an innate distaste for military life and a—highly civilized, they will tell you—aversion to military solutions.

Italian pacifism results in a continual search for compromise, often degenerating into a tendency to play both sides simultaneously in any international issue or conflict. This has earned the Italians a reputation as treacherous in both diplomacy and war. Over their history, ever since the confused fights between the Guelph and Ghibelline factions and subfactions in the Middle Ages, examples of signal treachery have been plentiful. Dante put quite a few wily thirteenth-century figures into the traitors' tier of his Inferno. Later, the name of Niccolò Machiavelli became the byword for cynically opportunistic policies. Of the many Italian leaders branded as Machiavellian at home or abroad, one was the very statesman who did the diplomatic spadework for unifying the nation, Benso di Cavour.

In the early twentieth century, Germany's chancellor Prince Bernhard von Bülow said in a crude comment on Rome's nimble waltzing between the Triple Alliance and its adversaries that Italy must decide whether she wanted to be "a wife or a whore." (The prince himself was married to an Italian.) And Antonio Salandra, Italy's government chief at the outbreak of World War I, spoke of the nation's "sacred egoism." He was quite right, but then again, when has altruism ever prompted the decisions of national governments?

Today, in recurrent manifestations of Italian pacifism, Rome will offer its good services to mediate in international controversies wherever they may occur. Sometimes such bids for conciliation are welcome or even requested; often they are felt to be superfluous and meddlesome. In many conflicts around the globe a superpower or a regionally predominant nation has a far better chance of bringing about a peaceful solution than does a secondary country that still has trouble being taken seriously. The Vatican, convinced that its moral authority can substitute for its lack of military or economic power, is encountering similar credibility problems in its frequent offers to act as an international peacemaker.

As for the Italian governing class, they might be well advised not to try too hard to live up to Garibaldi's admonition, "Be serious!" If Italy has earned prestige and even admiration during the last few decades, it has not been by puffing itself up and seeking military or diplomatic big-power status, but rather through the creativity of its people and the talents of innumerable individuals exercising that fine Italian hand.

10.

Virtuosos
Without Orchestra

It is a remarkable fact that the land of grand opera lacks a world-class symphony orchestra. Italy has produced great conductors from Toscanini to Giulini, Abbado, and Muti, great sopranos and tenors, but there is rarely excellence in ensemble work on the Italian stage or in the orchestra pit. Players in an Italian musical body—always referred to as the "professors of the orchestra"—dislike being subordinate to the conductor as much as local soldiers detest having to obey their sergeant or lieutenant; exhausting rehearsals until a score is rendered flawlessly by all instrumentalists the way the maestro wants are as incompatible with the Italian temperament as is close-order drill in the courtyard of the barracks compound. An Italian musician wants to be Paganini, not second fiddle.

Fellini depicted the breakdown of cooperation in a musical ensemble in his film *Orchestra Rehearsal,* using it as a sardonic metaphor for the anarchistic tendencies in Italian society: Players ignore the conductor, quarrel with one another, do their own thing (one couple is making love in a corner); they are intent on anything but preparation for a concert. The result is bedlam.

Repugnance to regimentation or merely coordinated procedures is observable in all sectors of Italian life, particularly labor and politics. Each of the dozen or so parties represented in Parliament is torn by factions and cliques that are forever plotting against one another and shifting allegiances.

Individualism has distinguished the Italians since the Middle Ages and has enabled them to score artistic triumphs while suffering military defeats. Such ingrained individualism makes it hard to explain how Mussolini managed to impose his will on his fractious nation for two decades. But did he? When the marble busts of Il Duce, the stone eagles, and all the other trappings of Fascism came crashing down, it was revealed that behind the facade of the seemingly monolithic dictatorship scores of local chieftains had been running their fiefs the way they liked. There were still a few faded inscriptions on house walls reading "Il Duce Is Always Right!" but it became clear that Mussolini had not known what was really going on in the country and had deluded himself for a long time about having changed the national character.

Once the Italians were freed from the shackles of Fascism, individual initiative and inventiveness performed wonders. The achievements of the black market, which not only kept the country alive but produced a semblance of well-being, were recalled in chapter 5. In the cities, many of which had been severely damaged by military action, people did not wait for municipal authorities to restore transportation systems; overnight, decrepit tricycles and minitrucks appeared, ferrying passengers from one point to another for moderate fares. In Rome a great number of improvising entrepreneurs were running their *camionette* (little trucks), fueled by black-market gasoline, along bus routes that had ceased functioning months earlier. The drivers called out the route codes, "NT" or "MB" for instance (for Nomentana to Trastevere, or Macao to Borgo districts), and travelers climbed aboard, stepping on little ladders or footstools put on the pavement for them by youngsters. The entire makeshift operation *alla garibal-dina* was cheerful and, in its own way, efficient and reliable.

No society seems better attuned to the free-enterprise system than that of the Italians; private initiative in many fields has indeed been the secret of the "Italian miracle" of speedy postwar recovery. The odd thing about that recovery is that so many of the little, independent business operators were voting Communist in election after election—as if, just escaped from Fascist regimentation, they craved another dictatorship. The Communist party was strongest in some of the richest areas of the country, like Emilia and Tuscany. It looked as if a great many Italians were convinced that the Soviet Union was going to triumph in the Cold War and this time wanted to be on the winning side.

Communists or not, those who brought about Italy's resurgence after World War II did not wait for state intervention but pursued their private interests like any capitalists. Caring for oneself and one's own without thinking much about the national community has long been an Italian characteristic. From the gloomy, ironic poet Giacomo Leopardi in the early nineteenth century to Alberto Moravia and other modern writers, Italian thinkers have deplored the lack of a pronounced civic sense in their compatriots.

Any first-time visitor to the country will notice many telltale signs of its inhabitants' exuberant individualism. Like the Italians' distaste for lining up in orderly queues, their driving habits are a symptom of their self-interest and their need to excel. "The Italian is an exhibitionist," says Vittorio Ghidella, who for eight years was chief of Fiat's automotive branch. "He wants to show off that he is more astute and speedier: hence he overtakes you just before an intersection and does similar daring feats."

Driving on Italian highways and in the congested cities is a highly competitive undertaking in which motorists continually muster all their skills and cunning, always prepared for the worst from everyone else on the road. Only the quick reflexes with which most Italians seem endowed keep the accident rate below the appalling figures of such other European countries as Belgium and Spain. Italian drivers are generally aggressive not only toward one another but, in the cities, also toward pedestrians, as if these were a contemptible species unworthy of any consideration. The average Italian motorist does not slow down when noticing someone in a pedestrian crossing but will, most likely, step on the gas pedal, if only to frighten the person on foot and send him or her running for safety on the sidewalk. Alas, the drivers often miscalculate, and every year a good many pedestrians are killed by cars in marked crossings. To less fatal effect, cities and towns are invaded by motorcycles and motor scooters that observe no traffic light or regulation and take shortcuts on sidewalks. Yet proceed from Como to Lugano on the far side of the Italian-Swiss frontier, and you will see motorists braking and halting at crossings whenever a pedestrian is in sight. Lugano is in the Italian-speaking canton Ticino and is geographically closer to Milan than to Zurich, yet even cars with Italian license plates will yield to pedestrians there: Their drivers know this is the way to behave in Switzerland.

In any big Italian city the dearth of civic virtues can be read from the state of public facilities like underpasses at busy intersections or subway passages. They sparkle when they are new, but a year later they look dismal: Burned out or broken neon tubes have not been replaced, walls are covered with graffiti (many of them obscenities), display windows have been shattered, the shelves behind them are empty, and the floor is covered with litter that nobody ever seems to remove. Pedestrians who want to get from one side of the street to the other have long given up using the underpass and brave heavy surface traffic. Similarly, the walls of public housing projects carry spray-can inscriptions with curses at some visiting soccer team or political slogans in the first week the tenants move in; soon the paint will peel and many windows in the stairwells will be broken.

During the Fascist era Italians used to say that theirs was a country of inaugurations, not of maintenance. Buildings that Il Duce himself had solemnly taken into state possession from the contractors were dilapidated a few years later (not only from vandalism but also because the building materials used were shoddy). Today, about once a month, especially during one of the periodic strikes by sanitation workers, the newspapers and television stations of Rome, Naples, Palermo, and other big cities wake up to the fact that the streets and housing are filthy; they fail to explain that the squalor is to a large extent caused by the carelessness of individual residents. (Just watch the abandon with which people throw empty cigarette packs or candy wrappers on the sidewalk a few steps from a garbage bin.) In the scruffy cities there are constant complaints that the municipal sanitation departments don't do their job properly; yet they might if the residents were neater and, among other things, curbed their dogs.

The mountaineers of the Italian Alpine provinces know they will have to comb their slopes, panoramic sites, and peaks at the end of summer because excursionists and picnickers from the nation's South will have left mounds of plastic bags, soft-drink cans, and other trash. Anyone pointing out the easily verifiable fact that Southern Italy with all its natural and artistic beauty is today more neglected and rundown than the country's North runs the risk of being branded a "racist." (A hill town in western Sicily, Erice, is nevertheless known as the "Sicilian Switzerland" because of the proverbial cleanliness of its sloping streets and well-kept buildings.)

Littering has nothing to do with ethnicity; it has to be

viewed in the context of education and cultural awareness. In the Renaissance, Italians were renowned for their tidiness and were horrified by the dirty habits of the Germans and other northerners. Things changed later. Dickens in his *Pictures from Italy* recounted seeing "disheartening dirt, discomfort and decay" on the Italian Riviera, and "depravity, degradation and wretchedness" in Naples; squalor was indeed anywhere up and down the peninsula. In Italy's North, decay and vandalism are today often blamed on newcomers from the Deep South. Yet urban neighborhoods in the United States that are mostly inhabited by descendants of immigrants from the Mezzogiorno stand out with the careful maintenance of their houses and gardens and their general neatness.

The ragged appearance of Italian cities, particularly in the South, is matched by their noise. In evenings during the warm season, when all windows are open, entire neighborhoods echo with a medley of programs from half a dozen television channels, the sound system of every set turned to maximum. Many Italians, it is true, seem to be able to take astonishing decibel levels, even to enjoy them, complaining that some outlying neighborhood is "dead" when it is just quiet. There are people sensitive to sound, but their neighbors will dismiss them as *matti* (crazies) and go right on letting their loudspeakers blare at full blast.

Motorcycles and motor scooters roar in the streets and piazzas until the early hours of the morning. They come from the factory equipped with mufflers, but their owners at once take the sound abatement devices off to gain maximum pleasure from their nocturnal carousals. Every now and then one reads that some exasperated resident, often an elderly man, has fired a shotgun into a cluster of youths who for months had been noisily congregating under his windows at night to have some fun with their thundering motorbikes or whining scooters. A friend of mine who was kept awake every night by the people living in the apartment above his because they used to come home late and walk around for hours in shoes that seemed to have iron spikes sent a set of felt slippers upstairs; the next day he found his gift thrown into the garbage bin in the courtyard, and his neighbors stopped greeting the *matto*.

If civic-mindedness is, to a great extent, instilled by parents and teachers, Italian "familism" and inadequate instruction in the schools must be considered responsible for tax dodging and for decay and neglect of towns and cities, especially in the Mezzogiorno. Excessive individualism and "familism" are compounded by widespread and deeply rooted enmity—sometimes open, often unconscious—toward the state and its institutions. The youth who unmuffles his motorbike, rips off the cord of a pay telephone, or sets fire to a trash can not only indulges in what he feels is virile fun but also vents his anger at society. So does the tax dodger: None of my money for that rotten system! Judging by the innumerable mufflerless motorcycles, vandalized pay phones, and scandalously false tax returns, there must be plenty of antisocial rage in Italy. The same, of course, can be said about vandalism in American cities, but evidence of hostility toward society is more surprising in a reputedly easygoing country such as Italy.

Until quite recently there has been a gaping void between family and state in Italy—there is hardly any associational life outside the Roman Catholic church, which has always pursued its own interests and cared little about the state (in fact, until the deal between Mussolini and Pope Pius XI in 1929 that created the State of Vatican City, the church was opposed to the unified kingdom). But now students and parents are electing their representatives for school councils, some neighborhood and block associations have sprung up, and new environmental and consumer groups are active. In Sicily churchmen and schoolteachers are taking an active part in the fight against the Mafia. Italy is undoubtedly on the road toward democratic maturity, and its people are becoming increasingly involved in public affairs.

The political parties have, since the collapse of Fascism, presumed to act as legitimate democratic intermediaries between the individual citizen and the state, but being essentially vote-getting entities, they have spawned an oligarchy of professional and part-time politicians, a group that the people at large call, usually with an expression of contempt, *la classe politica* (the political class). The average Italian is convinced and will vocally affirm on every occasion that the political class will always defend its own interests first—its constituents' relatively high pay, their railroad and airline passes, and particularly their reliance on graft (as long as it does not exceed certain acceptable dimensions; current Italian idiom has a neat geometrical term for a kickback or other income from corruption—*tangente*, tangent line). Talk to ten Italians, and nine will tell you that all politicians "are stealing." The tenth may himself belong to the political class, or hope to join it soon. There are, after all, plenty of posts to fill. Italy's national legislature—the Chamber of Deputies and the Senate—has double the membership of the U.S. Congress, even though the American population is four times Italy's. Then there are hundreds of seats in the twenty regional parliaments.

The Christian Democratic party, the nation's strongest political force since the end of World War II, seems a federation of unruly tribes that most of the time are scheming against one another in complicated power plays and reach a truce only before elections to display a semblance of unity for the benefit of voters.

The Italian Communist party—which was born in a split within the country's Socialist movement in 1921—reemerged from clandestine existence after Mussolini's downfall. For a long time it seemed a monolith. Its leadership professed the principle of "democratic centralism," meaning Leninist guidance of the rank and file by a small elite, and permitted no audible debate between party factions. Communist leaders used to enjoy a reputation for being comparatively untainted by corruption, but then they had fewer chances for receiving "tangents," having been barred from the central government since 1947. Still, many cities and towns had and have Communist mayors, and although Italy has managed to keep the Communist party, the country's second biggest political movement, out of the national power centers, it was never ostracized. Collaboration between non-Communists and Communists has in fact been going on in parliamentary committees, regional and city governments, and in many other areas within the state machinery, as well as in state-controlled industry, since the end of World War II.

Communist politicians and intellectuals are, after all, part of the nation's establishment. The system whereby the world's most powerful nongoverning Communist party is seemingly sidelined but actually all the time a partner in deals with the ruling groups may be the ultimate triumph of the Italian art of arrangement. Communists sit on all parliamentary bodies and preside over some of them, as trade-union leaders negotiate with the government and with the managers of private industries; Communists control municipal and regional administrations, are in charge of one of the three channels of the government television network, and have their representatives in many other public and semipublic institutions. And all along, the Italian Communist leadership has engineered its own "arrangement" in its relations with Moscow: It approved when Soviet tanks crushed the Hungarian uprising in 1956 but voiced criticism of the Soviet action to smother the "Prague Spring" in 1968, and it condemned the

Soviet invasion of Afghanistan in 1980. The late Italian Communist leader Enrico Berlinguer even told his party that the Soviet October Revolution of 1917 had "lost its thrust," meaning that Leninism had run out of steam.

Although the Communist leadership knows that the rank and file still include a hard core of Leninist-Stalinists, it has resolutely backed the reforms of Mikhail Gorbachev in the Soviet Union. The Italian Communists have also over the years swung from violent opposition to NATO toward tacit— occasionally even explicit—acceptance of Italy's membership in the Western Alliance. In the process of gradual accommodation to changes in the world and within Italy, the Communist party has started to look increasingly like the country's other political groups. A Stalinist old-timer on its central committee, Armando Cossutta, bitterly commented in 1989 that the party had undergone a "genetic mutation."

How real power is being managed behind the scenes of the noisy spectacle that the political parties and the clumsy government machinery continually present became visible, in glimpses, through the P2 affair of the early 1980s. P2 stands for Propaganda Two, a lodge of Italian Freemasonry that about fifteen years earlier had begun to separate itself from the mainstream of the fraternal organization and, in effect, become a secret society of influential people. Freemasons had been champions of the nineteenth-century Risorgimento; Garibaldi and other leaders in the fight for national unification and independence had belonged to the fraternity and were able to count on the support of fellow Masons in Britain and France. More recently, Italian Freemasonry split into two rival branches, each virtually a separate organization for mutual assistance among its members. The combined membership of all Masonic lodges in Italy today is estimated to be between 20,000 and 30,000.

The P2 lodge was founded by Licio Gelli, an affable businessman from Tuscany who had risen rapidly in Italy's Masonic community, reaching the rank of venerable grand master. He recruited high government officials, magistrates, generals, financiers, journalists, and other prominent people into his "covert," or secret, Masonic group. For some time Gelli held periodic initiation rites in his permanent suite at Rome's Excelsior Hotel. His name remained unknown to the Italian public until the mid-1970s, when the first hints of his role as a power broker appeared in the press. Eventually the media started mentioning him in connection with the sensational insolvency cases of two bankers, Michele Sindona and Roberto Calvi. Both died under mysterious circumstances—the first after drinking his morning espresso in the prison cell where he was being held on bankruptcy and other charges, the second found hanged beneath the Blackfriars Bridge in London.

In 1981 Milan magistrates investigating the Sindona case ordered the Finance Guard to search Gelli's villa near Arezzo. There the policemen seized membership lists of the P2 lodge, and the 962 names of alleged initiates contained in them were eventually released. High officers of every armed forces branch and of the secret services, the top civil servant in the foreign ministry, ambassadors, judges, politicians, bankers, and Prince Victor Emmanuel of Savoy, the exiled pretender to the Italian throne, were among them. Most of those on the lists denied that they had ever been P2 members, and many of them managed to get cleared by parliamentary or professional committees or by the judiciary. Gelli himself vanished, reportedly finding refuges in Latin American countries and in Florida.

In his absence, Italian magistrates charged the venerable grand master with plotting in collusion with rogue officers of the secret services and with right-wing terrorists. A special committee of the Italian Parliament investigated the P2 affair, hearing many witnesses and sifting heaps of documents. It concluded in 1984 that Gelli had been the kingpin of a conspiracy linking unidentified shadowy forces—conservative politicians? business tycoons?—with a subversive structure that represented a "metastasis of the institutions," a national cancer.

In 1983, four years after his disappearance, Gelli had been arrested by the Swiss police in Geneva as he was trying to collect a large sum of money from a bank. He escaped from prison with the help of a corrupt Swiss corrections officer and stayed at large for another four years. At last he surrendered in Geneva, pleading ill health and requesting hospital treatment. Gelli was eventually extradited to Italy and placed in a maximum-security prison, only to be released shortly thereafter pending court rulings on a variety of charges. By that time the nation had more recent scandals to talk about, and the P2 case seemed old hat. Presumed former members of Gelli's lodge stated publicly that nobody had been able to prove that any punishable crime had been committed. The P2 investigation at any rate showed again that behind the stage sets of the Italian democratic system there was, in the words of the parliamentary committee, "a picturesque and, in many ways, incredible world" of influence peddlers, power brokers, and fixers that provided "support, protection and *omertà*" to careerists, adventurers, and profiteers.

To millions of Italians the world of Lodge P2 and its affiliates was not incredible at all. They had always known that to get ahead in life one had to join some "mafia," not necessarily the Sicilian Mafia with its drug wars and sawed-off shotguns, but one or another of certain elusive groupings that trade favors in every government department, political party, business corporation, armed forces branch, or any other institution. One has to keep track of shifting alignments, watch who is rising and who declining, and get an early warning on who is going to betray whom. The fine Italian hand has forever to grope for new supports and crevices, like a climber on a rock face.

This all may sound perilous, yet for most Italians the need for continual maneuvering—at the wheels of their car, at the office or on the shop floor, in their love lives—seems to add zest to their existence. No one who falls appears to fall very hard; comebacks after disgrace are frequent, for individual Italians are as resilient as is their nation. One hears plenty of self-criticism in the country as newspaper editorials and garrulous passengers in railroad compartments complain about things being done *all'italiana*, yet the outsider who observes the country for even a short while starts wondering whether it actually does want fundamental changes. Do the Italians really desire to become "serious"? For that matter, do people in other nations want the Italians to become "serious"? Opinion polls appear to indicate that the majority answer to either question is no. There seems to be no desire, in or outside the country, for a national Italian "orchestra."

While fully acknowledging and possibly even exaggerating the seeming chaos at home, a great many Italians are ready to swear that despite—or perhaps just because of—its disorder there is no place on earth where one can live so well: Nowhere, according to them, are the cities and landscape so beautiful, the climate so agreeable, the food so tasty, the beaches and bays so inviting, men so virile and women so voluptuous. Nowhere is it so easy to get away with so much if one knows the ropes and is adept at "arrangements." Wine is flowing, people laugh and smile a lot, *amore* is more important than money. The longevity of many Italians has already been noted; the nation boasts also one of the world's lowest suicide rates—5 for every 100,000 deaths. (Inexplicably, a much higher proportion of Italians take their own lives in two very different places: Udine in the Northeast, one of the country's wealthier cities, and Gubbio in green Umbria.)

In seemingly every survey by social research institutions,

about four-fifths of Italians polled declare they would never abandon their country to live elsewhere because they cannot imagine a better place in the world. Foreign comparative evaluations of the quality of life in various nations consistently rank Italy among the most desirable, together with, say, Denmark. There are drawbacks, as this book has shown. But the Italians are virtuosos at coping with them.

INDEX

Abba, Marta, 119
Abbado, Claudio, 213
Abruzzi, 1, 151
Accius, Lucius, 200
Adenauer, Konrad, 14
Adultery, 118–23, 133
Aeschylus, 10
Afghanistan, 164, 222
African enterprises, 21, 199, 200, 206, 207
Agnelli, Giovanni (Gianni), 139–42, 144, 155
Agnelli, Umberto, 142
Agnelli family, 139, 143, 145
Agrigento (Akragas), xiii, 2, 4, 10
Agrippa, M. Vipsanius, 39
Albania, 151
Alexander VI, Pope, 28, 203
Algeria, 106
Alla garibaldina, 194, 215
All' italiana, x, 66, 225
Allum, P. A., 208
Alpine provinces, 96, 217
Amato, Giuliano, 195
Amatrice, 29
Amedeo, Prince, 116
Americans, 35. *See also* United States
Amodio, Massimo, 134

Anarchism, 82–85
Anastasia, Albert, 164
Andreotti, Giulio, 72
Angelis, Giulio de, 152
Anna Karenina (Tolstoy), 129
Aosta Valley, 9
Apennine Peninsula, 40
Apulia, 13, 41, 96
Aqua Virgo (Virgin Water), 39
Arabs, 10, 40, 105
Archimedes, 10
Arduino, Teresio, 36
Arezzo, 96
Argentina, 33
Ariosto, 53
Arlacchi, Pino, 164
Arrangements, 88–109, 137, 210, 221, 225
  cinema, 91–92
  and ENI, 103–6
  lines, 88–89
  and Naples, 92–96
  opera, 90–91
  parking, 89–90
  tax evasion, 97–102
Asians, 26, 175. *See also* East Asia
Aspromonte (Harsh Mountain), 150–51, 154
Atlantic Alliance, 105

Index

AT&T (American Telephone & Telegraph Company), 143
Augustus, Emperor, 39
Australia, xiv, 74
Austria, 8, 14, 50, 73, 108, 157, 201, 205–6
Austria-Hungary, 83, 206, 207
Automobiles, xiii-xiv, 66, 90. *See also* Driving

Baader-Meinhof gang, 180
Bahamas, 99
Bakunin, Mikhail, 83, 84
Balkans, 200
Banfield, Edward C., 112
Banks, 48, 76–77, 89
Barbara, Joseph, 164
Bari, 52, 63
Barista, 38
Barzini, Luigi, Jr., 7, 110–11, 117, 182, 203–4
Basile, Giambattista, 31
Basilicata, 10, 12, 13, 24, 112
Bassetti, Piero, 179
Battle of Fornovo, 203–4
Beffa, 108
Belgian Congo, 144
Belgium, 21, 76, 144, 216
Benetton, Carlo, 137, 138
Benetton, Gilberto, 137, 138
Benetton, Giuliana, 137–38
Benetton, Luciano, 137–38
Bergamo, 30
Bergman, Ingrid, 91–92, 122, 123
Berlinguer, Enrico, 222
Bernardinelli, Dante, 152
Bertolucci, Bernardo, 113
Birth control, 134–35
Birthrates, 134
Black Hand, 19
Blackshirts, 84, 173, 207, 211
Bocca, Giorgio, 200
Boccaccio, Giovanni, 88, 122

Bolivia, 183
Bologna, 1, 29, 72, 178, 201
Bonanno, Joe, 164
Borgia, Lucrezia, 27–28
Bossi, Umberto, 24
Bourbons, 7, 32, 157
Brancati, Vitaliano, 131
Braudel, Fernand, 151
Brazil, 33, 167, 192
Bresci, Gaetano, 83
Brindisi, 1, 12
Britain, 41, 46, 49, 59, 60, 68, 74, 76, 86, 118, 194, 195, 198, 207, 222. *See also* England
economy of, xii, 47, 100
Eighth Army, 208
Royal Army, 43
Bulow, Prince Bernhard von, 211–12
Burckhardt, Jakob, 151, 202
Bureaucracy, 48–54, 58–64, 65–75
Burgess, Anthony, 73
Buscetta, Tommaso, 167
Byron, Lord George, vii, 7, 129
Byzantines, 10

Cagliari, 51, 77
Calabria, 2, 4, 10–13, 17, 18, 58, 73, 101, 166, 168, 169
Calabrians, 164
and kidnapping, 23, 148, 150, 151–52, 154, 155, 169
Cala Ulloa, Pietro, 158
Caltanissetta, 3–4
Calvi, Roberto, 223
Camorra, 12, 155, 157, 159, 164, 169, 175
Campania, 13, 17, 24, 41, 155
Canada, 33, 161, 163, 195
Caporetto, 206–7
Carabinieri Corps, 54, 170–77, 188
Caranti, Biagio, 7
Carbonari, 7

Carducci, Giosuè, 198
Carlo Alberto, King, 205
Carpino, Giovanni da Pian del, 14
Casanova, Giacomo, 11
Castro, Fidel, 183
Catania, 1, 162
Catanzaro, 3, 51, 63
Catasto (real estate register), 66–67
Cavour, Count Camillo Benso di, 11, 198, 211
Cazzola, Franco, 179
Cellini, Benvenuto, 45
CENSIS (Center for Social Investment Studies), 62, 177–78
Chamber of Deputies, 117, 128, 156, 220
Charles V, Emperor, 202
Charles VIII, King, 202–3
China, 15, 94
Chinese, 27, 95
Christian Democratic party, 72, 103, 105–6, 114, 117, 220
Churchill, Winston, 199, 207
Ciano, Count Galeazzo, 126–27
Cicero, 5
Cinema, 91–92, 122–25
Cirillo, Ciro, 175
Cities, conditions in, 216–19
Cittanova, 11
Clement VII, Pope, 202
Clientela, 5
Clifford, Alexander, 45, 46
Colombia, 62, 155
Columbus, Christopher, 15
Commedia dell'arte, 92
Communist party, 72, 84, 94, 118, 180–83, 186, 190, 208, 215, 220–22
Comunità (Community), 143
Condottieri, 201, 202
Constitution of 1948, 81, 180, 209
Corporations, 54–55

Corriere della Sera, 30, 111, 126, 195
Corsica, 151
Cosa Nostra. *See* Mafia
Cosenza, 2
Cossiga, Francesco, 149–50
Cossutta, Armando, 222
Costa, Raffaele, 70
Costa Smeralda (Emerald Coast), 149
Court of Accounts, 67, 87–88
Court of Cassation, 63
Craxi, Bettino, 165
Cremona, 93
Crime, 177–91. *See also* "Crimes of honor"; Kidnapping
  in Mezzogiorno, 151, 155–57, 159, 179
Crimean War, 198
"Crimes of honor," 131–32
Cronin, Vincent, 204
Cuba, 183, 184
Cuckoldry, 132–33
Czechoslovakia, 184

Dalla Chiesa, Carlo Alberto, 156, 166
Dalmatians, 201
D'Annunzio, Gabriele, 129, 198
Dante Alighieri, 11, 53, 82, 121, 211
Da Ponte, Lorenzo, 16
Das Gupta, Sonali, 122
d'Azeglio, Massimo, 9
De Benedetti, Carlo, 49, 137, 138, 142–44
De Benedetti family, 142, 145
Debray, Régis, 183
De Gasperi, Alcide, 14
Deledda, Grazia, 150
De Mita, Ciriaco, 74, 87
Denmark, 226
De Sica, Vittorio, 122

d'Este, Duke Ercole I, 27
Dickens, Charles, viii, 218
Di Lelio, Alfredo, 46
Divine Comedy, The (Dante), 121
Divorce, 117–19
Doctor Zhivago (Pasternak), 124, 182–83
Dolce Vita, La (film), 124
Donat-Cattin, Carlo, 75, 190
Dottori (doctors), 56–57
Driving, 215–16
Drugs, 163–65, 174, 178
Dumas, Alexandre, 8
Dürer, Albrecht, vii
Duse, Eleonora, 129

Earnings Integration Fund, 80, 87
East Asia, xiv, 102
Eastern Europe, xiv
Eden, Anthony, 126
Education, 55–57
Egyptians (ancient), 86, 211
Eisenhower, Dwight D., 105
Elections, 3
Elisabeth, Empress, 83
Empedocles, 10
Engels, Friedrich, 84
England, 37, 205. *See also* Britain
ENI (Ente Nazionale Idrocarburi—National Hydrocarbons Agency), 103–6
Erice, 217
Ertl, Monica, 183
Esposito, Raffaele, 32, 33
Espresso, 35–39, 44, 69, 70
Ethiopia, 193, 198, 206, 207
Ethnic minorities, 9
Etna, Mount, 2, 23, 156
Etruscans, ix, xiii, 3, 40
Euripides, 10
Europe, patents in, 57. *See also* Eastern Europe; Western Europe

European Community, xv, 30, 100, 102, 179, 195, 196
European Court of Justice, 30

Faccendiere, 98
Facchineri family, 10–11
Faenza, 96
Fairbanks, Douglas, 46
Family, 111–45, 219
  and adultery, 118–23, 133
  businesses, 135–45
  and divorce, 117–19
  and sexual preoccupations, 126–35
Fanfani, Amintore, 117
Farewell to Arms, A (Hemingway), 206
Fascism, xi, 68, 84, 111, 181, 199, 200, 214
Father-daughter relations, 134
Federal Bureau of Investigation, 167
Fellini, Federico, 92, 123–24, 135, 213
Feltrinelli, Giangiacomo, 111, 180, 181–85, 209
Feltrinelli, Giannalisa, 111
Ferdinand II, King, 31, 157, 158
Fermi, Enrico, 57
Ferro, Vito Cascio, 162
Ferruzzi, Serafino, 145
Ferruzzi family, 145
Fiat Motor Company, 79–80, 103, 104, 139–43, 145, 165
Fila (lines), 59–62, 88–89
Filippo, 79–80
Films, 91–92, 122–25
Finance Guard, 98, 174, 223
Finance Ministry, 97
Fiora, Marco, 150
Florence, xii, 67, 112, 178, 201, 203

Florentine, ix, 68, 113
Fontana, Giovanna, 124–25
Fontana, Micol, 124–25
Fontana, Zoe, 124–25
Ford, Henry II, 140
Fortebraccio, Bernardino (Strong-arm), 203
France, xii, 7, 10, 21, 26, 49, 50, 74, 76, 108, 116, 118, 144, 157, 171, 192, 195, 198, 201, 205, 206, 209, 222
  academic unrest in, 55
  alcohol in, 37, 41
  automobiles in, 66
  civil service in, 68
  economy of, 47, 194
  invasion of Italy by, 202–4
  longevity in, 86
  railroads in, 73
  in World War I, 207
Francis of Assisi, St., 11
Franco, 135–37
Franz Joseph, Emperor, 205
Freemasonry, 222–23
Freight trains, 73
Friuli region, 30, 172, 178, 210
Front Line, 209

Galileo, 57
GAP (Proletarian Action Groups), 184–85
Gardini, Raul, 145
Gardner, Ava, 124
Garibaldi, Giuseppe, 7–8, 11, 16, 159, 182, 205, 212, 222
  followers of, 208
  monuments to, 192–93
  personality of, 193–94
Garofalo, Frank, 164
Gaspari, Remo, 54
Gelato, 39–40
Gelli, Licio, 222–24
Genoa, 29, 46, 75

Germany, 10, 34, 35, 37, 57, 60, 94, 172, 201, 202, 209, 218. *See also* Nazis
  and World War I, 206, 207
  and World War II, 196, 197
Getty, J. Paul III, 151–52
Gettys, the, 152
Ghibelline faction, 211
Ghidella, Vittorio, 196, 215
Giannini, Guglielmo, 119
Giannini, Massimo Severo, 58
Gibbon, Edward, 211
Giolitti, Giovanni, 84
Giotto, 11
Giulini, Carlo Maria, 213
Gladstone, William, 157
Godfather, The (Puzo), 20
Goethe, Johann Wolfgang von, vii, 93, 129
Gonzaga, Francesco, 203, 204
Gorbachev, Mikhail, 222
Goria, Giovanni, 49
Graziani, Rodolfo, 207
Greece, 10, 13, 137, 211
Greeks (ancient), xiii, 10, 31, 40, 159, 211
Gregory XI, Pope, 201
Gronchi, Giovanni, 105–6
Gubbio, 225
Guccis, the, 112–13
Guelph faction, 211
Guevara, Che, 183
Guiccioli, Countess Teresa, 129
Guttuso, Mimise, 114–15
Guttuso, Renato, 114–15

Hawkwood, Sir John, 201
Haydn, (Franz) Joseph, 16
Health service, national, 74–76
Hemingway, Ernest, 206
Hepburn, Audrey, 125
Herodotus, 10
Hitler, Adolf, xi, 127, 194

Index

Holy League, 203
Holy Roman emperors, 201
Honorable Society. *See* Mafia
Horace, 31, 41
Hospitals, 75–76
Hotels, 135–37
Hungarian uprising, 221

Income tax refunds, 65
Individualism, 213–26
Indonesia, 74
Innocent IV, Pope, 14
Invalidi, 86–88
Iotti, Leonilde ("Nilde"), 121
Iran, 44, 105
Irish, the, 19
Irish Republican Army, 180
Italian Association for Demo-
    graphic Education, 134
Italian Automobile Club, 66, 89
Italian Journey (Goethe), 93
Italian Riviera, 218
Italians, The (Barzini), 110, 111
Italy. *See also* Mezzogiorno;
    Northern Italy
  Armed Forces, 154, 209
  black economy in, 100–101
  budget deficits, 98
  cultural differences in, 5–6
  economy of, 48
  image of, 196
  immigrants from, 16–19, 33–34
  laws in, 6
  population of, xiii
  quality of life in, 226
  size of, xiii
  total output of goods and ser-
    vices, 177–78

James, Henry, vii, viii
Japan, vii, xiii, 34, 47, 49, 194, 197
  Ministry of International Trade
    and Industry, 48

Japanese, 79, 96
  patents of, 57
Jewish immigrants, 19
Juárez, Benito, 84

Khan, Aga, 149
Kidnapping, 23, 146–55, 178, 187–
    88
"Kidnapping, Inc.," 155, 169
Kingdom of the Two Sicilies. *See*
    Mezzogiorno
Kublai Khan, 15

Labor movement. *See* Strikes;
    Unions
Lambrusco wine, 42
Lamy, René, 144
La Palombara, Joseph, 99
Lateran Treaties, 8
Latin America, 62, 164, 173, 175,
    202, 209, 223
Latium, 29
Law enforcement, 170–77
Law No. 580, 30
Lazzaroni (idlers), 93
Lebanon, 70, 147, 164
Leninism, 221, 222
Leonardo da Vinci, ix, 11, 15, 68
Leopard, The (Tomasi di Lampe-
    dusa), 182
Leopardi, Giacomo, 53, 215
Leopold II, King, 144
Levi, Carlo, 12
Liberal party, 110
Libya, 104, 141, 193, 207, 208
Liechtenstein, 92, 99
Ligurians, 16
Lindstrom, Dr. Peter, 123
Lines (*fila*), 59–62, 88–89
Lombardy, xii–xiii, 24, 68, 179
Longanesi, Leo, 32
Longevity, 86–87, 225
Loren, Sophia, 31, 124

Lucheni, Luigi, 83
Luciano, Lucky (Salvatore Lucania), 162–63, 164
Lugano, 216
Luxembourg, 30

Macchinetta napoletana, 39
Machiavelli, Niccolò, 122, 211
Mafia, xi, 2, 5, 12, 13, 22, 49, 82, 91, 100, 106, 112, 171, 179, 180, 187, 190, 197, 199, 220, 224
  and drugs, 163–65
  fight against, 155–56, 162, 166–69
  and kidnapping, 147, 148, 152
  reputation of, 19–21
  structure of, 157–61
Magnani, Anna, 122–23
Magri, Lucio, 114
Mail. *See* Postal system
Malaparte, Curzio (Kurt Erich Suckert), 94
Malatesta, Giovanni ("the Lame"), 121
Malatesta, Parisina, 121
Malta, 60
Mantegna, Andrea, 204
Mao Zedong, 94
"March of the 40,000," 79
"March on Rome," 173
Marconi, Marchese Guglielmo, 11, 57
Margherita, Queen, 32, 33, 34
Maria José, Queen, 115
Marinetti, Filippo Tommaso, 198
Marshall Plan, 43
Marx, Karl, 84
Marzotto, Gaetano, 113
Marzotto, Countess Marta, 113–15
Marzotto, Count Umberto, 113, 115
Marzotto family, 113

Masonic lodges. *See* Freemasonry
Massa-Carrara, 83
Mastroianni, Marcello, 92
Mattei, Enrico, 103–7
Maximilian, Emperor, 84
Mazza, Pietro, 97–98
Medical profession, 99
Medici, Isabella de', 121–22
Medici family, 15
"Mediterranean diet," xiv, 43
Meinhof, Ulrike, 180, 184
Menelik II, Emperor, 206
Mengoni, Daniele, 53
Mercader, Maria, 122
Messina, 51, 77, 157
Mestre, xii
Metal Workers' Union, 79
Metastasio, Pietro, 15–16
Metternich, Prince Klemens von, 5
Mexico, xiv, 31, 73, 84, 117
Mezzogiorno, 14, 199, 210, 219
  background of, 7–8
  crime in, 151, 155–57, 159, 179
  "crimes of honor" in, 131–32
  immigrants from, 16–21, 33–34
  vs. Northern Italy, 2–5, 8–13, 22–25, 47, 50–51, 57–58, 87, 118, 175, 176, 217, 218
Michelangelo, 11, 68, 83, 177, 200
Middle East, 105, 165, 187
Milan, vii, xii, 1, 30, 35, 55, 63, 165, 179, 185, 201, 205
  Bourse, 145
  massacre, 180–81
Miltiades, 211
Ministry of Bureaucratic Reform, 67
Ministry of the Public Function, 67
Mondadori, Arnoldo, 113
Mondéjar, duke of, 155
Montagnana, Rita, 121
Montaigne, vii

Moore, Henry, vii
Moral Basis of a Backward Society, The (Banfield), 112
Moravia, Alberto, 113, 186, 215
Mori, Cesare, 162
Moro, Aldo, 187–88
Moslems, 40
Mother-son bonds, 133–34
Mozart, Wolfgang Amadeus, 16
Mozzarella, 33
Mussolini, Benito (II Duce), xi, xii, 8, 9, 12, 21, 68, 94, 104, 111, 124, 126, 173, 184, 189, 207, 208, 211, 217, 219, 221
  and carabinieri, 172, 174
  on discipline, 84
  father of, 84
  vs. Mafia, 162
  and national character, 214
  and "new Italy," 198–200
  sexual life of, 119–20
  in World War II, 194
Mussolini, Rachele, 119–20
Muti, Ricardo, 213

Naia, 210
Naples, 1, 2, 10, 12, 13, 27, 29, 34, 48, 52, 93, 101, 134, 157, 178, 203, 218
  arrangements in, 92–96
  espresso in, 38–39
  murders in, 166, 168
  pizza in, 31–33, 35
Naples, king of, 193
Napoleon, 6–7
Napoleon III, 205
Narcotics. *See* Drugs
National Institute of Statistics, 100
NATO (North Atlantic Treaty Organization), 180, 209, 222
Natural gas, 104
Nazis, 46, 142, 172, 181, 189, 193, 207, 208

'Ndrangheta, 12, 155, 159, 164, 169
Neapolitans. *See* Naples
Neo-Fascists, 85, 117, 180, 181, 187, 189
Netherlands, 106
Niccolò III, Duke, 121
Normans, 3, 10
Northern Italy, 6, 30
  crime in, 179
  immigrants from, 17
  vs. Mezzogiorno, 2–5, 8–13, 22–25, 47, 50–51, 57–58, 87, 118, 175, 176, 217, 218
  partisans in, 181, 208
Nozionismo, 55–56
Nuoro, 148, 149

Olbia, 77
Olivetti, Adriano, 143
Olivetti, Camillo, 143
Olivetti typewriters (company), 103, 143–44
Opera, 90–91
Orchestra Rehearsal (film), 213
Ordoñez, Miguel Angel, 195–96
Organization for Economic Co-operation and Development, 101
Orlando, Vittorio Emanuele, 161
Orsini, Prince Paolo Giordano, 121–22

Padua, 36
Paestum, xiii
Paganini, Niccolò, 213
Palermo, 1, 4, 23, 29, 48, 52, 157, 158, 163
  trial, 167–68
Pantheon complex, 39
Paparazzi, 124–26, 128
Pappalardo, Cardinal Salvatore, 167
Parking, 89–90

Parliament, 6, 54, 62, 117, 175, 188, 194, 214
  and education, 55
  and industrial relations, 79, 81
  and Mafia, 155, 156
  and P2 affair, 223–24
Pasolini, Pier Paolo, 113
Pasta, 26–30
Pasternak, Boris, 124, 182, 183
Patents, 57
Paul VI, Pope, 117
Pavoni, Desiderio, 36
Penmanship, ix
Pensions, 65, 86–88
Persians, 40
Peru, 31
Petacci, Clara ("Claretta"), 119, 120
Pickford, Mary, 46
Pictures from Italy (Dickens), 218
Piedmont, 5, 11, 22, 41, 198, 205
Pirandello, Luigi, 14, 119
Pirelli rubber and tire company, 145, 165
Piu, Francesco, 70
Pius IX, Pope, 8
Pius XI, Pope, 219
Pizza, 30, 31–35
Pizza Margherita, 32
Pizza a otto, 32–33
Pizzerie, 34–35
Platen, August Graf von, 129
Plato, 10
Poletti, Charles, 30
Police. *See* Carabinieri Corps; State police
Polish troops, 208
Political parties, 220–22
Polo, Marco, 11, 15, 27, 44
Pompeii, 31, 95, 127
Pontine Marshes, 199
Porpora, Niccolò, 16
Porto Torres, 77

Postal system, 48, 58, 73–74, 77
Posto, 52
"Prague Spring," 221
Prezzolini, Giuseppe, 18
Prisons, 63
Prostitution, 178
Provinces, xii
Prussia, 7, 206
P2 (Propaganda Two) affair, 222–24
Public Security Police, 171
Puccini, Giacomo, 11
Puzo, Mario, 20
Pythagoras, 10

Qaddafi-al, Muammar, 141
Questura (police headquarters), 61

Radical party, 128
Raffaele, Giovanni, 132
Railroads, 48, 72–73
Raphael, 11, 177
Raso-Albanese family, 10–11
Red Army Faction, 180
Red Brigades, 47, 85, 185–88, 190, 209
Reggio di Calabria, 2, 23
Renaissance, ix, 6, 121, 129, 201, 218
Ribbentrop, Joachim von, 127
Ricci, Matteo, 15
Rimini (town), 135, 136
Rimini, Francesca da, 121
Rinaldi, Ivano, 112
Risorgimento, 7, 8, 9, 204–5, 206, 222
Rissone, Guiditta, 122
Rizzoli, Angelo, 113
Rizzotto, Giuseppe, 158–59
Romagna Riviera, 135–37
Roman Campagna, 199

Roman Catholic Church, 15, 94, 117, 118, 219. *See also* Vatican
 in U.S., 19
Roman law, 6
Romans (ancient), 27, 40–41, 49, 127, 149, 205, 211
Rome, xiii, 3, 4, 8, 10, 35, 62, 67, 69, 75, 87, 94, 95, 129, 131, 138, 170, 192–93, 201, 203, 204, 206
 black market in, 214
 espresso in, 39
 as Hollywood on the Tiber, 124–25
 influence of, 5–6
 after liberation, 29–30
 population of, xii
 prostitution in, 178
 restaurants in, 45–47
Romeo, Rosario, 196
Rome Protocols, xv
Rome State University (La Sapienza), 56
Rossellini, Roberto, 91–92, 122–23
Rovigo, 112
Ruskin, John, vii
Russia, 83, 198. *See also* Soviet Union
Russo, Giuseppe Genco, 164

Sacco, Nicola, 83
Salandra, Antonio, 212
Salieri, Antonio, 16
San Marino, 117
San Martino Hospital (Genoa), 75
Saracens, vii
Saragat, Giuseppe, 150
Sardinia, 13, 77, 172, 184, 205
Sardinians, 23, 148–50, 152, 154, 169, 198
Savoy, House of, 32, 115–16
Scandinavian countries, 74
Schichi, Riccardo, 128

Schild, Rolf, 147
Schoental, Inge, 184
Schopenhauer, Arthur, 129
Schuman, Robert, 14
Sciascia, Leonardo, 186
Security Service, 176
Segni, Antonio, 150
Senate, 117, 156, 220
Senegalese, 101
"Seven Sisters," 105, 106
Sexual preoccupations, 126–35
Sforzas, the, 201
Sgroi, Vittorio, 177
Shah of Iran, 106
Shelley, Percy Bysshe, xiv
Shoes, 102
Sibari (Sybaris), 10
Sibling incest, 134
Sica, Domenico, 155
Sicilians, xi, 4, 5, 19, 23, 40, 180, 224
 image of, 17, 20
Sicily, vii, 2, 8, 10, 12, 13, 18, 27, 29, 40, 46, 58, 60, 73, 77, 87, 132, 217
 banks in, 101
 corruption in, 179
 and Mafia, 147, 155–69, 171, 187, 220
Siena, 72
Sindona, Michele, 223
Singapore, 74
Slovenians, 9
Small business, 102–3, 137
Smith, Denis Mack, 206
Socialists, 72, 84, 180, 220
Social Welfare Agency, 65
Société Générale de Belgique, 144
Sopramonte range, 150, 154
Southern Italy. *See* Mezzogiorno
South Tyrol, 9
Soviet Union, 41, 106, 113, 114, 196, 200, 202, 215. *See also* Russia

aggression of, 221–22
and *Doctor Zhivago,* 182–83
Spain, 10, 15, 50, 108, 124, 137, 157, 173, 195, 209, 216
aggression of, 201–3
Spanish anarchists, 83
Spanish Civil War, 207
Spengler, Oswald, 199
Stalinists, 222
Staller, Ilona Anna, 128
State police, 170–71, 173–74, 175, 176, 177, 188
Stendhal, vii, viii, 36, 129
Strikes, 77–82, 84–85, 89
Stromboli, 2
Suicide, 225
"Sunny" Italy, vii
Sweden, 35, 47, 70, 202
Swiss anarchists, 83
Swiss Guard, 176, 201, 202
Switzerland, 21, 47, 73, 74, 76, 107, 117, 142, 165, 177, 216, 224
Syracuse, 10, 60

Taormina, vii
Taranto (Taras), 10, 12, 46
Tax evasion, 97–102, 219
Taylor, Elizabeth, 125
Telephones, 48, 74
Terrone, 22, 23
Terrorism, 180–91, 208–9
Testa, Antonio, 31
Testa, Monsù, 31–32
Thatcher, Margaret, 179–80
Togliatti, Palmiro, 120–21
Tolstoy, Leo, 129
Tomasi di Lampedusa, Giuseppe, 182
Toscanini, Arturo, 213
Train à Grande Vitesse (France), 73
Transportation, xiii, 77

Trapani, 2, 158
Treasury, 98, 174
Treviso siblings, 102
Trieste, 9, 36
Triple Alliance, 206, 211
Trucking, 73
Tunisians, 101
Turin, 30, 48, 75, 139, 140, 141, 142
Turkey, 36, 164, 198
Turks, 40
Tuscany, viii, xiii, 1, 5, 29, 83, 148, 215

Udine, 225
Umberto I, King, 32, 83
Umberto II, 115, 116
Umbria, xiii, 1, 225
Unions, 78–79, 100, 137. *See also* Strikes
United States, vii, 29, 42, 47, 49, 67, 73, 74, 76, 83, 141, 175, 194, 208, 209, 218. *See also* Americans
birthrate in, 134
cars in, xiii
cities in, 219
Congress, 123, 220
criminal trials in, 6
divorce in, 118
immigration to, 16–21, 33, 34
and Mafia, 161–63, 168
as occupying power, 94–95
patents in, 57
Urbino, vii
Uruguay, 192
U.S. Central Intelligence Agency, 181
U.S. Drug Enforcement Administration, 167
Usciere (doorkeeper or office attendant), 89

Valentino, Rudolph (né Rodolfo
    d'Antonguolla), 130
Valletta, Vittorio, 140
Vanzetti, Bartolomeo, 83
Vatican, 15, 19, 48, 87, 95, 114,
    117, 170, 197, 219
    foreign legion of, 201–2
    as international peacemaker, 212
    and Lateran Treaties, 8
    police forces, 176–77
    wire communications of, 175
Venice, vii, 27, 30, 41, 68, 129, 178,
    201, 203, 206
    coffeehouses of, 36
    dialects in, 5
    gondolas in, 93
    population of, xii
Verdi, Giuseppe, 11
Verona, 41
Vespucci, Amerigo, 15
Vesuvius, Mount, 2, 31, 34, 96
Vicenza, 96
Victor Emmanuel II, King, 8, 198,
    204–6
Victor Emmanuel III, King, 116,
    172, 173, 192, 223
Victoria Arduino machine, 36
Vietnam War, 94
Villalba, 161–62
Virginity, 132
Vizzini, Calogero (Don Calò),
    161–62, 164

Volta, Alessandro, 57
Von Trotta, Margarethe, 180
Vulcano, 2

Wertmuller, Lina, 113
Western Alliance, 209, 222
Western Europe, xv, 73
West Germany, 21, 30, 49, 74, 86,
    194. *See also* Germany
    automakers in, 142
    cars in, xiii
    economy of, xii
    and European Community,
        195
    terrorism in, 180
Wine, 40–42
Workers' Statute, 79
World War I, 198, 206, 207
World War II, xi, 104, 120,
    172
    claims from, 88
    destruction of, 1, 9
    entry into, 207
    and Mafia, 162
    partisans in, 181, 189, 208–9
    recovery from, 46
    surviving, 196–97

Yugoslavia, 62, 73, 137, 206

Zaire, 144
Zwingli, Ulrich, 202